# Thinking and Writing About Literature

## The Story of **Starpath** Books

Starpath books are selected Prentice-Hall texts
that have been specially adapted to meet the needs
of high school students.

As originally published by Prentice-Hall's College
Division, these books have been widely used not only
in colleges but in high schools as well. Now, in
response to suggestions from many educators, Prentice-
Hall's Educational Book Division has prepared Starpath
editions of these titles, revised and rewritten for
use at the high school level.

The result is a series of widely acclaimed texts,
carefully adapted on the basis of extensive evaluation
by high school educators and specifically designed
to appeal to today's high school students.

STARPATH SERIES

# Thinking and Writing About Literature

**Edgar V. Roberts**

Herbert H. Lehman College

The City University of New York

Prentice-Hall, Inc., Englewood Cliffs, N.J.

**THINKING AND WRITING ABOUT LITERATURE**
(Adapted from *Writing Themes About Literature*)
Edgar V. Roberts


**Supplementary:** Teacher's Guide

10   9   8   7   6

ISBN 0-13-917518-0

Prentice-Hall International, Inc., London
Prentice-Hall of Australia Pty. Ltd., Sydney
Prentice-Hall of Canada, Ltd., Toronto
Prentice-Hall of India Private Ltd., New Delhi
Prentice-Hall of Japan, Inc., Tokyo
Prentice-Hall of Southeast Asia Pte. Ltd., Singapore
Whitehall Books Limited, Wellington, New Zealand

*For Nanette*

# Contents

# 6  THE THEME ABOUT SETTING                                        75

# 7  THE THEME DISCUSSING IDEAS                                     86

# 8  THE THEME ON A CLOSE READING                                   97

# 9  THE THEME ON A SPECIFIC PROBLEM                                107

# To the Teacher

This book provides a tested but fresh approach to writing themes on literary topics; it concentrates on literary problems *as* they bear on writing themes. I have tried to keep in focus the needs of students faced with difficult assignments, and I have emphasized how the assignments may be treated within the confines of a theme. This approach has worked; it has the virtue of making the theoretical discussion of a technique of literary criticism immediately vital to students. If they can see a literary problem in the light of their necessity to write about it, they are more likely to learn their lesson well. This book might be called a rhetoric of practical criticism for students.

Students need guidance before they write a theme about literature. It is a common complaint among teachers that students' papers on literary topics are not really to the point. The reason is simple: the majority of students asked to "analyze the structure of X play, or Y poem, or Z short story" do not really understand what structure is or how to go about analyzing it. Students asked to discuss "point of view in X literary work" are similarly handicapped, and so on. Under these conditions, teachers either take valuable time explaining theme assignments or else continue to receive inadequate student writing about literature. This book is offered as a solution. Its aim is to free teachers from the drudgery and lost time of making assignments and to help students by explaining and illustrating many approaches to literary technique in order to provide a sound basis for analysis. The practical aim of the book is to aid students in improving their reading and writing skills.

It has been many years since the first edition of this book was published in 1964. During the interval a number of books on the same general topic have appeared, evidence of a widening use of literature in composition exercises, and also evidence that professional literary criticism does not offer practical guidance for students who are about to write on literary topics. It no longer seems necessary, therefore, to justify the need for the approach found in *Thinking and Writing About Literature.*

Nevertheless, I should like to re-assert that each of the assignments in this book has been worked out in the classroom and has demonstrably helped students improve their themes about literature. Even though the assignments can stand alone, they may be used as bases for discussions before assignments are due or as supplements to the discussions. Of course, the assignments may be modified if you desire.

Each chapter is devoted to the consideration of a separate literary approach that creates a problem in composition. The method is to go from precept to example, in the belief that both will benefit a student more than each can separately. The first part of each chapter is thus a discussion of the problems raised by a particular assignment, and is followed by one or two sample themes illustrating a way of handling the problems in a theme-length form. The discussions are always focused on critical techniques as they bear on writing assigned to students. The sample themes show how the students themselves might handle the various assignments. Although some students will follow the patterns closely, others will wish to adapt the discussions and samples to their own needs.

The sample themes have been written in the belief that the word *imitation* does not have to be preceded by adjectives like *slavish* or *mere.* There is an additional question of how best to liberate the minds of our students. My belief is that liberation best occurs when students are freed from uncertainties about how to approach the problems they face. In other words, if students must search for the proper forms of expression, they will dissipate their energies and fail to devote themselves fully to the real problems at hand. But if they already know the forms in which to present their thoughts, they can focus directly on reading and interpreting the texts at hand. An immediate result should be superior themes about literature, and a longer-term result should be a step toward that goal we all seek: liberal education.

For illustrative purposes, the sample themes are slightly long, yet they are within the approximate lengths of many high school themes. Although the various lengths cannot always coincide with the word limits set by individual teachers, the organization and method of the sample themes should be, and have been demonstrated to be, helpful. These samples should be regarded both as goals toward which average students can work and as guides for more advanced students.

New in this edition are commentaries on each of the sample themes, for use as additional study guides. These have been added at the suggestion of many students. It is my hope that they will help students make the connection between the precepts in the first part of the chapter and the examples in the second part.

Some of the sample themes have been rewritten for this edition, and many new ones have been added. In some chapters I have included two sample themes when two different approaches have been clearly mandated by the theme types. Thus Chapter 12, on imagery, presents sample themes on imagery in a poem and symbolism in a story, and Chapter 1, on précis writing, presents themes on a story and on an article.

An important addition, in Chapter 10, is a sample theme on the technique of extended comparison and contrast. This example provides one way out of the pitfalls of plagiarism which are often encountered in the research paper. As an alternate long paper, the theme offers both the challenge of handling many sources — here mainly primary — and the requirement of dealing with documentation. In this theme there is an example of how reference works may be used for factual information, but the use of critical secondary sources has been avoided. If this approach is not followed, there is still Appendix C, which provides a perspective on research and which, if taken in conjunction with the chapter assignments, offers guidance for extensive research work.

An additional word seems necessary about the completeness of the various sample themes, for it has been suggested than an in-class impromptu theme cannot come anywhere near the scope and detail of the samples. The themes are guides, and as such they represent a *full* treatment of each of the various topics. If students are preparing their themes outside of class, they can readily approximate the scope of the sample. Even though the samples usually treat an average of three aspects of particular topics, there is nothing to prevent the assigning of only one, either for an impromptu theme or for an outside-class theme. If the subject is tone, for example, students may be asked to discuss only how the tone is shown through selected diction in the work assigned. This method of assigning papers would make for short, well-focused themes, and it could also be applied to paragraph-length assignments. On a day-to-day basis, the assignment of paragraphs can prove most useful, both as a method of assuring preparation for classroom discussions and as a means of keeping students in practice for longer assignments. If the sample themes are used in these ways — as a guide in a flexible system of assignments rather than as hard-and-fixed goals — their purpose will have been realized.

In the introduction to this edition of *Thinking and Writing About Literature* I have included a short description of the various genres; it seems necessary here to refer to the applicability of most of the chapters to the genres. Obviously, a few of the themes are more appropriate to some of the genres than to others. Thus Chapter 4, on character analysis, is most applicable to drama and narrative, where characterization is preeminent, but generally not to poetry and the essay. Chapters 5 and 6, on point of view and setting, are useful primarily for narrative but not for the other genres. One may readily grant that Chapter 14, on prosody, is exclusively the domain of poetry, while Chapter 15, on prose style, is designed for the other genres. (Even so, most of the approaches to studying prose style can also be applied to poetry.) Chapter 18, on film, is designed exclusively for writing themes about movies. All the other chapters, however, are useful for the study of any one of the genres. While imagery (Chapter 12) is probably best studied in poetry, it is an element in all literature and can profitably be analyzed in a story, essay, or play (the second sample theme is an analysis of symbolism in a story). The structure of anything (Chapter 11) can be studied, and anything written has some quality of tone (Chapter 13) that can be analyzed and described. Ideas may be found in all the genres (Chapter 7), just as a common element in any of the genres may be set up as the common ground for comparison and contrast (Chapter 10). The other chapters are equally applicable to all the genres.

In addition to the extensive changes already mentioned, the present edition contains many significant alterations and improvements. There is new material on documentation in Appendix B, and there are extensive changes in the discussion sections of the chapters. My general plan in revising has been to make things better wherever my experience, together with the helpful advice of many obliging users of the book, has discovered the need for improvement. Almost no chapter has remained untouched, and many have undergone great change. This edition also reflects a number of decisions about basic changes that were proposed but not accepted. In their effect, these decisions have significantly determined the shape of the book, although they must remain "unseen" to everyone but myself and a few advisers.

There are frequent references throughout the book to many literary works, and it is unlikely that any student will yet have encountered all. Because references cannot be justified unless they clarify, I have tried to make each one self-explanatory and have included enough details to achieve this end. Lack of familiarity with the particular work being discussed therefore should not deter a student from understanding the point of the reference. In addition, I have tried to refer to works that high school students are likely to encounter, if not in a general English class, then in a survey or honors course, or even, let us hope, in their own independent reading.

The chapters have been arranged in an order of increasing difficulty and technicality. With the précis theme in Chapter 1, students may begin with the simplest form of writing about any of the genres. The first three themes become progressively broader in scope. The next three are designed primarily for courses offering students an introduction to the study of narrative fiction. The next four, again applicable to any of the genres, provide a number of reading techniques that reach a climax in the comparison-contrast theme, a theme which could suitably focus all the various techniques that students have acquired to that point in the course. The remaining chapters are admittedly more difficult and in some cases more specifically "literary." They are nevertheless useful for students in basic courses, and I have been pleased to learn that many teachers have assigned them there with considerable success.

Although a full-year course could be devoted to the progression of themes from beginning to end, quite often only part of the class time is available. Whatever your situation, flexibility should always be your guide. For example, you may wish to assign the same type of theme on different works of literature until students show a mastery over that type, or you may assign separate types on the same work to show how compatible the different approaches are; you might also base theme assignments on single aspects of any one chapter. In addition, I believe that students beyond average ability will continue to find the book useful, because the advanced assignments here are on a level of difficulty and technicality suitable for upper-level courses.

The book offers a practical solution to a very real problem with many composition assignments. Composition is frequently regarded as a service, for it teaches writing techniques essential in all high school work. This need has forced the content in composition to cover too wide a range of subject matter. There can be little unity when students write themes on topics derived from many unrelated fields. All this material is usually taught by teachers who have been prepared by years of literary study. Here is the rub: although you yourself may want to teach literature as a discipline and as a pleasure, you know that your students must have intense work in composition for all their other high school work. One purpose of this book is to reconcile this conflict by unifying the course and making it challenging to you as well as to the student. Using assignments here, you can satisfy the needs of your course by teaching composition while you satisfy your own discipline by teaching literature and literary techniques. Although these assignments attempt to integrate the teaching of literature and composition, many have residual effect on other courses, and in this edition I have emphasized these relationships. Thus, Chapter 1 has a beneficial effect on study methods for any course. Chapter 2 contains a basic thematic method for assembling any body of material. The theme in Chapter 10 can be applied to any course where comparisons and contrasts are required, such as the heredity-environment controversy in science or social studies. In this way, I hope that the usefulness of the chapters will extend far beyond the immediate course.

An almost foolproof solution to another difficulty in teaching composition—plagiarism—is offered. During one year, for example, you might assign a theme about the main idea in "The Garden Party," whereas during the next you might assign a theme about the main idea in *Macbeth,* and so on. In high schools where a common syllabus is used in all yearly English courses, the same procedure could be followed uniformly. This plan, whereby the form of each theme is preserved while the subject matter is changed, could prevent students from copying papers written in the past. The possibilities for varied assignments are virtually endless.

Most important of all, however, is that the book is aimed at the appreciation of good literature. Literature is the property of all; its appeal is to all. But literature, as an art, employs techniques and offers problems that can be understood only through analysis, and analysis means work. The immediate aim is to help the student in this work, but the primary object of the book is to promote the pleasurable study and, finally, the love of literature.

# Introduction

The chapters that follow are theme assignments based on a number of analytical approaches important to the study of literature. The assignments are designed to fulfill two goals of English courses: (1) to write good themes, and (2) to assimilate great works of literature into the imagination. Negatively, the book aims to avoid your writing themes that are no more than retellings of a story, vague statements of like or dislike, or biographies of an author. Positively, the book aims to raise your standards of judging literature — and therefore your ability to appreciate good literature — by requiring you to apply, in well-prepared themes, the techniques of good reading.

No educational process is complete until you have applied what you have studied. That is, you have not really learned something until you can talk or write intelligently about it, or until you can apply it to some question or problem. The need for application forces you to recognize where your learning is complete or incomplete, so that you may strengthen your knowledge and supplement your deficiencies. Thus, it is easy for you to read the chapter in this book on *point of view*, and it is presumably easy to read, say, Thomas Mann's story "Mario and the Magician." But your grasp of point of view as a concept will not be complete — nor will your appreciation of at least one aspect of the technical artistry of Mann's story be complete — until you have written about point of view in the story. As you write, you may suddenly discover that you need to go back to the work, to study your notes on it, and to compare them with what you understand about the problem itself. In writing, you must verify facts, grasp their relationship to your topic, develop insights into the value and artistry of the work, and express your understanding in a well-organized and well-developed theme. After you

1

have finished a number of such themes, you should be able to approach other literary works with more certainty and skill. The more you know and the more you can apply, the more expert and demanding will be your critical taste.

## Reading Habits to Develop

The need to apply principles of literary study in writing themes should have a positive influence on your reading and study habits. The essential principle of being a good reader is to derive from the reading process a factual basis for emotional responses and intelligent interpretation. Each person goes about reading in his or her own way, but it stands to reason that casual readers may often read so superficially that their reactions to a work may be uncertain and unreliable. Preparing to write a theme on a work, however, should create the need for improved reading habits. Here are some habits that you should develop and always pursue:

1. Study each reading assignment carefully. Look up all words that you do not know.
2. Make notes on interesting characterizations, events, and ideas. If you like a character, say so, and try to describe what you like about that character. If you dislike an idea, say so, and try to describe what you dislike about it.
3. Try to see patterns developing. Make an outline of the story or main idea. What are the conflicts in the story? How are these resolved? Is one force, or side, triumphant? Why? Or is the conflict unresolved? Why?
4. With specific reference to your assignment, take notes on features of style and organization that seem to have an immediate bearing on your topic. If, as you read, you get ideas about how the topic can be handled, write a paragraph for later use or adaptation. Sometimes you may get good ideas as you are reading. Do not forget them.
5. Do you see anything in the story that you do not understand? Do not forget the difficulty; write a note about it and ask your instructor in class.
6. For further study, underline what seem to be key passages. Write some of these passages on cards, and carry the cards with you. Then, when you are going to or from school, or at other times, try to memorize key phrases and sentences and lines of poetry.

## What Is Literature?

It is not possible to make a definition of literature that pleases everyone. Some people who have studied literature all their lives hesitate to define it. It is therefore better to read individual works of literature and to experience them fully than to set up definitions that would exclude this or that work—and any definition invariably excludes something.

Nevertheless, you should be able to recognize a work of literature when you see one. Careful reading and comprehension being assumed, you should find something in the work that is of more than passing or specialized interest. The work should intrigue you, captivate you, stimulate you, or elevate you. When you finish reading it your awareness of life should be heightened. You may never discern that the work has changed you in any way, but in fact these changes do occur as a result of experiences in reading. Passages in the work should come back to your mind when you least expect them, for you will see in them, either consciously or incidentally, an expression of human aspirations, a dramatization of a permanent aspect of human conduct. Literature, like all art, is one of the essential things that make human beings human. In one way or another, everyone is touched by it.

## Types of Literature:
## The Four Genres

Technically, anything spoken or written down is literature. This would include everything from soap commercials to Shakespeare's sonnets. In practice, however, the works of literature you will be studying fall into four categories: (1) narrative, (2) drama, (3) poetry, and (4) non-fiction prose. To a greater or lesser degree, all these forms are designed to interest, entertain, stimulate, broaden, or ennoble. While a major purpose of non-fiction prose is to inform, the other genres also provide information, although this usually takes place unintentionally. All the genres share the characteristic of being art forms, with their own internal requirements of style and structure. In varying degrees, the forms are both dramatic and imaginative. Even a work of non-fiction prose designed almost purely to instruct will be unsuccessful unless it makes at least some appeal to the imagination.

### NARRATIVE FICTION

A narrative is a chronological account of a series of events, usually fictional, although sometimes fictional events may be tied to events that are genuinely historical. The two kinds of narrative fiction you will read most often are *short stories* and *novels; myths, parables, romances,* and *epics* are also part of the genre. A short story is usually about one or two characters undergoing some sort of difficulty or facing some sort of problem. The characters may go uphill or downhill, but they almost never remain the same, for even staying the same may usually be interpreted as either downhill or uphill. Although the characters will interact with other characters and with the circumstances surrounding them, usually these relationships are described fairly briefly, for the shortened form of the story does not permit a great deal of development about how human character changes in response to human beings and environment. The novel, on the other hand, permits a full development of these interactions, and its length is caused by this fullness of development. Like the short story, the novel usually focuses on a small number of characters, although the cast of secondary characters is often large, and the number of incidents is multiplied.

### DRAMA

A drama or play is designed to be performed on a stage by live actors. It therefore consists of spoken dialogue together with directions for action. Like narrative fiction, it focuses on a single character or a small number of characters. Drama does not rely on narration, however, but presents you with speech and action which actually *render* the interactions that cause change in the characters and that resolve the conflicts in which the characters are engaged. Drama shows you people talking and doing, whereas narrative tells you about these activities. (To the degree that short stories and novels actually include dialogue, they use the technique of drama.) A *film script* is like drama although films often require much unspoken action, therefore verging on *pantomime*. It is often difficult to read a dramatic text because you miss a good deal of what real actors could bring to their parts by way of interpretation. Reading a play therefore requires a good deal of imaginative reconstruction on your part.

The dramatic types are *tragedy*, *comedy*, and *farce*. In the face of human disasters, tragedy attempts to elevate human values. Comedy treats people as they are, laughing at them or sympathizing with them, but showing them to be successful nevertheless. Farce exaggerates human foolishness, gets the characters into improbable and lunatic situations, and laughs at everyone in sight.

### POETRY

*Poetry* is a broad term that includes a great number of separate sub-types, such as *sonnet*, *lyric*, *pastoral*, *ballad*, *song*, *ode*, *drama*, *epic*, *mock epic*, and *dramatic monologue*. Essentially, poetry is a compressed and often highly emotional form of expression. Each word counts for more than in prose, and the basic arrangement is separate lines rather than paragraphs, although *stanzas* correspond to paragraphs, and *cantos* sometimes correspond to chapters. Poetry relies more heavily than prose on *imagery*, that is, on a comparative, allusive, suggestive form of expression that is applicable to a wide number of human situations. It is this compactness of expression, combined with the broadness of application, that makes poetry unique. Because poetry is so compact, the *rhythms* of poetic speech become as vital as the emotions and ideas. Sometimes these rhythms are called the *music* of poetry. Some poetic forms are fairly free, particularly poetry written since the time of the American poet Walt Whitman. Other forms are carefully arranged and measured into definite, countable units, and often employ *rhymes* to affect the minds of the readers and listeners.

The topic material of poetry can be just about anything. Love, personal meditations, psychological studies, reviews of folklore, attacks on conspicuous consumption, religious worship, friendship, funerary occasions, celebrations of the seasons, observations on life in the streets or in the home—these are just a few of the topics you will find. While writers of narrative and drama confine themselves exclusively to these forms, poets are free to select any form they wish. Thus some of the best poetry is dramatic (for example, Shakespeare's plays) and narrative (Milton's epic poem *Paradise Lost*).

### NON-FICTION PROSE

This is a broad term referring to short forms like essays and articles, and to longer non-fictional and non-dramatic works. The essay or article is a form designed primarily to express ideas, interpretations, and descriptions. The topics of essays are unlimited; they may be on social, political, artistic, scientific, and other subjects. In an essay an author focuses on one topic such as the influence of diet on health or the contrast between envy and ambition. One of the very famous essays in the language, by Charles Lamb, is on the taste of roast pig. Another famous essay, by Jonathan Swift, compares human beings to a broomstick. The writer usually develops a single topic fully but not exhaustively. When exhaustiveness is the aim, the writer expands the essay into the form of an entire book, which retains the same centralized focus as the essay but permits a wide examination and application of the entire subject.

A form closely related to the essay is the *article*. An article is designed to explore and draw conclusions from facts, and sometimes is exclusively factual. Therefore the article is used in all scholarly areas, such as economics, chemistry, physics, geology, anthropology, and history. When an article is used exclusively for the reporting of research findings, it is distant from the essay in style, but when a writer combines

a consideration of factual material together with conclusions and inter-
pretatio is of the facts, the article form comes close to the essay. When
the scope of an article is enlarged, as with the essay, it becomes a book.

**What Is Literary Analysis?**

Analysis attempts to find truth. The process of analysis is to divide
a problem into various parts, which may then be examined more easily;
their natures, functions, and interrelationships may be more fully understood when they are examined one by one. For example, if you have
the problem in chemical qualitative analysis of discovering the elements
in a chemical solution, you can make only one test on the solution at a
time, because if you tried to make all your tests at once you would not
be able to control or distinguish your results.

Although the work of literature you are to analyze is an entirety,
you must make separate inquiries to discover its full meaning and to appreciate it fully. You could not talk about everything in *Paradise Lost* at
once, for example, without being guilty of the greatest superficiality. It
is better to narrow the scope of your topic by talking about the diction,
epic conventions, theology, or dramatic action. An attempt to discuss
everything at once would inevitably distort some things and omit others. Truth, however, can emerge only if all possibilities are considered.
So your problem in making an analysis is to make the subject small
enough so that you can go deeply into it.

A serious objection sometimes arises about literary analysis. Although scientific analysis is necessary, it is said that too much literary
analysis "spoils" appreciation of a work, or that in making an analysis,
you "murder" literature as you "dissect" it. This objection is not valid,
for the purpose of analysis is not to cut up literature like a frog and leave
it in pieces. No matter how completely you analyze a work, the work
will remain healthy and untouched. For example, the fourth voyage of
Swift's *Gulliver's Travels* has not been changed by all the critical essays
that have been written about it. But what has changed is what people
*see* in the fourth voyage. Critics at one time saw evidence that Swift
hated humanity. More recent analyses of the work have disclosed
evidence that Swift was a humanitarian urging human beings to
change their behavior by steering a course between emotion and
pure reason. Other analyses have seen the work as an appeal to follow religion. The effect of these and other analyses has been to uncover the work's rich complexity and its basic affirmation of life, and
ultimately to raise it in critical esteem. Such is the real business of
literary analysis. By pointing out the authors' insights into problems

of life, and by describing various aspects of their skill, literary analysis aims at the appreciation of literary excellence.

It is therefore important for you to keep literary analysis in perspective: analyzing a work is a *means* toward appreciation and evaluation, not an end in itself. It is an honest attempt by you, the reader, to discover the truth about a work and to base your appreciation on your own thought and discovery, not on a vaguely aesthetic reaction. If you analyze the work to know it better and to like it better, you have really dismissed the entire objection.

Another way to think of literary analysis is that it is a way of fulfilling the objectives of good reading. If you had a choice, you would no doubt prefer to be a good reader rather than a bad reader. Once you have finished the composition and literature activities you are now assigned, you may never again have to write a literary analysis. Invariably, however, you will continue reading and also talking about what you have read. If you establish good reading habits now, reinforced by the exactness of mind required for writing, then your future discussions will be forever improved. The themes you write today will have a residual impact on your future reading habits.

As you think about what to put into your theme, remember that literary analysis is a way of getting at the heart of the work. To this end, there are four broad areas that literary analysis explores: (1) meaning, (2) structure, (3) style, and (4) background and influences. There is usually overlapping among these; for example, in writing about point of view, you would emphasize its impact on both meaning and style. It is always wise, in fact, to emphasize that your particular topic has a relation to the entire work. In this way you are really demonstrating the relationship of literary analysis to literary appreciation, which is the goal implied in all intelligent discourse about literature.

One of the major problems in literary analysis is that you will somehow remain *outside* the work, and only with difficulty see the work as the author saw it. The goal is to try to recreate to some degree the way in which the author looked at the work, to see the blank page the author originally saw and to try to reconstruct the choices and ideas the author had. Thus you should exert a good deal of imagination when you read a work. If you had an idea about rendering a personality that is insecure and fearful, as Franz Kafka did in his story-fantasy "A Country Doctor," you might try to create such a story yourself. A clinician, for example, might give a straightforward report of a character suffering from a deep-rooted sense of inadequacy. But Kafka chose to represent this story from the point of view of the country doctor himself, describing his fears in the form of a fantasy, a dream in which mysterious horses appear to carry him off to a sickroom where a young man is ill of a disease he cannot initially diagnose. In considering this story you would serve your-self well if you tried to visualize what other ways this story could be told, what other organization could be used. In short, you should face the story as an open situation which offers innumerable possibilities.

If you can develop a capacity to look at works in this way, you can then understand better what the author has actually done. You will be in a position of both looking at the work as a finished product, and de-termining what the work is actually like, and you will also see it as a developing product that comes into being as a result of many artistic, conscious choices. The questions to ask as you prepare your themes are: How else could this be done? What would be the possible effects of some other method? In what way or ways is the method the author chose superior to these other ways? In answering these questions you are developing the objectivity necessary to evaluate works, but preserv-ing your sense of the work that is actually there. You may never need to include the answers to these questions, but the fact that you raised them will sharpen your own observations and interpretations.

**What Is a Theme?**

As you begin any of the assignments in this book, you should bear in mind the two basic requirements of themes. The first is the need for a *central idea* or *point*. A theme, like an essay, should be a short, accurate, and forceful presentation of ideas or descriptions, well con-trived as a totality or unity. A theme should not ramble in any way, but should be clearly united around a dominating central thought. A theme is a brief "mind's full" on any particular subject; that is, it presents and considers the subject in several of its various aspects. The theme cannot cover all aspects, as might a book or a long essay.

The second basic need is that a theme must have a *clearly dis-cernible organization*. Let's examine these two essentials in detail.

**The Central Idea or Point**

*Themes* are so named because throughout such a composition there runs a basic or central idea — a theme — that unifies the paper into a logical whole. On every subject you encounter there should be some dominating idea or mood that will suggest itself to you or one that you will derive from your own intensive concentration. For example, when you look at a room, you might feel that it is cheerful; when you listen to the latest news, you might decide that it is depressing. Were you to write a theme describing the room or another discussing the news, you would have to keep your central idea foremost in your reader's mind *throughout* your theme, or else you would not have a theme.

One of your first objectives should be to decide on a central idea for your theme. Usually you are working on an assignment from your teacher. With this problem or topic in front of you, your task will be to formulate a central idea that will in effect be your solution to the problem raised by the assignment. As always, study the work carefully and take notes describing the major actions and statements. If the author has stated an idea that is developed in the work, make a note of that. Then, consider your notes with care and try to work up a central idea on the basis of your observations and conclusions.

Let us assume, for the moment, that your assignment has been a "specific problem" theme, the question being: "In Katherine Mansfield's story 'Miss Brill', is Miss Brill worth your sympathy?" The following material represents a collection of notes and observations that are typical of what you yourself might write when reading the story for this assignment. Notice that page numbers are given, so that you could easily go back to the story to refresh your memory on any particular details when you start sketching out your theme.

p. 14   Miss Brill is introduced. She loves her fox fur, and lives alone. She is observant. Goes to the park often. Is familiar with the park and the band there.

p. 15   She eavesdrops, but not with a bad intention. She lives in others, not herself. She recalls a dull conversation of the week before.

p. 16   Many people are in the park, some seeming to be like Miss Brill. She is quiet and harmless, with no more aggression than a bag of popcorn. She is observant. Life seems to have passed her by, and therefore she enjoys looking at the people in the park. She seems to have some sympathy for the lady in the "ermine toque."

pp. 16–17   She discovers a way to identify herself with life in the park: she is an actress, with a part to play. She almost expects that everyone will join the band in singing. She would be a part of the choir.

p. 17   A boy and a girl come. They insult Miss Brill so that she can hear them.

pp. 17–18   She goes home to her small, dark room. She cries. Her emotions have gone from calm, to excitement, to being terribly hurt, to being just about heartbroken. She is like a hurt bird, a helpless victim. She is a nobody, but a nobody I feel sorry for. Her real sorrow results from the fact that the insults make her aware of just how insignificant she is. The only joy she knew is taken away from her. What more would she have? Not much.

In response to the assignment question, this set of notes leads naturally to the following central idea: "Miss Brill is worth my sympathy." The conclusion is not startling in any way, and a reader might just as easily have arrived at it without the system of notes. The virtue of the notes, however, is that they will provide a factual basis for developing the theme.

Once you have established the central idea, you should concentrate on the use you can make of it. All the ideas you now bring out about the work you have read will be related to the central idea. When you finally write your theme you should state the idea in your introduction, for you should leave your reader in no doubt about what you wish to assert. Also, throughout your theme, you should think about reminding your reader that references to the story or poem, and all conclusions you are drawing, are relevant to the central idea. Anything not related to this point will not belong in your theme.

The need for a central idea will also make you aware of the need for paragraph transitions, because you are proving or showing *one* central idea, not a *number* of ideas. Transitions form bridges to connect one part of the theme with another; having a central idea always in mind makes continuity between paragraphs both essential and natural.

## Organizing Your Theme around the Central Idea

The next job is to establish a clearly ascertainable organization for your theme. You should look carefully again at your notes and at any ideas they suggest. It may be that some ideas have already come to you, for quite often people decide even before they have finished reading the assigned work that they would like to write on such or such a point. Get these ideas down on paper, for when you can see them in front of you, you can work with them. If you try to keep them only in your mind, you may forget them. Here are some raw thoughts on the subject of the story we have been examining. They represent a stage beyond the first stage of note taking. Each one of the topics could make separate parts of a possible theme.

1. Miss Brill has little human contact except what she imagines.
2. She is lonely and vulnerable.
3. She doesn't have much insight into her life until the end of the story, or else she is self-indulgent.
4. She is no threat to anyone in the park. Therefore the young people who insult her must be at least somewhat unkind if not vicious.

5. The author views Miss Brill with apparent understanding and kindness, but she underplays the ending.

6. If Miss Brill can keep people at a distance, she seems to function fairly well. When they get close, they hurt her.

These are six possible thoughts on the story. Working with these, together with others that may occur as you go along, you should create topics that will serve as the basis for developing the entire theme. Let us say that you choose number 4 as a topic, then number 2, and then number 5. These topics may be entitled: (4) harmlessness, (2) loneliness and vulnerability, and (5) artistic treatment. If you arrange these topics in 1, 2, 3 order, you now have the material for a potential thesis sentence and an outline.

## The Thesis Sentence

A thesis sentence is like an itinerary of a journey, a plan of action. Just as few people would ever think of taking a trip before planning a route, so you should never start to write before having a clear notion of the topics you will consider. The thesis sentence does just that; it connects the central idea and the plan of topics. The first thing to do, then, is to put the central idea together with the topics, in order to plan the form of the thesis sentence. Again, let us use the materials that have been developed thus far:

| CENTRAL IDEA | TOPICS |
|---|---|
| Miss Brill is worth my sympathy. | 1. harmlessness |
| | 2. loneliness and vulnerability |
| | 3. artistic treatment |

From this arrangement we can now write the following thesis sentence:

My feeling of her worthiness results from her harmlessness, from her loneliness and vulnerability, and from Katherine Mansfield's skillful treatment of her plight.

## The Topic Sentence

Just as the entire theme is to be organized around the thesis sentence, each of the paragraphs should be organized around a topic sentence. The topic sentences are derived, grammatically speaking, from the topics in the predicate of the thesis sentence. Thus, the first topic will be Miss Brill's harmlessness. But something more must be done than just announcing the topic; the topic must be shown to have a bearing on the central idea. Let us suppose that the original raw thought can be brought back into consideration here, so that we can create the following topic sentence:

> Her harmlessness [topic] makes the hurt done to her seem unjustified and unnecessarily cruel [connecting topic to central idea].

Notice that the words "unjustified" and "unnecessarily" indicate a judgment by you the writer which is related to your conclusion that Miss Brill is worthy of your sympathy. With such a judgment you could then write a paragraph in which you might develop an argument like this one: "Unjustified and unnecessary hurt done to anyone makes me defensive and sympathetic to the person receiving the hurt." In such a way the topic sentence eventually enables you to expand upon the central idea, and at the same time it channels your thoughts into a development related to the central idea.

You should follow the same process in forming the other topic sentences, so that when you finish them you can put them together in the form of an outline. The particular type of outline that we have been developing here is the "analytical sentence outline." This type requires (1) that the central idea be modified so that it can be used in the grammatical subject of the thesis sentence, (2) that the topics in the predicate of the thesis sentence become the subjects of the topic sentences, and (3) that the predicates of the topic sentences have a clear bearing on the central idea. Such a plan will ensure that you are always thinking within a clear, definite pattern of organization.

As an optional final part of the outline, there may be a concluding or summarizing sentence, which should generally govern the conclusion of your paper. Because this sentence is not derived from the predicate of the thesis sentence, it is technically independent of the material to be included in the body of your theme. But it is a part of the thematic organization, and hence should bear a close relationship to the central idea. It may represent a summary of some of the leading ideas; it may suggest an evaluation or a criticism of some of these ideas; it may also suggest further avenues of exploration that you did not examine in the body of the theme.

As you plan your outline and start to write, bear in mind that writing is in many ways a process of discovery. New ideas often come as you write. If these ideas do not conform to your original plan, change the plan to accommodate them.

When completed, the analytical sentence outline should have the following appearance:

THEME:     ***Miss Brill as a Sympathetic Character***

Paragraph 1     INTRODUCTION containing CENTRAL IDEA and THESIS SENTENCE

CENTRAL IDEA:   Miss Brill is worth my sympathy.

THESIS SENTENCE:   My feeling of her worthiness results from her harmlessness, from her loneliness and vulnerability, and from Katherine Mansfield's skillful treatment of her plight.

BODY containing three TOPIC SENTENCES

Paragraph 2     TOPIC SENTENCE:   Her harmlessness makes the hurt done to her seem unjustified and unnecessarily cruel.

Paragraph 3     TOPIC SENTENCE:   Her loneliness and vulnerability make her pitiable.

Paragraph 4     TOPIC SENTENCE:   Katherine Mansfield's skillful treatment of Miss Brill's plight encourages the right proportion of sympathy.

CONCLUSION

Paragraph 5     TOPIC SENTENCE:   Sympathy for Miss Brill is the dominant effect of the story.

By the time you have created an outline like this one, you will have been thinking and organizing for a considerable time, and you should be well prepared to write your theme. The outline should now be put into operation. In your introduction you should include both the central idea and the thesis sentence. The various topic sentences will belong at the beginnings of the paragraphs in the body of your theme.[1] You may, of course, use the sentences just as they are, or you may, as you become more experienced as a writer, wish to modify them to make them seem less obvious. "It is the purpose of art," said one very wise person, "to hide art." If the machinery of your themes is creaky at first, your experience and development may eventually oil it and allow it to run smoothly and noiselessly.

## The Sample Theme

So that you may see more clearly the relationship of the outline and the theme, the following theme is based on the material we have been discussing. It is drawn mainly from the ideas contained in the

[1]For illustrative purposes, in all the sample themes in this book the central ideas and thesis sentences are in italics and are identified by an asterisk or a dagger. Topic sentences are italicized in the sample themes for Chapters 2–8.

notes, and is wholly dependent for its structure on the analytical sentence outline.

### Miss Brill as a Sympathetic Character

[1] To raise the question of whether Miss Brill, of Katherine Mansfield's story "Miss Brill," is sympathetic is to imply that there are reasons for which a reader may be put off by her. There are a number of reasons. Objectively, Miss Brill is an odd person, one of the many scarecrows sitting on the park benches. She is not communicative; she does not lead an exciting or interesting life; she is simple and almost verges on stupidity; and finally, she is self-indulgent to the point of being almost unconnected with reality. Despite these bad qualities, *Miss Brill is worthy of sympathy.** *My feeling results from her harmless character, from her loneliness and vulnerability, and from Miss Mansfield's skillful treatment of her plight.†*

\*Central idea
†Thesis sentence

[2] *Miss Brill's harmlessness makes the hurt done to her by the young couple seem unjustified and unnecessarily cruel.* Her manner, her thoughts, and her activities all make a person feel that she is to be let alone and tolerated, but never to be harmed. If she eavesdrops on people in the park, the simple solution would be for the offended people to move to another bench, perhaps with a glare on their faces but with no other expression of anger toward her. She does not mistreat anyone, or lure any small children to their destruction. Nor could she do so. In view of these facts, the hurt done her by the young couple is far beyond anything she deserves. It seems almost calculated to hurt her in the worst possible way. Even if people did not like Miss Brill, their hearts would have to go out to her as a result of the insult. Mine does.

Topic sentence

[3] *She is, then, no threat to anyone, and she is made to seem even pitiable because of her loneliness and vulnerability.* The thought of this lone creature imagining herself part of the park scene, and almost believing that everyone in the park will join the band in singing, makes one realize just how solitary she is. She has almost nothing. The best one could claim for her, even by stretching the imagination, is that she is a nobody. She has no one, and no one cares. All of her joy, pathetic as it is, hangs from the very thin thread of her imagination. With only that, she is defenseless and alone, like a hurt bird. There can be no delight, but only sorrow, when the defenseless are destroyed.

Topic sentence

[4] *This is not to say that the story is a sentimental one, for Katherine Mansfield's skillful treatment of Miss Brill's plight encourages exactly the right proportion of sympathy.* Particularly crucial in this regard is the treatment of Miss Brill when she returns home after the insults. She does not buy her honeycake, but rushes home. As she puts away her fur she is crying, but Katherine Mansfield does not overdo her tears. Instead she makes the reader figure out what is happen-

ing. This brief moment, when the reader ponders just whom Miss Brill hears crying, is enough to keep everything from going overboard. Also, the story ends abruptly at this point, with the reader being left to imagine the life that Miss Brill will have afterward, with no more of the joys she had experienced before the insults. There is no indulgence, but there is great sympathy here.

[5] Sympathy, rather than deep sorrow, is the major effect of the story. Miss Brill is shown realistically as a person of solitude and harmlessness. Her faults are at worst those of an eccentric, and her happiness is marginal and fleeting. If people have many things and lose one of them, the loss causes little sympathy or grief. But if they have only one thing, and that is taken from them, as joy is stolen from Miss Brill, then those people have nothing. Is Miss Brill worthy of sympathy? She most certainly is.

## Main Problem in Writing

Once you have understood and applied the principles of thematic development and thesis-sentence organization, you will still be faced with the problem of how to write well. There is little difficulty in recognizing superior examples of student writing when you see them, but there is usually much difficulty in understanding precisely what constitutes the superiority. For this reason the most difficult and perplexing questions you will ask as you write are these: (1) "How can I improve my writing?" or (2) "If I got a C on my last paper, why wasn't the grade a B or an A? How can I improve my grades?" These questions are really both the same, with a different emphasis. Your concern is with improvement.

As a high school student, you should not be offended if you are told that you probably have not yet acquired a great deal of knowledge and understanding of literature. Your mind is growing, and it still has many facts to assimilate and digest. As you accumulate these facts and develop your understanding, you will find that ease of expression will also develop. But at the moment your thoughts about literature might be expressed thus: "When I first read a work, I have a hard time following it. Yet when my teacher explains it, my understanding is greatly increased. I would like to develop the ability to understand the work without my teacher's help. How can I succeed in this aim? How can I become an independent reader?"

In answer, you can start trying to overcome this problem the day you start your English class, provided you have a sincere desire to improve. Bear in mind also that education is a process, and that what baffled you in junior high school may seem child's play when you are in high school. But in the meantime you want to know how to assist growth. There is no magic answer, no shortcut to knowledge. You must work constantly to develop the habits of the good reader described earlier.

The second major obstacle to writing well is inexperience. As a result, when you start you may be tempted simply to retell a story or do no more than list the ideas in an argument. Even when you begin with specific approaches, you may wind up retelling the story. This is really the path of least resistance, but it is inadequate for most of your themes.

Your education is aimed first at acquiring knowledge and second at digesting and using knowledge. Retelling a story indicates only that you have read the material. To show your understanding of it, you must also show that you can put what you have read into a meaningful pattern.

The theme assignments in this book are designed to help you do just that. As you work out each assignment, you will be dealing with particular methods of assimilating and using knowledge. In only one assignment are you asked to retell a story or rephrase factual material; this is the *précis theme* (Chapter 1), and even here at least one purpose is to establish in your mind the distinction between retelling a story and carrying out the analysis necessary for a theme. In all the other assignments you are asked to concentrate on a particular point raised in the study of literature. In every case it is important that you read and follow the work, but it is more important that you show you understand the work.

There are a number of ways in which you may set up patterns of development that can assist you in showing your understanding. One way is to make a deliberate point of referring to events or statements in the work in a reverse order. Talk about the conclusion or the middle of the work first. But rarely should you refer first to the opening of the work. Beginning your discussion with references to parts of the work other than the opening will almost force you to discuss your understanding of the work rather than to retell events. If you look back at paragraph 2 of the sample theme on "Miss Brill," you will see that this technique has been used. One of the last events in the story, Miss Brill's being insulted by a young couple, is the main reference material of that paragraph, yet the paragraph is the first in the body of the theme. You can see that this technique permits you to impose your own organization on your theme and frees you from the organization of the work being analyzed.

Another important method is to consider the reader for whom you are writing your theme. Imagine that you are writing to other students like yourself, students who have read the assigned work but who have not thought very much about it. You can immediately see what you would write for such mythical readers. They know the events or have followed the thread of the argument. They know who says what and when it is said. As a result, you do not need to tell these readers about everything that goes on, but should regard your role as that of an explainer or interpreter. Tell them what things mean, but *do not tell them the things that happen.*

To look at the situation in still another way, you may have read stories and novels about Sherlock Holmes and Dr. Watson. Holmes always points out to Watson that all the facts are available to both of them, but that, though Watson sees, he does not observe. Your role is like that of Holmes, explaining and interpreting facts, and drawing conclusions that Dr. Watson has been unable to draw for himself. Once again, if you look back at the sample theme on "Miss Brill," you will notice that everywhere *the assumption has been made that the reader has read the story already.* References to the story are thus made primarily to remind the reader of something he or she already knows, but *the principal emphasis of the theme is to draw conclusions and develop arguments.*

### Using Literary Material as Evidence

The analogy with Sherlock Holmes should remind you that whenever you write, on any topic, you are in a position much like that of a detective using clues as evidence for building up a case, and also like that of a lawyer using evidence as support for arguments. If you argue in favor of securing a greater voice for students in school government, for example, you would introduce evidence in support of your claims, such as past successes with student government, increased maturity of modern-day students, important contributions students have made to the school, and so on. Writing about literature requires evidence as well. *For practical purposes only,* when you are writing a theme, you may conveniently regard the work assigned as evidence for your arguments. You should make references to the work not for their own sakes but as a part of the logical development of your discourse. Your objective is to persuade your reader of your own knowledge and reasonableness, just as lawyers attempt to persuade juries of the reasonableness of their arguments.

The whole question of the use of evidence is a far-reaching one. Students of law spend years studying proper uses of evidence. Logicians have devised the system of syllogisms and inductive reasoning to regulate the use of evidence. It would not be logical, for example, to conclude from Shakespeare's play *Macbeth* that Macbeth behaves like a true friend and great king. His murders, his rages, and his pangs of guilty conscience form evidence that makes this conclusion absurd. A more difficult problem in evidence concerns Hamlet, one of the most universally admired of Shakespeare's characters. At the end of the play, after Hamlet has died, it is claimed that he would have made a great king had he inherited the throne of Denmark. But even here there is evidence that has been used as a counter-claim: some critics have asserted that Hamlet is too introspective, too hesitant, to have carried out the action necessary for being a great king. But other critics have pointed out specific instances in which Hamlet does act, and have cited other evidence to explain why he hesitates. How should the apparently contradictory evidence be reconciled? As yet, there is no consensus on this question.

To see how evidence may be used as part of a theme, let us refer once again to the sample theme on "Miss Brill." The fourth paragraph is about how Katherine Mansfield's artistic skill keeps a balance in the reader's sympathy for Miss Brill. The writer uses the conclusion of the story as the main evidence in his argument. The event at the conclusion is this: Miss Brill returns to her room and thinks she hears "something crying," but the reader immediately perceives that Miss Brill herself is the one crying. Notice again how the paragraph from the sample theme uses this rather simple and brief episode as evidence. It is clear that the writer's argument is more important to him than a description of the episode. In this sense, the literary work has become evidence for argument.

It is vital to use evidence properly if you wish your reader to follow your ideas. Let us look briefly at two examples to see how writing can be made better if the writer truly considers the needs of the reader. These examples are from themes analyzing Thomas Hardy's story "The Three Strangers."

1

After a short lapse of time, the second stranger enters to seek shelter from the rain. He is a rather full-fleshed man dressed in gray, with signs on his face of drinking too much. He tells the guests that he is en route to Casterbridge. He likes to drink, exhausting the large mug full of mead that is offered to him, and quickly demanding more, which makes Shepherd Fennel's wife extremely angry. With the mead going to his head and making him drunk, he relates his occupation by singing a song in the form of a riddle. This second stranger is a hangman who is supposed to hang a man in Casterbridge for stealing a sheep. As he reveals his occupation, stanza by stanza, an increasing air of dismay is cast over the guests. They are horri-

2

Hardy uses the second stranger — the hangman — to produce sympathy for the shepherds and distrust of the law. By giving the hangman a selfish thirst for mead, which drains some of the Fennels's meager supply, Hardy justifies Mrs. Fennel's anger and anxiety. An even greater cause for anxiety than this personal arrogance is the harsh legal oppression that the hangman represents to the shepherds. Indeed, the shepherds were already sympathetic to the plight of Summers, the first stranger (whose crime seems rewardable, not punishable), but the domineering manner of the hangman clearly makes them go beyond just sympathy. They silently decide to oppose the law by hiding Summers. Hardy thus makes their obstructionism during the later

fied by the hangman's description of his job, but he makes a big joke about all the grim details, such as making a mark on the necks of his "customers" and sending them to a "far countree."

manhunt seem right and reasonable. Perhaps he has stacked the deck against the law here, but he does so to make the reader admire the shepherd folk. In this plan, the hangman's obnoxiousness is essential.

Although the first example has more words than the second (174 words in column 1, 151 in column 2), it is not adequate, for it shows that the writer felt only the obligation to retell the story. The paragraph is cluttered with details and it contains no conclusions and no observations. If you had read the story, the paragraph would not provide you with a single piece of new information, and absolutely no help at all in understanding the story. The writer did not have to think much in order to write the paragraph. On the other hand, the second column is responsive to the reader's needs, and it required a good deal of thought to write. Phrases like "Hardy thus makes" and "In this plan" show that the writer of the second theme has assumed that the reader knows the details of the story and now wants help in interpretation. Column 2 therefore leads readers into a pattern of thought that may not have occurred to them when they were reading the story. In effect, column 2 brings evidence to bear on a point and excludes all irrelevant details; column 1 provides nothing more than raw, undirected evidence.

The answer to that difficult question about how to turn *C* writing into *A* writing is to be found in the comparison of the two columns. Besides using English correctly, superior writers always allow their minds to play upon the materials. They always try to give their readers the results of their thoughts. They dare to thrust their responses and are not afraid to make judgments about the literary work they are considering. Their principal aim in referring to events in a work is to develop their own thematic pattern. Observe this quality again by comparing two sentences which deal with the same details from the story:

1

He likes to drink, exhausting the large mug full of mead that is offered to him, and quickly demanding more, which makes Shepherd Fennel's wife extremely angry.

2

By giving the hangman a selfish thirst for mead, which drains some of the Fennels's meager supply, Hardy justifies Mrs. Fennel's anger and anxiety.

Sentence 1 is detailed but no more. Sentence 2 links the details as a pattern of cause and effect within the author's artistic purpose. Notice the words "By giving" and "Hardy justifies." These indicate the writer's *use* of the facts to which he is referring. There are many qualities in good writing, but perhaps the most important is the way in which the writer uses known facts as evidence in a pattern of thought that is original. Always try to achieve this quality in all your writing about literature.

**Keeping to Your Point**

Whenever you write a theme about literature, then, you must pay great attention to the proper organization and to the proper use of references to the work assigned. As you write, you should try constantly to keep your material unified, for should you go off on a tangent, you are following the material rather than leading it. It is all too easy to start with your point but then wander off into a retelling of events or ideas. Once again, resist the tendency to be a narrator rather than an interpreter.

Let us look at another example. The following paragraph is taken from a theme on the "Idea of Personal Responsibility in Homer's *The Odyssey*." This is the third paragraph; the writer has stated his thematic purposes in the first paragraph, and in the second has shown that various characters in *The Odyssey* believe that people are responsible for their actions and must bear the consequences. In the third paragraph he writes:

> More forcefully significant than these statements of the idea is the way it is demonstrated in the actions of the characters in the epic. Odysseus, the hero, is the prime example. Entrapped by Polyphemus (the son of Poseidon the Earth-Shaker by the nymph Thoosa) and threatened with death, Odysseus in desperation puts out the eye of his captor, who then begs his father Poseidon for vengeance. Answering his son's anguished curse, Poseidon frustrates Odysseus at every turn in the voyage back to Ithaca, and forces him to wander for ten years before reaching home.

This paragraph shows how easily people may be diverted from their objective in writing. The first sentence adequately states that the idea is to be demonstrated in the actions of the epic. That the remainder of the paragraph concentrates on Odysseus is no flaw, because the writer concentrates on other characters in following paragraphs. The flaw is that the material about Odysseus does not go beyond the story itself; it does not come to grips with the announced topic of personal responsibility; it does not indicate understanding. The material may be relevant to the topic, but the writer does not point out its relevance. Remember always that in expository writing you should not rely on making your meaning clear simply by implication; you must make all relationships explicitly clear.

Let us see how this problem can be solved. If the ideal paragraph could be schematized with line drawings, we might say that the paragraph's topic should be a straight line, moving toward and reaching a specific goal (explicit meaning), with an exemplifying line moving away from the straight line briefly in order to bring in evidence, but returning to the line after each new fact in order to demonstrate the relevance of this fact. Thus, the ideal scheme would look like this:

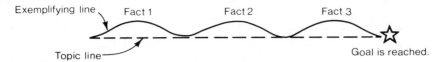

Exemplifying line    Fact 1            Fact 2            Fact 3

Topic line                                           Goal is reached.

Notice that the exemplifying line, or the example or the documenting line, always returns to the topic line. A scheme for the above paragraph on *The Odyssey*, however, would look like this:

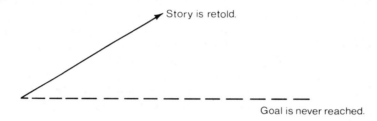

Story is retold.

Goal is never reached.

How might this paragraph be improved? The best way is to reintroduce the topic again and again throughout the paragraph to keep reminding the reader of the relevance of the exemplifying material. Each time you mention the topic you are bringing yourself back to the line, and this practice should prevail no matter what the topic. If you are analyzing *tone*, for example, you should keep pointing out the relevance of your material to the tone of the work, and the same applies to *structure* or whatever aspect of literature you are studying. According to this principle, we might revise the paragraph on *The Odyssey* as follows, keeping as much of the original wording as we can. (Parts of sentences stressing the relationship of the examples to the topic of the paragraph are italicized.)

> More forcefully significant than these statements of the idea is the way it is demonstrated in the actions of the characters in the epic. Odysseus, the hero, is the prime example. When he is entrapped and threatened with death by Polyphemus (the son of Poseidon the Earth-Shaker by the nymph Thoosa), Odysseus in desperation puts out the eye of his captor. Though his action is justifiable on grounds of self-preservation *he must, according to the main idea, suffer the consequences.* Polyphemus begs his father Poseidon for vengeance. Poseidon hears, *and accordingly this god becomes the means of enforcing Odysseus' punishment,* since Odysseus, in injuring the god's son, has insulted the god. The Ithacan king's ten years of frustration and exile are therefore not caused by whimsy; *they are punishment for his own action. Here the idea of personal responsibility is shown with a vengeance;* despite the extenuating circumstances, *the epic makes clear that characters must answer for their acts.*

The paragraph has been lengthened and improved. You might object that if all your paragraphs were lengthened in this way your theme would grow too long. The answer to this objection is that it is better to develop a few topics fully than many scantily. Such revision might require you to throw away some of your topics or else to incorporate them as subpoints in the topics you keep. This process can only improve your theme. But the result of greater length here is that the exemplifying detail points toward the topic, and the paragraph reaches its goal.

The same need for sticking to your point is true of your entire theme, for you will not be successful unless you have thoroughly convinced your reader that your central idea is valid. The two following themes should illustrate this truth. The theme on the left is only rudimentary. The writer suggests at the outset that he will explore the harm the parents cause their children in the two plays being compared. Although occasionally he gets back to this point, the theme rarely gets above the level of synopsis. The theme in the right-hand column is superior because the writer announces his central idea and pursues it throughout. As in the earlier paragraph, those parts of the following themes that emphasize the central idea will be italicized. The type of theme is *comparison-contrast* (Chapter 10), and the assignment was made specifically on Arthur Miller's *All My Sons* and Tennessee Williams's *The Glass Menagerie*.

| THEME 1 | THEME 2 |
|---|---|
| A Comparison of Two Plays | The Destruction of Children by Parents in Two Plays |
| Miller's *All My Sons* and Williams's *The Glass Menagerie* are the two plays being compared. Both plays have the family as the center around which the characters revolve. In both families, *the parents hurt the children.* Miller writes of a well-off, factory-owning family; Williams of a low-class family. | In both Miller's *All My Sons* and Williams's *The Glass Menagerie,* the family is the center of the action. Miller's family is well off; Williams's is lower class. This difference is not material in view of the fact that both dramatists demonstrate the *destructive effects of parents upon children,* regardless of class. It is true that these parents were once children themselves, and that presumably they were recipients of *equally destructive effects from their parents.* This element gives both plays direct, universal appeal: that is, both plays dramatize the process by which our society is *generally hurt by what,* to the dramatists, *are outmoded economic and social values, transmitted by parents to children.* The fathers, mothers, and children will be discussed in that order. |

The comparison of the families may start with the fathers. Joe Keller of *All My Sons* is an ambitious, conniving, and good businessman. He allows a defective shipment to go through because, as he says, he could not let forty years' work go down the drain. He also says to Chris that he did what he did because he wanted Chris to have something for his future, a business. Not much is mentioned of the father in *The Glass Menagerie*, but from what is given the reader, we picture him as a worthless drunkard. He had no purpose in life and consequently was a poor provider for his family. One should not condone Keller for what he did, but at least Keller had some initiative and foresight whereas the Wingfield father had nothing. *Both fathers hurt their children.*

Next we can compare the mothers in the two works. In Miller's play the mother is a sensitive, unyielding, and loving person. It is she who stands firm in her belief that Larry is still living. By doing this she prevents her other son Chris from marrying Ann. In a sense, she is looking out for her son's interest because if Larry was ever to return, chaos would result. Amanda, the mother of *The Glass Menagerie*, is a very sociable person. Her daughter is unbelievably shy. The mother attempts to help her daughter. She does, also, what she thinks will be in the interests of her daughter. Therefore she concludes that marriage is the answer to Laura's problems. We can see how two different mothers with the same goals—

The fathers in both plays seem to be the ones *first to do hurt*, because they both lack responsibility and social conscience. Joe Keller is shown as ambitious and conniving—qualities which in America go to form the good businessman. The Wingfield father, never seen except in portrait but only described, is a drifter and worthless drunkard. *Both are irresponsible. Joe's unscrupulousness causes the death of twenty-one boys who flew in airplanes made defective by his deliberate negligence.* The Wingfield father simply *abandons his family.* The trouble is that both characters are simply pawns in a game much larger than themselves. Joe's defense of his action, for example, makes good sense. *His motives are not bad* from a short-term point of view. He really did not want to let forty years of work go down the drain, and he really did want to give Chris (and Larry) a thriving business. His means, however, *were selfish and hurtful—primarily economic rather than human and loving*—just as the Wingfield father causes his family *untold damage* by abandoning them for a life that to many might seem very pleasant.

While less *creators of hurt* than *agents of it*, the mothers in both families also *cause much damage*. Kate Keller, while sensitive and unyielding, is nevertheless loving. Her firm belief that her son Larry is still alive is caused, we ultimately learn, by a defense against her awareness of *Joe's great crime*, but *the end result is the unhappiness of her son Chris.* Her love is mixed with a *deliberately unreal outlook*. While superficially different from Kate, *Amanda is similarly destructive.* Attempting to look out for the interests of her daughter, she tries to make a carbon copy of herself, even though her background is dead as far as her daughter is concerned. Her failure is that she does not see her daughter as an individual happiness for their children — *achieve the opposite results because they fail to attend to the needs and desires of their children.*

Lastly, the children will be compared. Chris is both an idealistic as well as realistic person. He tries to think the best of people, as he does with his father. When he finds out otherwise, he *is terribly shocked and disappointed.* Much the same thing happens when Laura finds out that Jim is going to get married; her reaction is one of *disappointment and withdrawal.* Just when she has finally gotten socially involved with someone, he leaves. So we see how both children have to put up with *disappointments;* one finds out his father is a murderer, while the other loses the first person she ever loved.

Through comparing and contrasting the members of each family we have been able to see how these families are different and how they are similar. In both *families, however, the children are hurt by well-intentioned* but foolish parents.

with separate and distinct needs. Laura's reaction to her mother's manipulation is *withdrawal,* but Amanda cannot see any *harmful effect.* Both mothers, desiring to make their children happy, *produce the same unhappy results.*

The full effects of *these destructive parents are felt by the children.* Larry, we learn, *has killed himself because of shame for his father's deed.* Chris, we see demonstrated, *is shocked, angered, and embittered by it.* Laura is disappointed, ostensibly by hearing that Jim is going to marry another, but ultimately by having been brought up *without a father and with her mentally disjointed mother.* Tom simply leaves, but he remembers his mother objectively and his father condescendingly. *While a bang marks the destruction* in *All My Sons,* one might say that a sigh — or a whimper — marks it in *The Glass Menagerie.* But the effects of the parents on the children, and beyond that of the society on its members, are the same — *destruction and decay.*

Comparing and contrasting the two families in this way finally brings out their basic similarities. The parents in both families are interesting and not particularly abnormal. In both groups of parents there are strongly contrasting values which contend to *the destruction of children.* In the Kellers it is *money against humanity.* In the Wingfields it is *social position against individuality.* In both families *everyone really loses,* because neither family is clearly enough committed to the idea of humanity and individuality. Though the relevance of this theme to society at large has been only mentioned, the implication in both plays is that our society must make a commitment to human and individual values if it is to survive. If people do not make this commitment, *the destructive patterns in the Keller and Wingfield families will continue.*

There is another reason why the theme on the right is superior. In addition to sticking to the point, the writer in a number of spots suggests that the harmful influences of the parents are related to impractical or unjust economic values. At the end, the writer interprets his central idea by stating that society at large needs to commit itself to human values. In short, *the writer has made his idea grow.* He has not simply exemplified it but has tried to delve into some of its implications. You should be trying, always, to develop your central ideas in a similar way. Admittedly, in a short theme you will be able to move only a short distance with an idea, but you should never be satisfied to leave an idea exactly where you find it. Nurture it and make it grow. Constantly adhere to your topic and constantly develop it.

### Using Accurate and Forceful Language

The best writing has a quality of accuracy, force, and insight. Quite often the first products of our minds are rather weak, and they need to be rethought, recast, and reworded. Sometimes this process cannot be carried out immediately, for it may take days or even weeks for us to gain objectivity about what we say. As a student you usually do not have that kind of time, and thus you must acquire the habit of challenging your own statements almost as soon as you write them. Ask yourself whether they really mean what you want, or if you can make a stronger statement than you have.

As an example, consider the following statement, a central idea about E. M. Forster's short story "The Machine Stops," an allegory about a future world in which people are completely dependent on machinery but perish when the machinery breaks down.

> The central idea of this story is that because of the machine and its marvelous powers, the people place their total dependence on it.

This central idea could not carry you very far if you were writing a theme based on it. But try to restate and strengthen the essential material in the sentence. Two possibilities are as follows:

1. Forster shows that human beings, by accepting the machine and by becoming hostile to Nature, have alienated themselves from their environment and are therefore responsible for their own destruction.

2. Forster shows that the pursuit of ideas and technology to the exclusion of Nature has led human beings to destroy themselves.

Either of these two sentences would be more helpful as a statement of a central idea than the first example.

It is also true that sometimes, in seeking to say something, we wind up saying nothing. Here are two sentences from themes about Robert Frost's "Stopping by Woods on a Snowy Evening."

1. It seems as though the author's anticipation of meeting with death causes him to respond as he does in the poem.

2. This incident, although it may seem trivial or unimportant, has substantial significance in the creation of his poem; by this I mean the incident which occurred is essentially what the poem is all about.

The vagueness of sentences like these must be resisted. A sentence should not end up in limbo the way these do. The first sentence is satisfactory enough up to the verb, but then it falls apart. If Frost has created a response for the speaker in the poem, it is best to describe *what* that response is rather than to state simply that there *is* a response. A more forceful restatement of the first sentence may thus be, "It seems as though the author's anticipation of meeting with death causes him to think about the need to meet his present responsibilities." With this revision, the writer could go on to a consideration of the meaning of Frost's final stanza and could relate the ideas there to the events and ideas described in the first part of the poem. Without the revision, it is not clear where the writer would go.

The second sentence is so vague that it confuses rather than informs. Essentially, such sentences hint at an idea and claim importance for it, but they never directly define what that idea is. If we adopt the principle that it is always better to name the specific things we are talking about, perhaps the second sentence could be revised as follows:

Although stopping by the woods to watch the snow fall may seem trivial or insignificant, the incident causes the poet to meditate on beauty and responsibility; the important thoughts in the poem thus grow from the simplest of events.

When you write your own sentences, you might test them in a similar way. Are you referring to an idea? State the idea directly. Are you mentioning a response or impression? Do not say simply, "The poem left me with a definite impression," but describe the impression: "The poem left me with an impression of sympathy," or "of understanding of the hard lot of the migrant farmer." Similarly, do not rest with a statement such as "I found this story interesting," but try to describe what was interesting and why it was interesting. If you always confront your impressions and responses by trying to name them and to pin them down, your sentences should take on exactness and force. Naturally, your teacher will probably tell you whatever you have accomplished or failed to accomplish. Good writing habits that you develop from these criticisms of your work, and from discussions with your teacher, will help you to write more forcefully and accurately.

Whenever you write a theme, then, keep these ideas in mind. Keep returning to the point you wish to make; regard the material of the work you have read as evidence to substantiate your arguments, not as material to be described. Keep demonstrating that all exemplifying detail is relevant to your main point. Keep trying to develop your topic; make it bigger than it was when you began writing. Constantly keep trying to make your statements accurate and forceful. If you observe these precepts, you should be well on the way toward handling any of the following theme assignments successfully.

# 1

# *The Précis, or Abstract*

A PRÉCIS is a shortening, in your own words, of the text of a written work. In writing a précis you describe, as accurately as possible, what happens in a story or play, or you briefly restate, abridge, digest, or encapsulate the substance or main ideas in an essay, article, or poem. Other words that describe the précis or abstract are *paraphrase, condensation,* and *epitome.* All these words suggest a shortening or a highlighting of only the most significant details and sections of a work.

The length of your précis depends on the extent of the original work and the approximate length of your assignment. Thus, a 3,000-word story might be condensed into 100 or 1,000 words. The amount of detail to include naturally depends on the desired length of the précis. The 1,000-word précis would contain much detail, whereas the 100-word précis would not contain much more than the main headings.

## Uses of the Précis

The précis is important in the service of study, research, and speaking and writing. One of the best ways to study any work is to write a précis of it, for by so doing you force yourself to grasp each of the various parts. Also, referring to your précis later helps to bring the entire work back to your memory. There are few better ways to study any subject.

When you do research, you must take notes on the material you find. Here the ability to shorten and paraphrase is essential, for it is impossible to reproduce everything in your notes. The better you are able to write a précis, the better and more efficient will be your research.

In discussions, you will improve your arguments if you refer briefly but accurately to sections of the work being discussed. When you are writing a theme, particularly a longer one, it is often necessary to remind your reader of the events or facts in the work. Here the need is not to tell *everything*, but just enough of the significant material so that your conclusions will be self-sustaining. In an argumentative or persuasive speech or theme, when you are trying to convince your listener or reader of the validity of your conclusions, it is necessary to get the facts straight in order to eliminate objections that may arise about your use of detail.

For all these occasions you will profit from being able to paraphrase or abstract written material. Although you will sometimes need to condense an entire story or epitomize an entire argument, most often you will need to refer only to parts of works, because your arguments will depend on a number of separate interpretations. No matter what your future needs are, however, your ability to write a précis will be constantly helpful to you.

## Problems in Writing a Précis

1. ACCURACY.   Just as the précis is important in establishing a "handle" on the facts, one of the first problems in writing a précis is to make certain that you get the facts straight. You should make no unwarranted statements. Let us suppose that you are writing about so simple and well-remembered a story as "Hansel and Gretel." Suppose you write that "the children eventually overcome the witch by thrusting her into the oven." This statement is only partially true, and it might possibly lead to unjustifiable conclusions, say about the resourcefulness of the two children. In fact, it is not *both* children who defeat the witch, but Gretel alone, for Hansel is locked up in a cage at the time the witch and Gretel are preparing the oven. If you think only casually about what to write, however, it would be natural to say that "the children" are both agents of victory. It is important to resist such inaccuracies, and you should go over the first draft of your précis carefully to make sure that all you say is factually correct.

2. USING YOUR OWN WORDS.   Another problem is the difficulty you may find in using *your own* words in your précis to replace the words and ideas in the original. Here you may be helped by the need for condensation, for the need to shorten the original can help you find verbal independence. If you get bogged down in looking for your own words, then you may introduce some of the original wording *in your first draft*. Be especially careful, however, to underline, star, or otherwise mark these borrowed words, and then try to make changes by using your own words when you revise for your second draft. If it seems im-

possible to make changes of some words, you may preserve a small number of the originals, but be sure to include them within quotation marks.

3. SELECTING DETAILS.   A third problem is that of determining what details to select. Try to pick out only those details that are of greatest significance. A writer may tell about two people who, in a restaurant, order a wide variety of dishes and engage in lengthy conversation. Obviously, in a précis you do not want to mention each item of food and drink. If one of the characters gets drunk, however, it might be important to state that the character drank too much. Similarly, you would not need to report all the conversation, but only that part which contained the important details, such as that a character was profoundly happy or unhappy. The reporting of detail becomes a critical aspect in the way your précis will be judged. Some things are more important in literary works than others, and you must select details according to this scale of importance.

4. AVOIDING CONCLUSIONS. Surprisingly, a major problem in a précis is the need to avoid making conclusions. In every other kind of writing about literature that you will be called on to do, you will be encouraged to draw conclusions and you will be graded on the quality of these conclusions and on the validity of the arguments you introduce to support them. But in a précis you should resist conclusions. You are trying to get at facts, and the goal is to achieve an accurate and impartial report. The following columns will show the difference between unsuccessful and successful technique:

| THEME A<br>*with* conclusions | THEME B<br>*without* conclusions |
|---|---|
| Gretel fulfills her plan to overcome the witch by pretending ignorance. Thus she confesses her inability to open the door, in this way leading the witch to doom. Angered by Gretel, the witch demonstrates the proper way to open the door. Gretel, having seen the success of her plan, quickly pushes the witch into the fire and rescues Hansel. | Because Gretel states that she is unable to manage the oven, the witch angrily goes to the door and demonstrates the proper way to open it. Gretel then quickly pushes the witch into the fire and rescues Hansel. |

Often, of course, it is necessary to draw general conclusions about details in the work. Let us suppose that your story contains many details which demonstrate that a character is cheerful. It is proper to state generally that the character is cheerful, for you may make that conclusion fairly and it is essential to be as brief and as comprehensive as possible.

But it would be improper here to add your own conclusions, such as that "this cheerfulness shows the character's courage in the face of danger." The conclusion may be the right one, but you should not offer interpretations of this type in a précis.

5. AVOIDING CHOPPY SENTENCES. Although you concentrate on essential details in your précis, you should avoid the temptation to fall into a pattern of short, choppy sentences. Here is an example of what to avoid:

> It is December, just before Christmas. Phoenix Jackson is beginning to walk to Natchez. She is a black woman. She is old but cheerful. She walks with a cane. She has walked this way many times.

Here there are six sentences, all very short and beginning with the subject followed immediately by the verb. Sentences like these are almost impossible to read for an entire paper. A revision should reduce the number of sentences but keep the same details, as in the following:

> Just before Christmas, Phoenix Jackson begins her familiar walk through the country from her home to Natchez. She is a poor and old black woman, who needs a cane for support, but she is cheerful.

**Your Theme**

In your précis you should stick as closely to your work as possible. Bring out details about a character or an argument only as the author brings them out in the work. Thus, in her story "A Worn Path," Eudora Welty reveals in the last page that the main character has gone into town to get medicine for her infirm grandchild. It would be helpful to introduce that detail at the start of the précis, but because the author has included it only at the end of the story, it is proper to bring it in only at the comparable stage of the précis.

If your précis is to be very short, say 100 to 150 words, you might confine everything to only one paragraph. If you have a longer word limit, say from 200 to 500 words, it is good to arrange your paragraphs according to the natural divisions in the original work. Thus, if the work has parts or sections, you might devote a paragraph to each of these divisions. If an undivided story moves from place to place, as in the first sample theme below, you might provide a paragraph for events occurring at each place. Or if the story takes place in only one location, you might use paragraphs to describe (1) the events leading up to the main action, (2) the action itself, and (3) the consequences of the action. If you are writing a précis of an essay or article, you might organize according to the author's main divisions, such as the background of the problem, possible solutions, and consequences. Whether you are writing about fiction, drama, poetry, essay, or article, however, follow the general principle of letting the work itself be your guide about paragraphing.

FIRST SAMPLE THEME (SHORT STORY)

### A Précis of Eudora Welty's "A Worn Path"

[1]    Just before Christmas, Phoenix Jackson begins her familiar walk through the country from her home to Natchez. She is a poor and old black woman, who needs a cane for support, but she is cheerful. She releases herself from a thorny bush, climbs a high hill, and finds her way through areas with no marked path. She is attacked by a large dog, and falls into a ditch, but soon is assisted by a young white hunter, who frightens off the dog. Phoenix sees the man drop a nickel before he chases the dog; she recovers it and hides it. Though the man advises her to go back home, Phoenix resolutely continues on her way toward Natchez.

[2]    As she enters town, she is successful in getting a white lady on the street to tie her shoes, for she states that neatly tied shoes are essential for going to an important building. Almost without thinking about where she is going, she climbs many stairs to find the medical office in the building, and then she sits down there, blankly.

[3]    While an attendant asks her about her business, a nurse enters and reveals to the attendant that Phoenix has come to get medicine for her grandson, who two or three years earlier had drunk lye and is now totally disabled. Phoenix receives the free medicine, and the attendant gives her five pennies. With these, together with the nickel she had recovered earlier, Phoenix states that she will buy a little paper windmill for her grandson. She then leaves the office.

★COMMENTARY ON THE THEME

Though many details from the story must necessarily be eliminated, each paragraph concentrates on the major actions that occur in each of the main locations in the story. The sample theme is about 250 words long, and therefore it is possible to include some of the details about Phoenix when she first reaches Natchez. With a shorter word limit it would be necessary to eliminate these details and instead concentrate on the events in the medical office, for these concluding details are more important than what occurs to Phoenix on the Natchez streets.

The précis is successful as a précis for the foregoing reasons and

In *Thirteen Stories by Eudora Welty*, ed. Ruth M. Vande Kieft (New York: Harcourt, Brace & World, 1965), pp. 59–68.

also because it includes most of the details that in the story itself are the basis for Eudora Welty's portrait of Phoenix. She is cheerful even though she has suffered great sorrow and poverty, and her lot in life will not change. She is dependent, forgetful, kind, and trusting, with a harmless trace of larceny. She is both strong and simple. Eudora Welty uses the events in the story to bring out all these traits, and the précis, by the presentation of the same events, could be used as the basis for such conclusions about the character of Phoenix.

---

SECOND SAMPLE THEME (ARTICLE)

---

### A Précis of Evelyn Shaw's Article, "Fish in Schools"

[1]    Schooling in fish is common. About 4,000 varieties stay in schools during their entire lives, including anchovies, tuna, herring, cod, and striped bass, and 12,000 other species school as young fish. A school may vary in size from two to millions. There are no leaders in a school; those in front find themselves in back when the school changes direction.

[2]    Schooling is instinctive, programmed in the genes of the fish, for fish of the same species seem to recognize each other, and begin schooling without being taught by other fish. In a school, the fish are "polarized"; that is, they move at the same speed, in the same direction, and keep a uniform distance from each other. When the school changes direction or speed, all change together, for the fish try to maintain polarization constantly.

[3]    Fish preserve their schooling formations by sight, smell, and sound, and they also possess a unique sensing system, named the "lateral line," that makes them sensitive to changes in the pressure and the currents of surrounding water. Adult fish maintain a space of half a body length from other fish, a distance at which the "lateral line" apparently works best. Through all these means, fish in a school can respond within a fraction of a second to changes of the entire school. This speed accounts for the apparent immediacy with which the school reacts to changing conditions.

[4]    Fish benefit from schooling. They use less oxygen, tolerate worse water conditions, and learn faster than fish by themselves. They escape predators more readily, and find food more easily than when alone. Schools of prey fish move slowly to avoid predators, while schools of predators swim rapidly to increase sightings of prey. Prey fish in schools confuse predators because they all look alike, and hence there are no apparently weak or slow fish which predators usually select. When for some reason the school is momentarily broken up, the individual members are easy prey until they reshape the school. A final advantage is that school-

*Natural History*, 84, no. 8 (October 1975), 40–46.

ing fish conserve energy because they swim in each other's wake. Thus they have a reserve of strength to handle emergencies.


★COMMENTARY ON THE THEME

This précis, about 350 words long, is successful because it covers the major details in the article. The four paragraphs are devoted to the four major topics treated by the author. These are: (1) commonness and size of schools of fish, (2) descriptions of typical schools, (3) causes for schooling and characteristics of schools, and (4) benefits of schooling for the fish. If you are assigned a précis of a scientific article, try to find the principles by which the article is organized, and devote a paragraph to each of the main topics, as is done here.

# CHAPTER
# 2

# *The Summary Theme*

THE SUMMARY THEME is a step beyond the précis. Like the précis, it concentrates on the details in a work, but unlike the précis, it requires the basic thematic structure of a central idea, a thesis sentence, and topic sentences. Because of these requirements, the summary theme demands that you make judgments about the work you are summarizing. To this degree, you are beginning to write criticism.

This criticism is not just "literary," however; it is characteristic of the mental processes that you must employ in any of your college courses. For example, in a history course you will rarely be requested simply to present a list of facts; you will be required to show how the facts are related to a dominating idea or "tendency" in history. Here is a short paragraph showing how historical details can be placed in the context of an idea; the technique is that of the summary theme:

> The major fault of the British government — and one of the major causes of the Revolutionary War — was not that it imposed taxes, but that it did so without consulting the Colonials. This was true of the Stamp Act, which the British withdrew in 1766 after fierce riots in the colonies. It was also true of the commodities taxes, like those on glass, paint, and tea, which were imposed late in the 1760's. There was a need for these taxes, but the Colonials did not share in the acts which imposed them, and it was resentment over this, rather than taxation itself, which led to the Boston Tea Party in 1773.

Notice here that the major idea — that there was no consultation — controls the presentation of the facts. This idea is stressed throughout the paragraph. The need for relating facts to a dominating thought is a primary characteristic of any good writing. Writing a summary theme thus should provide you with a basic technique you can apply in your other high school courses when extensive writing is required.


## What Do You Summarize?

The summary theme presupposes that you have been able to create a précis of the work assigned, whether it is a story, a play, a longer poem, an essay, or an article. Once you have reached this level, you will be faced with the major problem of organization — that is, of fitting your materials into a pattern. There is much in the work itself that can help you. If your work is fictional or dramatic, you should recognize a distinction between *story* and *plot*. The story is the set of events, details, or speeches in the work as they appear in narrative order or act-by-act sequence. It is the story that you condense as you write a précis. The plot is something more. It is the reasons or the logic underlying the story and causing it to take the form in which it appears. The essence of plot is the existence of a *conflict* between opposing forces — human beings against themselves, against other human beings, or against some natural or supernatural force. The conflict produces those actions and interactions that culminate in a *crisis* or *climax*, in which one person, force, or idea is triumphant.

There is little question, of course, about what happens in the story, since all the events are before you. But there is room for interpretation and subjectivity about the plot, because the reasons why characters do things are not always clear, even to the characters themselves, and also because a particular work of literature may mean many things at once, all equally discoverable in the story.

If you can make a brief description of the plot, however, you can use it as the central idea of your theme. If you were writing about F. Scott Fitzgerald's story "Babylon Revisited," for example, you might take a number of conflicts which could be treated as descriptions of the plot: (1) The past constantly influences the present. (2) Human beings must answer for their acts even though they are driven by uncontrollable forces. (3) Wealth destroys human values and perspectives. Each one of these statements could serve as a satisfactory central idea for a summary theme on the story. If you glance ahead at the first sample theme, you will note that the central idea is stated as a conflict or contrast in the first paragraph:

> Welty shows that Phoenix possesses great personal strength and cheerfulness despite the grimness of her life.

There could of course be other central ideas, for good stories are as complex as life itself. Regardless of what you perceive as the plot, however, the important thing is to use the description of the plot as your own central idea. Do not worry about the "rightness" of your interpretation; just concern yourself with making it the basis for unifying theme.

If you have been assigned a non-narrative work such as an essay or article, you may look for the same sort of help in the work itself. You have, first, the details in the work—similar to the events in a story—and second, the author's central idea, such as "Running for political office is grueling" or "Many poor countries of the world are experiencing a severe shortage of fuel." The author's main idea here is analogous to the plot in a story or play, and you may use it as your own central idea in your summary. Thus, the central idea of the second sample theme is a restatement of the main idea by Carson McCullers in her essay on "Loneliness":

> In her essay "Loneliness . . . An American Malady," Carson McCullers asserts that loneliness—"an involuntary and fearful thing"—is a byproduct of the normal human "quest for identity."

The rest of the theme is a development of this central idea; that is, details in the essay by McCullers are shown to have a direct relationship to this central idea.

## Planning the Theme

The first thing to do is carefully study your notes on the work. Try to determine how the events or details fit into a pattern that you can describe as a central idea. In the famous ancient Greek play *Oedipus the King* by Sophocles, for example, it is possible to determine that the events occur as illustrations of the *pride* of Oedipus. That is, the events are caused by his belief that he was superior to his fate. Thus, he killed a stranger on the road when he knew that he was foredoomed to kill his own father, and he married a widowed queen when he knew that he was fated to marry his own mother. Somehow he believed that he was above these deeds and could avoid them. But he could not, and the ancient play shows how Oedipus learns that he, like everyone else, cannot change his fate. In a theme on this play it would be necessary to show how during most of the action Oedipus tries to avoid this realization, thus preserving for a time, at least, his sense of his own importance—his pride. In this manner, for any work, look at the details carefully and try to find some common denominator that will help you launch your theme.

## Choosing and Limiting Details

You need include only enough detail to bring out your central idea. Let us suppose that you are writing about *Huckleberry Finn* and you establish a central idea that the book is about "the growth of the individual to maturity." You develop the following thesis sentence: "This growth is shown, negatively, by Huck's experiences under the care of the Widow Douglas and, positively, by his trip on a raft with the runaway slave Jim." In developing a theme from this thesis sentence you would not have to include all the details from the early part of the book, but only those that seemed especially foolish or unreasonable to Huck, such as being told by Tom that a Sunday-school picnic was really a meeting of Arabs. Similarly, you would need to include only those incidents on the river which had a positive bearing on Huck's growth; thus you would emphasize details that show his increasing sense of obligation to Jim. You might rightfully claim that there is a great deal in the novel that you would be leaving out. That is exactly the point. You should include in a summary theme only enough detail to substantiate your central idea, and no more. Your job is to write a well-organized theme that will give your readers a sense of what to expect from the work should they start to read it.

## Organizing Your Theme

Usually there will be two parts in a summary theme, the introduction and the summary itself.

### PART I: INTRODUCTION

The introduction identifies the work, the most significant character or characters, and the general situation; it is the place for your central idea and thesis sentence. In the introduction you should also describe the most noticeable physical characteristics of the work — that it is a play, story, essay, article, or novel; that the work is mainly in dialogue, or narration; that the narration of events is accompanied by descriptions of the hero's thoughts; that the story is told by the hero personally; that the description of present events is augmented by reminiscences of past events; that the reader must infer the relationships among the characters; that much of the story is in dialect; that the author relies on the research of others, and so on.

### PART II: THE SUMMARY

The summary itself grows out of your thesis sentence. The development of your theme should follow the form of the work that you are summarizing. That is, you should present the main events as they occur in the story, even if much of the story is related by a flashback method; you should try to recreate the actual movement of the story itself. Remember, however, that what characterizes your theme *as a theme* is your central idea — your general interpretation of the work — and your guiding topic sentences that give unity to each of your paragraphs. Remind yourself constantly as you write that (1) you should closely follow the work you summarize, (2) you should write accurately, precisely, and vividly, and (3) you should use an occasional word, phrase, or passage from the work in order to give your reader a taste of the original.

---

FIRST SAMPLE THEME (SHORT STORY)

---

### A Summary of Eudora Welty's "A Worn Path"

[1]       In "A Worn Path," a story of about 3,500 words, Eudora Welty describes a brief incident in the life of an old but almost timeless black woman, Phoenix Jackson. *Welty shows that Phoenix possesses great personal strength and cheerfulness despite the grimness of her life.\** The story is mostly narrative, with dialogue when characters other than Phoenix appear, and with monologue as Phoenix herself addresses animals, a thornbush, birds, a scarecrow, and herself. *Her spiritual strength and optimism are shown in her walk through the countryside to Natchez, her brief experience on the streets in town, and her meeting with the medical personnel in the office building.†*

[2]       *Her walk to Natchez, by far the longest section of the story, demonstrates Phoenix's strong determination.* Just before Christmas she is walking on a way through the countryside that she obviously knows well. This is the "worn path." She conquers a long hill, extricates herself from a prickly thornbush, balances on a log across a creek, and crawls through a barbed wire fence. Having no one to speak to, she carries on a cheerful monologue with the creatures and objects around her, thus overcoming her loneliness. When she is attacked by a large black dog she falls in a ditch, from which she is pulled by a young white hunter. He is impressed with her single-mindedness and bravery, although he advises her to go back home and stay out of danger. A trace of minor larceny is shown by Phoenix when she steals a nickel the young man had dropped as he left her to scare away the dog which previously had threatened her, but she is honest enough with herself to realize that this "theft" is a violation of her integrity.

[3]       *Once Phoenix reaches Natchez, she has left the danger of the countryside and expects only friendliness on the streets.* She sees a white woman carrying Christmas bundles, and persuades this woman to tie her shoelaces, a task which the woman obligingly performs. Phoenix's confidence in this instance is rewarded.

In *Thirteen Stories by Eudora Welty*, ed. Ruth M. Vande Kieft (New York: Harcourt, Brace & World, 1965), pp. 59–68.

*Central idea.       †Thesis sentence.

[4]      *After Phoenix finds the building that marks her destination, the perspective of the story changes to make plain the grim personal adversity against which she must struggle daily.* This section is written mainly in dialogue between the attendant and the nurse. The nurse has known Phoenix for a long time and reveals to the attendant that Phoenix's grandson had drunk lye two or three years before and is now an incurable invalid whom Phoenix must attend alone. Phoenix had come for a soothing syrup, which the nurse gives her, while the attendant gives her five pennies. Phoenix resolves to buy a paper windmill with her money and to take it to her grandson, and it is on this note of her confidence and resolution that the story ends.

★COMMENTARY ON THE THEME

To clarify the distinction between a summary theme and a précis, this summary theme is about the same story that is discussed in the first sample theme in Chapter 1. The summary theme contains a paragraph of introduction, in which details about the physical appearance of the story are included. The first paragraph also contains a central idea and a thesis sentence. A précis contains none of this material.

The second paragraph begins with a topic sentence about Phoenix's determination, and all the details in the paragraph are related to her character. The paragraph thus shows that she *conquers* a hill, that she *overcomes* loneliness by speaking to her surroundings, that she is *single-minded* in her discussion with the hunter, and even after stealing the nickel, that she is aware of a breach in her *integrity*.

In each of the remaining paragraphs the details are similarly related to positive aspects of Phoenix's character. The theme is therefore unified by means not expected of a précis. A summary theme, like any fully developed theme, will be unsuccessful unless the central idea is emphasized throughout.

SECOND SAMPLE THEME (ESSAY)

*A Summary of "Loneliness . . . An American Malady,"*
*by Carson McCullers*

[1]      *In her essay "Loneliness . . . An American Malady," Carson McCullers asserts that loneliness — "an involuntary and fearful thing" — is a byproduct of*

In *The Conscious Reader,* ed. Caroline Shrodes, Harry Finestone, and Michael Shugrue (New York: The Macmillan Company, 1974), pp. 31–33. Parenthetical page numbers refer to this edition.

*the normal human "quest for identity."** The essay is short, and in it Mc-Cullers deals with general principles. The reading is therefore hard, but it repays careful study. *In developing her ideas, McCullers illustrates that the individual seeks identity both as a person and as part of a group, and she specifically claims that the American quest for identity is a constant and lonely process.*†

[2]     *McCullers devotes more than half of her essay relating loneliness to the individual's desire to seek identity both as a person and as part of a group.* From infancy, babies distinguish the differences between their bodies and "the objects around [them]" (p. 32). Through the resulting consciousness of self, at each stage of development, they are able to find their place in the world, ultimately achieving maturity and a strong sense of individual identity when they are sure of the relationship. Loneliness comes, according to McCullers, when individuals try to place themselves in a group. Failure to do so produces loneliness. With love, however, individuals can merge with the group and overcome loneliness. Love is thus a "bridge that leads from the *I* sense to the *We*" (p. 32). McCullers also shows that the absence of love produces many related bad conditions. Without love people are in fear and will see themselves negatively and defensively. Thus the destructive conditions of "snobbism, intolerance and racial hate" and xenophobia are produced by loneliness (p. 32).

[3]     In the last four paragraphs McCullers deals with the type of American loneliness which she feels results not from fear or xenophobia but rather from traditional American individualism. Although Americans are "an outgoing people," they "tend to seek out things as individuals, alone" (p. 32). To McCullers, this national character trait literally enforces a degree of loneliness in Americans. Two typical Americans she cites are Thoreau and Thomas Wolfe, who confronted "the pastoral joys of country life" and "the labyrinthine city" (p. 33). While completing the first part of their quests for identity, she implies, neither man went the remaining distance to become a *"We"* person. Both men were thus seekers, like most Americans, who today "wander" and "question" while they travel the path toward belonging. But their journey is solitary. On this note, Mc-Cullers ends her discussion of loneliness.

★COMMENTARY ON THE THEME

This summary theme is about an essay, and therefore the factual basis is a set of ideas rather than a narrative, as in the theme on "A Worn Path." The same organizational principles may be seen in the second sample theme, however: The central idea follows Carson McCullers' idea that loneliness is a quest for identity, and each of the paragraphs in the body of the theme is developed on the basis of this idea. Paragraph 2 explains how loneliness is a failure to blend with

---

*Central idea.     †Thesis sentence.

others, and paragraph 3 shows how two American writers—like Americans generally, according to McCullers—have loneliness built into their lives because of national character. The theme thus follows the original essay quite closely while maintaining its own rhetorical coherence.

# *The Report*

THE REPORT is usually assigned in this way: "Write a report or paper about —— (story, novel, poem, play, or other work)." Assignments of this sort are made not only in English classes but in many others, so it is important to have a sense of what is expected in a general book report.

As you begin to think and to write, you should consider the subject of your theme in the following light: your teacher, though having made a general assignment, probably wants to see evidence that (1) you have read and followed the work, (2) you have understood it and can say something intelligent about it, and (3) you have reacted to it in some way and have formed an opinion about it. If your report is otherwise well written, your grade will depend on the success with which you fulfill these three requirements.

## Questions as a Means of Analysis

The report stands at a midpoint between the summary theme and the various sorts of analyses, including evaluation and appreciation. That is, you will need to write a summary that is a quick, thumbnail sketch of a work, while also dealing with the principal objects of writing about literature, namely, analysis and evaluation.

For a report you should be concerned with literary analysis in a general sense only. You do not need to exhaust all the possibilities of a particular analytical approach. In fact, you may be able to make your analysis mainly by answering several major questions. Here are some of them. Do not feel limited by them, but go further and raise some of your own:

1. Did you notice if the author emphasized any particular ideas? To deal with such a question, you must (a) state the idea, (b) show its importance in the work as a whole and describe its relationship to the layout or form of the work, and (c) evaluate the idea; that is, is the idea good, bad, helpful, dangerous, harmless, and so on?

2. Did you notice the form or organization of the work? Describe the various parts and their relationships. Try to explain what you think are the reasons for the relationships.

3. Did the work contain a great deal of dialogue, or narration? Was the dialogue well written? In what way? Did the narration hold your attention? How did it do so? Can you provide any information about particularly interesting passages and supply reasons for the interest?

4. Was the work written to satisfy any specific need or demand at the time it was first published? For example, Walt Whitman's poem "When Lilacs Last in the Dooryard Bloomed" was written in reaction to the assassination of President Lincoln. If you can point to an occasion or demand, try to state whether the writer dealt successfully with the issues faced as a result of the occasion.

5. Can you engage in any other kinds of analysis that will show that you have made an effort to comprehend the work? For example, in poetry it is sometimes helpful to count stanzas, lines, and words, for by determining the positions of things you can also determine developments of ideas and relationships of one part to another. Analyzing or parsing sentences may also yield insights that you did not have when you first read through the work. Studying words to see whether they are vivid or nondescriptive, specific or general, may give you an insight into the author's style.

If you try to write full answers to all these questions, you may find your report becoming too long. Pick and choose. The experience of many students has shown that in a free choice, most students will discuss ideas or "meaning." Perhaps the ideas you choose to discuss may have social importance, or political or personal significance. Whatever the import, always try to focus your attention on the areas in which you feel the ideas have the greatest bearing.

## Organizing Your Theme

You should include the following parts in your report: (1) an introduction, (2) a short summary, (3) an analysis, and (4) your reaction or responses.

### INTRODUCTION

Here you should name the work, the author, and any relevant data about the writing and reception of the work. Be brief on biographical and background information, however, for these matters can easily divert you from talking about the work itself. Begin describing the main characteristics of the work. Is it a novel, an essay, a long poem? Is it written in narrative, dialogue, argument? Does it contain dialect, slang? Is there anything else a general reader should know about it? After dealing with questions like these, move to your central idea and thesis sentence.

### A SHORT SUMMARY

The summary will be evidence that you have read the entire work. Concentrate on a short, succinct summary, not to take up more than about one-fifth of your theme. (This proportion will be smaller in longer reports, in which most of your attention should be devoted to analysis.) Remember that an intelligent summary should be interpretive in a limited way; this one should almost exclusively summarize plot as distinguished from story. If the work you are reporting on is divided into parts, chapters, stanzas, or some other ascertainable divisions, your summary should take these matters into account.

### AN ANALYSIS

Here you analyze the principal meanings and qualities of the work. This section should occupy the largest part of your theme. Since your teacher will likely place greatest weight on the skills you show in this section, you should demonstrate that you have examined the assigned text closely.

You might try to answer many questions like those listed above, or you might deal with only one, depending on the nature of the questions and your interest in them. If you deal with a question about ideas, for example, your analysis might very well be taken up entirely with that question. You may prefer to write on style, structure, and meaning separately. One thing to bear in mind is the general nature of the assignment: if you discuss a main idea, it is wise to show how that idea affects and is affected by the style and structure. You are concerned here with the general techniques of literary analysis. The more specific and detailed techniques will come later. Show that you are a good, alert reader and your book report will have achieved its aim.

You can make this section unnecessarily difficult if you allow yourself to wander. Always remember that a theme, even a report, should have a *thematic development* (see the Introduction, pp. 8–15). Your analysis should therefore be tied to the summary, perhaps by an introductory remark like, "This work's outstanding quality, which my summary cannot show, is the uncanny way Y author's style creates powerful anxiety in the reader. . . ." (Then would follow an analysis of how that effect is created, together with other related matters.) Throughout this analytical section, always make sure that your sentences are relevant to your central idea. All your insights, word counts, and general interpretations will lose effect if they do not cohere to a definite point. In short, your analysis should show continuity and development.

### FINAL SECTION: YOUR RESPONSES

Your theme should conclude with an explanation of your responses to the work (about one-fourth to one-eighth of your theme). Although this may be a short section, it is nevertheless important. Your remarks here should take on greater weight because of your work on the analysis. Your responses should be based on calm, rational thought, not prejudice. (Prejudice is usually the result of unconsidered emotion. It might lead to your rejecting a poem "because I don't like poetry." A considered opinion, on the other hand, is the result of thought; it might result in your criticizing a work because it does not succeed in doing what it tries to do.)

In expressing your responses to the work, you should try to answer questions like these: How did the literary work affect you? Did you feel satisfied, complete, happy, after reading it? Did you think that the work was good? Bad? Did you feel that the author should have done something more? What? This section is the place for your personal thoughts and reactions. Do not be afraid to speak your mind — provided you have a sound basis in ideas from the text. If the particular work did not interest you, it is your duty to say so, but try to assess the cause for your dislike properly: Is it a result of a failure of the author? If so, what could have been improved? Also, would you be willing to admit that you may have missed some of the author's major ideas, or that your response is based on simple differences of opinion? In dealing with these questions, you will perhaps learn something about yourself, but you will also be dealing with questions of evaluation and appreciation, which are fundamental to the study of literature.

## Precautions

As you write your report, remember that your teacher is interested in seeing (1) the evidence of your general analytical ability, and (2) the nature and degree of your individual reactions. Remember that good writing is always your aim. Make your theme coherent; be sure that your paragraphs start with transitional phrases. Your theme will have four parts, but do not make them seem like four lumps. Work out a good thesis sentence that will help your reader to understand the organization and plan of your paper, and write a brief but interesting introduction. In short, keep in control at all times.

Keep in mind that this·suggested organization should be adapted to the specific directions of your teacher. If there are no other directions, the four parts of the general critique should give you an acceptable organization and should enable you to write a well-rounded theme.

### The Report and the Review

If you are writing your report in a general English class the form as described in this chapter should be sufficient for your purposes. For more advanced classes, however, you should consider writing a review rather than a report (see Chapter 17). The review is similar to the report in that it is a general piece of writing about literature. The review, however, assumes more experience in analyzing and discussing literature than is assumed for a report.

---

FIRST SAMPLE THEME (SHORT STORY)

### *A Report on Ralph Ellison's Story "Flying Home"*

[1]      "Flying Home" was first published in 1944, during World War II. At that time, according to Ellison, blacks were trained as pilots but were not actually sent into combat. This fact provides the cause of the frustration of the major figure in the story, a young black pilot named Todd. The story has about an equal amount of dialogue and narration, and is not marked by sections or divisions. *Ellison's principal idea in the story is that a black person's ambitions are straitjacketed in a predominantly white society.** *This point is made clear in the principal action and the major characters, and it is made emphatic by the disturbing power of the story.†*

[2]      *The difficulty of being black in a white society is made clear in the principal action of the story.* Todd is black, and on a training mission has crashed his plane in a white man's field in Alabama. Seriously injured, he is consoled by an aged black named Jefferson, whose young son Teddy goes to find help. Todd is fearful that he might be seen as a failure by white people for having crashed. When Jefferson diverts him from his pain by telling a story, the story is about the difficulty of the blacks. Specifically, Jefferson's tale is about how he was ordered out of heaven by a white St. Peter. Todd is racked with pain, and, prompted by this and by Jefferson's narrative, he thinks about how, even from earliest youth, he had

---

In *Dark Symphony: Negro Literature in America,* ed. James A. Emanuel and Theodore L. Gross (New York: The Free Press, 1968), pp. 254–270. Parenthetical page numbers refer to this edition.

*Central idea.      †Thesis sentence.

wanted to fly but had been told that such aspirations were inappropriate for a black. At this point the owner of the field, a white named Graves, appears with two attendants who put Todd in a straitjacket, saying he couldn't let the black "git up that high without his going crazy" (p. 269). After enjoying his "joke," Graves orders Todd off his property, and the blacks, not the whites, carry him off. The action shows the hostility and indifference of whites to blacks.

[3]     *In presenting the black characters, Ellison shows that they have been limited by the same racial hostility and indifference.* Todd is young and determined, and is trying to cope in the real world of the air force. Jefferson is old and also determined, but his efforts to cope have turned mainly to fantasy. Todd's crashing and Jefferson's being turned out of heaven for "speeding" suggest how normal aims and aspirations, which may reach fruition for whites, always are thrust against a barrier for blacks. Todd has been given a plane but not allowed to fight during the war, while Jefferson, in his dream, has been given wings but not allowed to fly. By this means Ellison shows that both men have the ability to function well — just as by implication all blacks, like all human beings, have this same ability — but because they are black they will not be allowed to.

[4]     *A similar parallel is drawn between Todd and Teddy, the young son of Jefferson.* First, of course, their names are similar. Second, even though Teddy does not figure prominently in the story — during most of it he has been away getting help for Todd — Ellison brings out details about him that show his similarity to Todd. Teddy is a competent boy, being entrusted to get help and to carry Todd on the stretcher. He has strength of character similar to that of Todd, whose childhood dreams of being a pilot are so important in the story. If the parallel is followed, of course, much the same kind of frustration that happened to Todd and Jefferson will be the lot of Teddy.

[5]     *Because of these parallels, it seems to have been no accident that Ellison created the three black persons as possessing youth, maturity, and age.* All have the same past, present, or future — namely, being frustrated or truncated. The three whites in the story, by contrast, are all in the full power of their maturity, which is the apparent inheritance of the white race in the social structure criticized by Ellison. Interestingly, too, the whites do not directly assist Todd from the field. They provide the stretcher, but make sure that Jefferson and Teddy do the actual carrying. If there is to be any improvement for blacks, Ellison may be suggesting, it will be brought about only by blacks of all ages pulling cooperatively together.

[6]     *Primarily because of such a clear, direct view of the predicament of the black in the society geared to whites, this story is compelling but also disturbing.* If people are injured to the extent of having a broken ankle, as Todd is, it should be a human thing to help them. Yet Ellison shows that the attendants put a straitjacket on him in an enactment of Graves's grim joke. This incident is powerfully disturbing as a symbol: when people fall into quicksand they need help, not a push. Yet the effect of the symbol is that Todd gets a push. Because of the outrageousness of this action, together with the aspirations so clearly portrayed by Ellison, such as the letter of Todd's sweetheart and the story of

Todd's grasping at the empty sky for an airplane, "Flying Home" is deeply moving. Here is a story with a coherent, richly symbolic texture. The study of almost any passage is illuminating and most rewarding.

★COMMENTARY ON THE THEME

This sample report, with six paragraphs, is longer than the earlier sample themes, in keeping with the more extensive assignment. Even though the report requires four separate parts — introduction, summary, analysis, and response — it is still governed by a dominating, central idea. Note that the summary in paragraph 2 is kept short. The longest section of the theme, the analysis, is contained in paragraphs 3, 4, and 5. Paragraph 3 deals with two characters, paragraph 4 with one. Paragraph 5 deals with all three major characters together. Observe that each of these paragraphs emphasizes the theme's central idea by developing contrasts between the aspirations of the characters and a "barrier" (paragraph 3), "frustration" (paragraph 4), and a state of being "truncated" (paragraph 5). The last paragraph pursues the central idea by emphasizing the power of the story to disturb one's emotions because it contrasts the need for help and sympathy with the actual cruelty practiced by Graves.

Note that this theme assumes that the reader knows the major incidents in the story. For this reason the writer can refer to events without retelling the story in full. Notice this sentence:

> Todd's crashing and Jefferson's being turned out of heaven for "speeding" suggest how normal aims and aspirations, which may reach fruition for whites, always are thrust against a barrier for blacks. (paragraph 3)

This sentence refers to two incidents in the story, but it is important to observe that the incidents are used as part of a point and are not described for their own sakes. In your theme, always try to use details from the story in the same way.

SECOND SAMPLE THEME (NON-FICTION)

### *A Report on Loren Eiseley's* The Invisible Pyramid

[1]       *The Invisible Pyramid,* published in 1970, is subtitled "A Naturalist Analyzes the Rocket Century." The naturalist is Loren Eiseley, who at the time of publication was "Benjamin Franklin Professor of Anthro-

Loren Eiseley, *The Invisible Pyramid* (New York: Charles Scribner's Sons, 1970). All page numbers in the theme refer to this edition.

pology and the History of Science at the University of Pennsylvania" (p. 175). The book is a collection of seven essays on the topic of human responses to modern science. *Eiseley's main idea is that human beings are constantly erecting "invisible pyramids" of science and technology to escape from earthly confinements, but that the earth is nevertheless a very good place on which to stay.** One may follow this idea in a short summary of the book, in a description of Eiseley's concept of the "invisible pyramid," and in a tribute to the interesting qualities of the book.†*

[2]     *It is difficult to describe the entire book briefly, because the seven essays are on separate topics, but one can see a number of unifying threads that are related to the main idea.* Throughout the essays, for example, Eiseley mentions Halley's comet, which he uses to contrast the permanence of nature with the shortness of human life. The "invisible pyramid" idea is repeated frequently also, as an example of how the human race is trying to move upward, like the Apollo astronauts, out of confinements. In the second essay, "The Cosmic Prison," Eiseley exemplifies this confinement by comparing our attempts to understand the universe to one white blood cell trying to understand the entire body of which it is a part. From beginning to end, the essays have many such interesting comparisons, all related to the main idea.

[3]     *While there are many ideas in the essays, the idea of the "invisible pyramid" dominates Eiseley's thought.* To Eiseley, in an essay entitled "The Spore Bearers," the "Great Pyramid at Gisa" in Egypt required a tremendous "outpouring of wealth and inventive genius" (p. 87). Modern industrialized human beings, in their attempts to follow science, specifically the investigation of outer space (and the inner space of the atom), are committing themselves to an equally great effort. The "invisible pyramid" therefore means that human beings are willing to devote huge amounts of energy and money in search of ideas, outer space, and a better tomorrow. There is a sense that great accomplishments are just ahead of us, around the corner, and the pyramid represents our attempts to realize these goals.

[4]     *But Eiseley does not commit himself blindly to the building of the pyramid.* He also stresses the practical limitations of human dreams, and he also emphasizes the constant role that chance plays in human affairs. His first essay, for example, entitled "The Star Dragon," suggests that the extinctions of "many big mammals — mammoth, mastodon, sloth, long-horned bison" (p. 25) at the end of the ice age may have been caused by a "giant solar flare activated for only a few moments" at some remote time (p. 26). Eiseley does not claim absolutely that such a flare occurred (even though moon explorers have found evidence for it in "glazed droplets" on moon rocks [p. 26]), but he does say that, whatever the cause, the extinctions of many animals forced human beings "to turn to plant domestication [agriculture] to survive" (p. 25). He goes on to

*Central idea.      †Thesis sentence.

say that agriculture is the "primary road to a settled life" that produces civilization (p. 25). The point is that a chance happening — the extinctions — produced a change in human life that pushed us toward the present time. A similar chance is that early ancestors of human beings climbed trees, and as a result evolved the upright spine and the "far-ranging 'eye brain' of the higher primates, including man" (pp. 44–45). This circumstance distinguished them from creatures on the ground, like dogs, who developed strong senses of smell and therefore pursued a different path of evolution from human beings. The idea is that no matter how high human beings may aim, their achievement may be shaped or limited by "cosmic" forces that operate by chance. For this reason, humanity is locked in a "cosmic prison" (the title of the second chapter) that constantly limits not only human imagination but the materials which furnish our imagination.

[5] *The book is everywhere thought-provoking in this manner.* Reflecting on the machine age, Eiseley constantly points out the origins of human aspirations, and causes the reader to think about the reverse side. It would be too much to say that the work is a satire on far-fetched dreams — it is too mild and tolerant for that — but Eiseley does effectively show the impossibility of much of what people dream about. On interplanetary space exploration, for example, he has the following thought:

> There are far more stars in the heavens than there are men upon the earth. The waste to be searched is too great for the powers we possess. In gambling terms, the percentage lies all with the house, or rather with the universe. Lonely though we may feel ourselves to be, we must steel ourselves to the fact that man, even far future man, may pass from the scene without possessing either negative or positive evidence of the existence of other civilized beings in this or other galaxies.
>
> — p. 79

[6] *There are many similarly wise passages in the book that make it excellent reading.* The emphasis is not that it is ridiculous to dream but that it would be best to be constantly realistic. Eiseley summarizes this idea at the end of "The Last Magician," the concluding essay in the book. Here he tells of Apollo 13, which broke down on its way to the moon, and which limped back to earth. Here the beauty and protection of earth — "a love for the green meadows we have so long taken for granted and desecrated to our own cost" (p. 156) — was foremost in the minds of everyone who hoped that the disabled crew would return safely. Eiseley's essays finally focus on this idea: the world is a beautiful, sheltering, creative place; we are lucky to have it for ourselves, and we should do everything possible to preserve it. The top of the pyramid reaches a point, but its base is always on the earth; no matter how high we rise, we always depend on the earth, and we can never really leave it. Thoughts like these make Eiseley's book invaluable.

★COMMENTARY ON THE THEME

The introductory paragraph briefly identifies the author and the nature of the book. After the central idea, the paragraph concludes with a guide to the remainder of the report. Paragraph two is a brief summary. Since the book is a collection of seven separate essays, the summary can do no more than refer to common, unifying references in the book. [By contrast, notice that for a shorter work like Ellison's "Flying Home" (in the first sample theme), a complete summary is possible.] Paragraphs three and four are devoted to a discussion of Eiseley's main concept in the book, that of the "invisible pyramid." The aim of these paragraphs is not to analyze or criticize Eiseley's idea, but instead to provide the reader with an understanding of the idea. Paragraphs five and six constitute a discussion of the ways in which Eiseley's book provokes thought, and therefore the paragraphs are a "tribute" to the book.

# 4

# The Theme of
# Character Analysis

THE ANALYSIS OF CHARACTER is an extremely popular theme subject, particularly in courses on drama and on the novel. Writers in ancient times wrote character sketches and novel-like stories, and many medieval and Renaissance writers, like Chaucer, were adept at creating character, but real interest in particularized fictional characters did not develop until the seventeenth century. In the eighteenth century the novel emerged as an important literary form. With the advent of modern psychology, interest in patterns of human behavior has come of age. Of course drama, with its emphasis on a main character, has been popular since the time of the ancient Athenians. In our own times it is one of the more vital literary forms.

If you think of some of the novels and dramas with which you are familiar, you will realize that they are about characters, their reactions to an extended series of actions, and their attempts to shape those events. The novel and the drama are similar in showing the interactions of character and action in rather full detail. Epic and narrative poetry also center on character and action. Short stories and poems do not aim at the broadness and fullness of the larger forms but concentrate instead on the essential high points of human experience.

### What Is Character?

Although sometimes we use the word *character* synonymously with "person," "human being," and "literary figure," more often we use it in reference to an individual's personal qualities and characteristics. Other words used as either equivalents or modifications of character are *psyche, soul, ego, consciousness, moral fiber, being,* and many others.

No matter what one calls it, character in literature is an author's representation of a human being, specifically of those inner qualities that determine how an individual reacts to various conditions or attempts to shape his or her environment. Choices and actions indicate character. Thus, if we know that John chooses to work ten hours a day to get ahead while Tom puts in only two, we have the basis for drawing conclusions about their respective characters.

You may assume that in literature the author will provide you with only the significant details of this sort. Thus you read about important events like a decision to go on a journey, the encounters with people on the journey, and the effects on the character's life and outlook. Or you read about the romantic affairs of a character, or the problems faced when a job is lost, or the joy experienced when things go right. From these details you make inferences about what the character is like, and in effect determine the "character" of the character.

In forming a coherent picture of a literary character, you should try to figure out the character's outstanding trait or traits. As in life, characters may be lazy or ambitious, anxious or serene, pugnacious or fearful, self-assertive or bashful, confident or self-doubting, adventurous or timid, noisy or quiet, truthful or mendacious, conscientious or careless, reasonable or hotheaded, fair or partial, straightforward or underhanded, "winners" or "losers," and so forth. With a list like this, you can start to approach a study of character. In viewing Jay Gatsby in F. Scott Fitzgerald's *The Great Gatsby,* for example, you might determine that Gatsby combines the contradictory aspects of a powerful drive for self-improvement but a profound doubt of his own self-importance. On the one hand he is confident but on the other he is self-doubting. It would be possible to develop a theme based on these conflicting qualities.

## Appearance, Action, and Character

When you consider character, you should take into account any physical descriptions of the character, but try to relate the physical to the mental. Herman Melville, in the long story *Billy Budd,* spends considerable effort describing Billy as a physically attractive man; this description is not an end in itself but is indicative of Billy's inward character as a perfect, Christlike individual. Similarly, when you treat an author's description of a character's physical appearance, you should try to move from what a character *looks like* to what that character *is.* The same applies to your treatment of a character's actions. Get beyond the actions themselves and indicate what they show *about* the character. Always try to get from the outside to the inside, for it is on the inside that character resides.

## Character Traits and Character Development

There is of course a great deal of interaction between character and the outcome of any story or drama. In some types of literature certain character traits are essential. In cowboy or detective stories, for example, it is essential that the main characters be strong, tough, steadfast, and clever, so that they may overcome the obstacles before them or solve the crime. In Greek tragedy a fatal flaw of character is the ultimate cause of the hero's downfall. In these cases there are consequences that proceed logically and almost inevitably from certain traits of character; the characters stay the same throughout the work and therefore cause their own success or failure.

In many works, however, you will perceive a change or a development of character, and therefore an outcome that might have seemed inevitable will change. You may decide for yourself whether human character is capable of radical change, or whether change is really to be described as growth or development. If people who as children were very combative become successful and peaceful as adult lawyers, they may simply have transferred their combativeness into the acceptable arena of legal wrangles and tangles. Was there a change or was there a development? Similarly, Shakespeare's Juliet is a young, impressionable girl at the start of *Romeo and Juliet,* but by the end of the play she is a determined, resolute woman. Does her character change, or does it develop? It is more important to observe and discuss such character modifications accurately than to take an arbitrary position on whether you have change or development. Of course some authors arrange their characterizations as an embodiment of either change or development. If the position of the author is clear to you, you must take this view into account in your analysis of the character.

## How Is Character Disclosed in Literature?

Before you prepare to write your theme, you should know the four ways in which a writer usually indicates characters to you:

1. By what the characters themselves say (and think, from the author's third-person omniscient point of view).
2. By what the characters do.

3. By what other characters say about them.

4. By what the author says about them, speaking as either the story-teller or an observer of the action.

These four points require amplification.

1. What particular characters say may frequently be accepted at face value, but just as often it may be only a reflection of their intellectual and emotional state at a given moment. If characters in deep despair say that life is worthless, for example, you must balance that statement with what the same characters say when they are happy. Then too, you must consider the situation when a statement is made. If characters voice despair at the start, but are cheerful (or sad) at the end, there has been a development, or change in the characters' view of life. In *Crime and Punishment,* for example, Raskolnikov is convinced of his right to make judgments on the lives of other people, but at the end of the novel he doubts his right. A. shift has occurred that any analysis of his qualities must consider.

2. Although an author may often show characters behaving consistently with what they say, just as often the author may create a character who professes honesty, yet does dishonorable things. Iago in Shakespeare's *Othello* is such a character. He professes to be Othello's friend and companion, but secretly he does everything in his power to bring about Othello's destruction. In analyzing what characters do, you must ask whether the characters' actions are consistent with their words. If not, why not? What does the author indicate about characters by revealing inconsistencies? The writer might wish to expose hypocrisy, for example, or to illustrate ideas like "Human beings have a great capacity for self-deception," or "Human beings are weak."

3. In literature, as in life, people are always talking about other people. What they say of course raises the problem of *point of view,* because the character and motivation of a person will condition whatever that person says about someone else (see Chapter 5). You know, for example, that the word of a person's enemy is usually biased against that person. Therefore an author may frequently give you a favorable impression of characters by having a bad character say bad things about them. Similarly, the word of a close friend or political manager may be biased in favor of particular characters. In short, you must always consider the context and source of all dramatic remarks about particular characters.

4. What the author says about a character is usually to be accepted as truth about that character. Naturally, authors must be accepted absolutely on matters of fact. But when they *interpret* the actions and characteristics of their characters, they themselves assume the role of critic,

and their opinions are open to question. For this reason authors frequently avoid making overt interpretations, and devote their skill instead to arranging events so that their conclusions are obvious to the reader.

## Character, Reality, Probability, and Decorum

We are entitled to expect that the characters in a novel or play will be true to life. That is, the actions, statements, and thoughts of a particular person must all be what a human being is *likely* to do, say, and think under given circumstances. This is the standard of *probability*.

The phrases "true to life" and "given circumstances" need explanation, for they are vital to the concept of literary character as distinguished from real-life character. There are major differences between literature and life. First, literature presents a highly selective view of reality, even in the most "realistic" of works. That is, each action performed by a character within a work has organic significance; it may be interpreted as a facet of character or as an example of an author's philosophy of life; those things in life that seem unpredictable, whimsical, and unaccountable are made to seem meaningful in literature. For example, in real life people sometimes simply "make conversation"; yet the conversation of the soldiers on the watch at the opening of *Hamlet* is there for a reason. Along with having a functional role in the exposition of the play, the talk shows the nervousness of the men, some of their characteristics, and their attitudes as midnight—the time the ghost walks—approaches. The speeches represent the way in which soldiers would likely talk under these circumstances; their speeches are not accidental, but are *probable* and relevant to the entire play.

In studying the characters in each work of literature, you should imagine what very different kinds of persons would do under exactly similar circumstances and with the same mental and philosophical outlooks. Look carefully at the early parts of the work in order to see what tendencies the characters have exhibited. With these characteristics in mind, then ask yourself, "Is the subsequent action a logical consequence of this character's qualities?" In the early scenes of *Macbeth*, for example, Shakespeare demonstrates that Macbeth is a loyal, strong, valiant, and almost foolhardy warrior; that he is ambitious; but that he is also kind and gentle. In view of Macbeth's later responsibility for a series of deaths and for a brutally oppressive regime as king, the question is how to reconcile his characteristics with the subsequent action.

A second condition that you will meet in literature is that not all works are the same nor do they present probability or reality in the same way or in the same aspects. Fiction attempting to mirror life—the realistic, naturalistic, or "slice of life" type of fiction—sets up conditions and raises expectations about the characters that are different from fiction attempting to portray a romantic, fanciful world. A character's behavior and speech in the "realistic" setting would be out of place in the romantic setting.

But the situation is more complex than this, for within the romantic setting, a character might reasonably be *expected* to behave and speak in a fanciful, dreamlike way. Speech and action under both conditions are therefore *probable* as we understand the word, although different aspects of human character are presented in these two different types of works. The same principle is applicable in farcical works, where foolish character traits are shown.

It is also possible that within the same work you might find some characters who are realistic but others who are not. In such works you have contrasting systems of reality. Shakespeare creates such a contrast in *Richard II*. Richard is a person with unrealistic expectations of himself and those around him; he lives in a dream world and is so out of touch with his surroundings that ultimately he is destroyed. You might also encounter works where there are mythical or supernatural figures who contrast with the realism of the other characters. In judging characters in works of this type, your only guide is that of probability.[1]

Concern for probability in literature is not new. In the Renaissance and eighteenth century, awareness of the need for adapting the conditions of life as described in various types of works led literary critics to extol the concept of *decorum,* or appropriateness. Authors of the period followed this principle in making their characters speak and act according to their class and circumstances and according to the type of literature in which they appeared. Thus, Shakespeare gave his noblemen elevated diction in poetic accents but gave his country bumpkins the slang of the Elizabethan streets.

Writers in the modern period have abandoned decorum as a practicing principle, but they still observe decorum to the extent that it coincides with common sense and also to the extent that their interest in various aspects of character leads naturally into certain types of literature. For example, modern psychology has had a far-reaching effect on this interest, and hence on the novel. Freud's metapsychology has led writers to explore means of delineating those aspects of character that in earlier fiction were not expressed except as they appeared in behavior. James Joyce's *A Portrait of the Artist as a Young Man* relies

---

[1]You may reasonably wonder about how you should judge the character of gods, or devils, for that matter. Usually gods embody the qualities of the best, most moral human beings, although the ancient Greeks sometimes attributed to the gods some of the same follies and faults that beset humanity. To judge a devil, try thinking of the worst human qualities, but remember that the devil is often imagined as a character with many engaging traits, the easier to deceive poor sinners and lead them into hell.

heavily on an "interior monologue" that takes place within the mind of the young Stephen Dedalus; much of the earlier part of the novel is written as the expression of Stephen's conscious observations and reflections as they cause new thoughts and associations to develop within his mind. This technique would not have developed had it not been for psychology.

The drama has also been heavily influenced by the altered and modified ideas of reality provided by modern psychology. Eugene O'Neill's massive drama *A Long Day's Journey Into Night*, for example, is not realistic by our everyday standards, but is realistic nevertheless because the members of the troubled family represent enlargements of human character; through these characters the anguish and disappointments of life are focused. Recent dramatists like Samuel Beckett and Harold Pinter do not aim at everyday realism; instead, they focus on the abstract aspects of human character and personify these parts through their stage figures. The resulting characters are still realistic, but realistic in the way that a microscopic view of the skin of a frog is realistic.

## Judging the Completeness of Character Development

With all these considerations in mind, you can see that literary characters should be true to life, under given circumstances and within certain literary specifications. The key to your study of character should always be to discover if the character—whether intended by the author to be a complete, lifelike person, a romantic hero, or an absurdist abstraction—does and says what you believe human beings might do and say under the exact conditions presented by the author. Does the character ring true? Come to life? Illustrate many qualities that add up to a really complete representation of a human being? Or does the character seem to be one-dimensional? The degree to which an author can make a character come alive is a mark of skill, and if you think that your author is successful in this regard, you should say so in your theme.

## Organizing Your Theme

### INTRODUCTION

As always, your theme should have a clearly stated central idea that runs throughout the entire character analysis. Your central idea will be whatever general statement you make to describe the character.

Your thesis sentence must be a brief statement of the main sections of your theme.

### BODY

The organization is designed to illustrate and prove your central idea. You have much freedom in organizing your main points. Some possible methods are the following:

1. Organization around central characteristics, like "kindness, gentleness, generosity, firmness," or "resoluteness of will frustrated by inopportune moments for action, resulting in despondency, doubt, and melancholy." A body containing this sort of material would demonstrate how the literary work brings out each of these qualities.

2. Organization around a development or change of character. Here you would attempt to show the character traits that a character possesses at the start of the work, and then describe the changes or developments that occur. Try to determine the author's view on such changes; that is, is the change a genuine change, or does the author establish latent traits in the character which are brought into prominence as the story progresses?

3. Organization around central incidents that reveal primary characteristics. Certain key incidents will stand out in a work, and you might create an effective body by using three or four of these as guides for your discussion, taking care to show in your topic sentences that your purpose is to illuminate the character you have selected, not the incidents. In other words, you would regard the incidents only as they bring out truths about character. In a discussion of the character of Stephen in *A Portrait of the Artist as a Young Man,* an effective arrangement might be to select the incidents of the pandybat and the young girl standing in the water.

Naturally, with this arrangement, you would have to show how the incidents bring out the characteristics and also how they serve to explain other things the character might do.

### CONCLUSION

The conclusion should contain your statements about how the characteristics you have brought out are related to the work as a whole. If people were good but came to a bad end, does this discrepancy elevate them to tragic stature? If they were nobodies and came to a bad end, does this fact cause you to draw any conclusion about the class or type of which they were a part? Or does it illustrate the author's view of human life? Or both? Do the characteristics explain why the people help or hinder other characters? Does your analysis help you to clear up any misunderstanding that your first reading of the work produced? Questions such as these should be raised and answered in your conclusion.

## Precautions

1. DICTION.   In view of the closeness between character analysis and psychology, you must realize that for a literary theme it is best to avoid technical psychological terms. Even if you have acquired much skill in using these terms, your instructor will probably not receive them sympathetically if you substitute them for thoughtful analysis. Always explain yourself, and do not descend to jargon, as there is great danger of doing in this theme. Some words from psychology are admissible without much amplification—words like *disturbed, frustrated,* and *anxiety* are satisfactory because they are in common use—but if you use words like *complex, neurosis,* and *psychosis,* you should explain the concepts. Be cautious, and use common sense. If you have any question about a word, ask your teacher.

2. ANALYZE CHARACTER, NOT ACTIONS.   Be especially careful to distinguish what characters do from what they are. Here is an example illustrating the problem:

> At the end [of D. H. Lawrence's story "Shades of Spring"] Syson has had the sad satisfaction of knowing he has triumphed over Hilda, and will continue to dominate her forever. He will continue to correspond with her, but they will never get together on a permanent basis.

A revision requires a reordering of the material so that a trait of character will be emphasized—in this case a desire for domination to the extent that human relationships are hurt:

> At the end Syson has again asserted his desire for domination. In fact, this desire is so overwhelming in him that it has ruined whatever chances for love he and Hilda might have had. He was always more involved in his own concerns than in hers, and as a result his domination represents a hollow triumph. He has had his victory but he is also alone; his desire for control is therefore self-destructive.

As in this sample revision, always try to make your material point toward character traits. Do not just retell events.

SAMPLE THEME

### The Character of Jim
### in Joseph Conrad's Lord Jim

[1]         Jim is difficult to understand. He is seen mainly through the eyes of Marlow, who imparts his own values to much of the story. He is also the

Joseph Conrad, *Lord Jim* (New York: The Modern Library, 1931). Parenthetical page numbers refer to this edition.

subject of much interpretation by other informants in the story, so that we receive many views of him. In addition, Jim is the principal figure in a richly symbolic tapestry, so that much of what he does and says is relevant to most people at most times. In this respect his individuality is sacrificed to his existence as a symbol. Despite these difficulties, however, Jim emerges as a fully developed individual. He is basically a dreamer, a "romantic" in Stein's words, who is capable of imagining the best in himself and in others, but who is incapable of acting up to his ideals. *He is therefore human, for his growth to success is not a gift, but must be created out of guilt and regret, like the growth of most human beings.\* Conrad symbolizes his development as a character by three incidents involving leaps or jumps that Jim fails to make, makes inadvertently, and makes deliberately.†*

[2]         *The first opportunity to leap, which Jim does not take, reveals the gap between his conscious ideals and his absence of courage and commitment to others.* Imbued with the British ideals of manhood and adventure in the days of the naval empire, he has been dreaming of his own "devotion to duty" in a way "as unflinching as a hero in a book" (p. 6). But when the opportunity comes to join in a rescue operation, for some unexplained reason he literally and figuratively misses the boat. Not only does he fail to jump into the boat when the others are rowing off, but he envies and minimizes the success of one of the rescuers. The point about Jim's character is that he had not realized his incapacity before this missed opportunity, for he had never been tested. The missed leap therefore reveals a void in his character. Despite his inward claims of personal integrity and his dreams of his own potential greatness, his commitment to others is not powerful enough to outweigh his reluctance to act. This one incident, in short, explains the moral laziness that finally causes him to ship aboard the rust-eaten vessel, the *Patna*.

[3]         *The bubble of Jim's self-esteem is totally destroyed by his second jump — from the* Patna *when it is listing heavily and supposedly near sinking.* This jump is the major incident in the novel, since it brings out the depths of Jim's being, that inner panic that destroys all his conscious dreams by causing a single cowardly act despite his good intentions. Symbolically, this downward jump suggests a low point in his character; it takes him away from honor and responsibility. Whereas the first jump indicated only a certain lack of capacity and could easily be dismissed as simple bad luck, this second jump openly reveals, for all the world to see, a basic cowardice. With his depths thus exposed, Jim feels morally naked; he no longer can rationalize to himself his own inconsistencies, because the proof of his cowardice is known by everyone. His flight from recognition all over the Indian Ocean area is therefore natural enough. It is an attempt to restore his public reputation even though he cannot escape his private humiliation.

[4]         *But the public nature of the* Patna *jump also makes Jim begin to grow inwardly.* He has a high sense of justice, and before he flees he faces trial, which can end in nothing but his dishonor and disgrace. His conscious

*Central Idea.     †Thesis sentence.

dream of what is right has enabled him to face the consequences of his real guilt. This facing of the trial when all the other deserters flee is the start of Jim's awareness, acted upon but never clearly stated by him, that life constantly demands expiation for guilt that is caused not entirely by our own choice.

[5]     *Jim's final leap results from his own choice, however, and as such it demonstrates that his character has reached a high point of development.* The jump is a kind of triumph, for being upward, it represents the affirmative power of his character. Leaping over the fence enclosing Rajah Allang's courtyard, he allies himself with Doramin and proceeds quickly to justify the title "Lord Jim" by acting wisely, in concert with Doramin, in governing the forlorn outpost of Patusan. He is convinced of the value of his dream, and always behaves with justice, honor, and firmness, yet always with forgiveness. These are the conscious virtues, to which Jim adheres closely, since they are the embodiment of his character as a dreamer.

[6]     *This adherence explains why he accepts the final responsibility for the death of Dain Waris.* Beyond question, his third leap has enabled him to dedicate himself to the good life in Patusan as expiation for his guilt in the *Patna* episode. The personal quality of this dedication should be stressed, however, and contrasted with the quality of Jim's feelings after Gentleman Brown commits his treacherous act. In this affair Jim is responsible only for not having destroyed the Gentleman *before* the murder is committed. Yet, in Gentleman Brown, Jim apparently sees that the cowardly depths are common to all mankind, not just to himself. So Jim faces Doramin in expiation, just as he had earlier braved the court and the subsequent disgrace. But as Jim sacrifices himself, the best in him, his capacity to dream, triumphs over whatever it was that made him leap from the *Patna*. He is genuinely great at that moment of sacrifice.

[7]     Admittedly, Jim is a puzzling character, since his characteristics show that human life is a mystery and since we never really get inside him. *But Conrad uses him to demonstrate that, if life has its depths, it also has its high points.* At the highest point, a human being willing to live out his dream, if this dream has value and ennobles mankind, can justify the claim that life is elevated and great. Jim, with all his frailty, is a truly great representation of a human being, since he has met and conquered life's greatest obstacle—the deflation of one's own high self-esteem.

## ★COMMENTARY ON THE THEME

This theme shows two separate systems of organizing a theme on character. One is that of development or change of character. Thus, paragraphs 2 and 3 of the body show the low points from which Jim's character grows, and paragraphs 4, 5, and 6 describe the growth.

This tracing of character development is tied to a series of similar but contrasting incidents, and these incidents form the second system of organizing and tightening the theme. The low points of Jim's character are therefore linked to the first two jumps, one which he fails to make and the other which he makes inadvertently. The development of character is traced to consequences of the second jump, however (paragraph 4), and the high points of character are related to the third jump, which Jim makes deliberately (paragraph 6). The virtue of using incidents from the work as focal points for a theme on character is that the discussion of character, which may easily become abstract, is always tied to the work itself.

# CHAPTER
# 5

# The Theme About Point of View

POINT OF VIEW is the position from which details in a literary work are perceived, considered, and described. Some alternative terms are *viewpoint, central mind, unifying voice, persona, center of attention,* and *focus.*

First and foremost, point of view is a method of presentation, the selection of a particular voice (or *persona, speaker,* or *mask*) with which to tell a story, define a problem, or describe a state of mind. You might respond that authors are *always* using their own voices; they are the ones who write the story or the poem, aren't they? While it is obviously true that authors write the work, it does not necessarily follow that they always use their own voices. It is not easy to determine just exactly what one's "own voice" is. Test yourself: When you speak to your teacher, to your friend, to a child, to a person you love, or to a distant relative, your actual voice always sounds the same. But the personality — or persona — that you employ changes according to the person you are speaking to. All the personae are you, but which one is really you?

## Point of View and "Throwing the Voice"

The same complexity may be seen in the creation of a work of literature, with the added dimension that authors may also deliberately *choose* to express themselves in voices that are not their own. In any literary work there is an intricate blending of speaker, situation, subject material, intention, and audience. Most writers select a voice representing a phase of personality that is appropriate given all the circumstances. Often, of course, the speaker may actually be the author, as nearly as that identity can be determined in light of all the complex shades of human personality. But just as often the voice may be a separate and totally independent character, consciously imagined and consistently maintained by the author.

Point of view is hence an imaginative "throwing of the voice" by authors. You might imagine that authors are like ventriloquists who are speaking through characters who for the entire work are perched on their knees. The characters are the ones you hear, but the authors are the ones who manipulates the characters and make them believable, consistent personalities. Suppose for a moment that you are an author and are planning a set of stories or discussions. Try to imagine the kinds of speakers you would create for the following situations:

A happy niece who has just inherited $25 million from an uncle recalls a childhood experience with the uncle years ago.

A disappointed nephew who was cut off without a cent describes a childhood experience with the same uncle.

A ship's captain who is filled with ideas of personal honor, integrity, and responsibility describes the life of a sailor who has committed a despicable, cowardly act.

A person who has survived a youth of poverty and degradation describes a brother who has succumbed to drugs and crime.

An economist looks at problems of unemployment.

A person who has just lost a job looks at problems of unemployment.

In trying to create voices and stories for the various situations, you will recognize the importance of your *imagination* in the selection of point of view. You are always yourself, but your imagination can enable you to speak like someone else totally distinct from yourself. Point of view is hence an imaginative creation, just as much a part of the author's work as the events narrated or the ideas discussed.

## Point of View as a Physical Position

Thus far we have considered point of view as an interaction of personality and circumstance. There are also purely physical aspects, specifically (1) the actual place or position from which speakers or narrators see and hear the action they are describing, and (2) their capacity as recipients of information from others. Narrators are firsthand witnesses in most cases, and they gain credibility because they are reporting events they actually saw or heard. If they are on the spot of an action, they may have acquired their knowledge because they were participants; or they could have been in a building and looked out a window just as the action began; or they might have been looking through a keyhole at action in another room. If they are not on the spot, they must get their information in believable ways: They could hear it from someone who was there; or they could receive an informative letter; or they could overhear a conversation between firsthand witnesses or participants. Sometimes the unidentified voice of the author comes from a person who seems to be hovering somehow right above the characters as they move and speak. This speaker is able to be present everywhere, unnoticed, and hence is a constantly reliable source of all information presented in the narrative.

## Kinds of Points of View

The kinds of points of view may be classified fairly easily. You may detect the point of view in any work by determining the grammatical voice of the speaker. Then, of course, you should go on to all the other considerations thus far discussed.

### FIRST PERSON

If the story is told by an "I," the author is using the *first-person* point of view, usually a fictional narrator and not the author personally. First-person speakers can report everything they see, hear, and think, as they do so they convey not only the action of the work, but also some of their own background, thinking, attitudes, and even prejudices. The speaker's particular type of speech will have a great effect on the language of the work itself. A sailor will use many nautical terms, just as a sixteen-year-old boy may use much slang. For these reasons, first-person speakers are often as much a subject of interest as the details they describe. Nick Carraway in F. Scott Fitzgerald's *The Great Gatsby* is such a speaker. Nick is ostensibly a minor character in the action who tells what is happening in the lives of Gatsby and the Buchanans. Sometimes the "I" narrator is the major character in the book, like Mark Twain's Huckleberry Finn or Swift's Gulliver. Often seemingly minor characters who happen to be narrators may be seen as major characters because of their interest and involvement in the action, like Joseph Conrad's Marlow, the narrator of the story "Youth," and of the novels *Heart of Darkness* and *Lord Jim*.

### THIRD PERSON

If the narrator is not introduced as a character, and if everything in the work is described in the third person (that is, *he, she, it, they*), the author is using the *third-person* point of view. There are variants here.

The third-person point of view is called *omniscient* when the speaker not only describes the action and dialogue of the work, but also seems to know everything that goes on in the minds of the characters. In the third person omniscient point of view, authors take great responsibility: by delving into the minds of their characters they assume a stance that exceeds our ordinary experience with other persons. Like God, the writers attempt to show the inner workings of characters' minds, workings that may be obscure even to those characters themselves. If you encounter the omniscient point of view, you may be sure that the writer is displaying great concern with psychological patterns and motivations. Writers like George Eliot, Dostoyevsky, Dickens, and Dreiser employed the omniscient point of view often. You may detect it whenever you see phrases like "He thought. . . ." or "As she approached the scene, she considered that. . . ." and so on.

If an author uses the third person but confines the narration mainly to what one single character does, says, and sometimes thinks, then you have the third-person *limited* point of view. While the omniscient point of view gathers in the thoughts of most of the characters, the limited focuses on only one. The limited viewpoint is thus midway between the first- and the third-person points of view. In Hemingway's story "Big Two-Hearted River," Nick Adams is the entire focus of the action. Hemingway confines his descriptions to what Nick sees and does, only occasionally referring to what he feels. Similarly, Joyce in *Dubliners* includes a number of stories (such as "A Little Cloud," "Counterparts," "The Dead") that are focused on the actions and thoughts of a major figure, while the reports on the other figures are confined to actions and statements.

### DRAMATIC

Writers using the *dramatic* point of view confine their work mainly to quotations and descriptions of actions. They avoid telling you that certain characters thought this or felt that, but instead allow the characters themselves to voice their thoughts and feelings. Often, too, authors using the dramatic point of view will allow certain characters to interpret the thoughts and feelings of other characters, but then attitudes and possible prejudices of these speakers enter into your evaluation of their interpretations. The key to the dramatic point of view is that writers present the reader with action and speech, but do not overtly guide the reader toward any conclusions. Naturally, however, the conclusions may be readily drawn from the details presented. Guy de Maupassant is famous for creating stories rendered in the dramatic point of view, as are Hemingway and Sherwood Anderson.

It goes virtually without saying that many novels, being long works, often have an intermingling of viewpoints. In a largely omniscient narrative, the writer may present a chapter consisting only of action and dialogue — the dramatic point of view — and another chapter that focuses entirely on one person — the limited. Writers of short stories, on the other hand, usually maintain a consistent and uniform point of view.

## Point of View and "Evidence"

When you write a theme about point of view, therefore, you should try to consider all aspects that bear on the presentation of the material in the work you have read. You may imagine yourself in a position somewhat like that of members of a jury. Jury members simply cannot accept testimony uncritically, for some witnesses may have much to gain by presenting misstatements, distortions, or outright lies. Before rendering a verdict, jury members must consider all these possibilities. Speakers in literary works are usually to be accepted as reliable witnesses, but it is true that their characters, interests, capacities, personal involvements, and positions to view action may have a bearing on the material they present. A classic example is the Japanese film *Rashomon,* in which four separate persons tell a story as evidence in a court, and they each present a version that makes them seem more honorable than they actually were. William Faulkner, in the novel *The Sound and the Fury,* similarly presents a story told by four characters, one of them being an idiot. While most stories are not as complex as these, you should always be on the alert to consider the character of the speaker before you render your verdict on what the story is about.

## Organizing Your Theme

In a theme on point of view, the areas of concern are language, selection of detail, characterization, interpretive commentaries, and narrative development. Your theme might be organized to include analysis of one, a few, or all of these elements. Generally you should determine how the point of view has contributed toward making the story uniquely as it is, and also toward your interpretation of the story. In what way has the author's voice entered into your response to the story? Are there any special qualities in the work that could not have been achieved if the author had used another point of view?

### INTRODUCTION

In your introduction you should get at the matters that you plan to develop. Which point of view is used in the work? What is the major influence of this point of view on the work (for example — "The omniscient point of view causes full, leisurely insights into many nuances of character," or "The first-person point of view enables the work to resemble an exposé of back-room political deals.")? To what extent does the selection of point of view make the work particularly interesting and effective, or uninteresting and ineffective? What particular aspects of the work (action, dialogue, characters, description, narration, analysis) do you wish to analyze in support of your central idea?

**BODY**

The questions you raise here will of course depend on the work you have studied. It would be impossible to answer all of the following questions in your analysis, but going through them should make you aware of the sorts of things you can include in the body of your theme.

If you have read works with the first-person point of view, your analyses will necessarily involve the speakers. Who are they? Are they major or minor characters? What are their backgrounds? What are their relationships to the persons listening to them (if there are listeners)? Do they speak directly to you, the reader, in such a way that you are a listener or an eavesdropper? How do the speakers describe the various situations? Are their methods uniquely a function of their character? How reliable are they as observers? How did they acquire the information they are presenting? How much do they disclose? How much do they hide? Do they ever rely on the information of others for their material? How reliable are these other witnesses? Do the speakers undergo any changes in the course of the work that have any bearing on the ways they present the material? Do they notice one kind of thing (e.g., discussion) but miss others (e.g., natural scenery)? What might have escaped them if anything? Do the authors put the speakers into situations that they can describe but not understand? Why? Are the speakers ever confused? Are they close to the action, or distant from it? Do they show emotional involvement in any situations? Are you as a reader sympathetic to their concerns or are you put off by them? If the speakers make any commentary, are their thoughts valid? To what extent, if any, are the speakers of as much interest as the material they present?

If you encounter any of the third-person points of view, try to determine the characteristics of the voices employed by the authors. Does it seem that the authors are speaking in their own voices, or that they have created a special voice for the narrators? You can approach this problem by answering many of the questions that are relevant to the first-person point of view. Also try to determine the distance of the narrator to the action. How is the action described? How is the dialogue recorded? Is there any background information given? Do the descriptions reveal any bias toward any of the characters? Are the descriptions full or bare? Does the author include descriptions or analyses of a character's thoughts? What are these like?

Do you see evidence of the author's own philosophy? Does the choice of words direct you toward any particular interpretations? What limitations or freedoms devolve upon the story as a result of the point of view?

### CONCLUSION

In your conclusion you should evaluate the success of the author's point of view: Was it consistent, effective, truthful? What did the writer gain (if anything) by that selection of point of view? What was lost (if anything)? How might a less skillful writer have handled similar material? After answering questions like these, you may end your theme.

### Problems in Writing Your Theme

1. In considering point of view, you will encounter the problem of whether to discuss authors or their voices as the originator of attitudes and ideas. If the author is employing the first-person point of view, there is no problem. Use the speaker's name, if one is given (e.g., Nick Carraway, Huck Finn, Holden Caulfield), or else talk about the "speaker" or "persona" if the speaker is not named. You face a greater problem with the third-person points of view, but even here it is safe for you to discuss the "speaker" rather than the "author," remembering always that authors are manipulating their narrative voice. Sometimes authors emphasize a certain phase of their own personality through their speaker. There are naturally many ideas common to both the author and the speaker, but your statements about these must be inferential, not absolute.

2. You may have a tendency to wander away from point of view into retelling the story or discussing the ideas. Emphasize the presentation of the events and ideas, and the causes for this presentation. Do not emphasize the subject material itself, but use it only as it bears on your consideration of point of view. Your object is not just to interpret the work, but also to show how the point of view enables you to interpret the work.

Obviously you must talk about the material in the work, but use it only to illustrate your assertions about point of view. Avoid the following pattern of statement, which will always lead you astray: "The speakers say this, which means this." Instead, adhere to the following pattern, which will keep your emphasis always on your central idea: "The speakers say this, which shows this about them and their attitudes." If a particular idea is difficult, you might need to explain it, but do not do so unless it illustrates your central idea.

3. Remember that you are dealing with point of view in the *entire* work, and not simply in single narrations and conversations. For ex-

ample, individual characters have their own points of view when they state something, but in relation to the entire work their speech is a function of the dramatic point of view. Thus, you should not talk about Character *A*'s point of view, and Character *B*'s, but instead should state that "Using the dramatic point of view, Author *Z* allows the various characters to argue their cases, in their own words and with their own limitations."

4. Be particularly careful to distinguish between point of view and opinions or beliefs. Point of view refers to the total position from which things are seen, heard, and reported, whereas an opinion is nothing more than a thought about something. In this theme, you are to describe the author's method of narration, not the ideas.

---

SAMPLE THEME

---

### Shirley Jackson's Dramatic Point of View in "The Lottery"

[1]       *The dramatic point of view in Shirley Jackson's story "The Lottery" is essential to the success with which the author is able to render horror in the midst of the ordinary.** The story is not just a horror story; it could also be called a surprise story, an allegory, and a portrayal of human obtuseness, passivity, and cruelty. But the validity of all other claims for "The Lottery" hinges on the author's establishing the horror as stemming from a seemingly everyday, matter-of-fact situation—a situation that could not easily be maintained if another point of view were used. *The success of Shirley Jackson's rendering of horror is achieved through her rudimentary but expert characterization, her almost clinically detached selection of details, and her deceivingly simple diction.†*

[2]       *The villagers are depicted as ordinary folks attending a normal, festive event—in contrast to the real horror of their ultimate activity.* Because of the dramatic point of view within the context of a brief narrative, Jackson prevents all but the most essential aspects of character from emerging. She chooses to see things from the outside, almost as though she is adopting the pose of a villager who is detached and emotionally uninvolved with the events that are unfolding. Her speaker thus records details about the villagers and reveals a certain knowledge of local gossip. The speaker presents enough background information about Mr. Summers, for example, to permit the conclusion that he is a middle-aged, pillar-of-society type who is the usual community leader. Tessie Hutchinson is the principal character in the story, but we learn little more about her than that she is chatty, illiterate, and relatively inarticulate—all facts

Shirley Jackson, "The Lottery," in *The Lottery* (New York: Avon Books, 1969). Parenthetical page numbers refer to this edition.

*Central idea.        †Thesis sentence.

that are essential to her behavior at the end of the story when she objects
not to the lottery itself but to the "unfairness" of the drawing. So it is
also with the other characters—and there are surprisingly quite a few—
who appear in the story. Their brief conversations are recorded but no
more. We see them from a distance, as we would likely see any representative group of human beings in a gathering that is too formal to
permit intimacy. This distant, reportorial method of illustrating character is fundamental to the dramatic point of view, and the twist of
cruelty at the end depends on the method.

[3]      *While the dramatic point of view could theoretically permit the introduction of many details, Jackson's method in "The Lottery" is to concentrate
almost clinically on only those details that bring out the horror.* Because her
speaker is removed from the immediate emotions of the scene, we learn
just enough detail, but no more. At the beginning of the story there must
be at least some information about the background of the lottery so that
the reader can make some sense out of it, but there should be absolutely
no disclosure about the consequences of drawing the black spot. Thus, the
speaker establishes that the villagers are gathering rocks, but includes
no mention of why. The short saying "Lottery in June, corn be heavy
soon" is mentioned as a remnant of a more ritualistic kind of scape-
goatism, but the speaker does not go into any sort of explanation (p. 215).
All such references are at first presented innocently, and it is only after
reading the ending that a reader can feel their sinister qualities.

[4]      *Without exaggeration, if there had been more detail in the story, contrast
could not have been brought out so well.* The selection of some other point of
view would inevitably have required more detail. A first-person narration, for example, could not have been credible if it had not explained
the situation in advance, or at least if it had not described some attitude that would have anticipated the conclusion. An omniscient narrator would necessarily have expressed some commentary on the reactions of the townsfolk. But the dramatic point of view permits just
enough detail to inform the reader, but not so much as to spoil the surprise conclusion.

[5]      *Appropriate to the conclusion, and to the graceless, simple, unquestion-
ing, overly conservative nature of the villagers, is the diction.* The language is
uncolored and unemotional, sufficiently descriptive but not elaborate.
When Tessie Hutchinson appears, she dries "her hands on her apron"
(p. 213)—a description that is functional and no more. Much of this sort of
diction may be seen as a means by which Jackson uses point of view to
delay the reader's understanding of what is happening. The piles of stones,
for example, are to be used in the ritual stoning of Tessie Hutchinson, yet
one could never draw this conclusion when they are first described:

> Bobby Martin had already stuffed his pockets full of stones,
> and the other boys soon followed his example, selecting the
> smoothest and roundest stones; Bobby and Harry Jones and
> Dickie Delacroix—the villagers pronounced this name "Della-
> croy"—eventually made a great pile of stones in one corner of
> the square and guarded it against the raids of the other boys
> —p. 211

The speaker's references to the nicknames, and to the association of the stones with apparently normal boyhood games, both divert the reader's attention and obscure the horror of the fact that within two hours the stones will be used to kill someone. Even at the end, Tessie Hutchinson's son Davy is given a few "pebbles"; the implication of this word is that the boy is going to a game!

[6]        *Because of such masterly control over point of view, it is obvious that Jackson has created a supremely successful story.* Her objective is to establish a superficial appearance of reality, which she maintains up to the last few paragraphs. Indeed, she is so successful that a possible response to the conclusion is that "such a killing could not take place among such common, earthy folks as the story presents." Yet it is because of this reality that a reader sees the validity of Jackson's vision. Horror is not to be found on moors and in haunted castles, but among the people we see everyday, like the villagers in Tessie Hutchinson's hometown. The story thus expands, and supports many applications to human life in general. Without Jackson's skill in controlling point of view, there could be little of this power of suggestion, and it would not be possible to claim such success for the story.

## ★COMMENTARY ON THE THEME

For illustrative purposes, this theme analyzes the dramatic point of view as it affects the characterization, description, and diction in "The Lottery." In your theme you might wish to consider all these aspects or only one, depending on the length of your assignment.

In the paragraph about the characters (paragraph 2), notice that the aim is not to present a full character study, but rather to discuss the ways in which the characters are rendered. The only idea about the characters that is needed for the paragraph is that they are to be judged not as complete human beings but as "ordinary folks." Once this idea is established, then the thrust of the paragraph is to show how the point of view is used to keep the reader at a distance sufficient to draw this conclusion.

In the same way, the paragraphs about the selection of detail (paragraphs 3 and 4) emphasize the sparseness of detail in keeping with the dramatic point of view. Note here that the dramatic point of view is contrasted with other points of view that might have been used. This way of developing a discussion might be helpful for you to adopt, for by imagining how the events might be described in another way you can better perceive the method used by the author you are studying.

The third section of the body (paragraph 5) emphasizes the idea that the diction defers the reader's awareness of what is happening in the story. Thus the point of view of the detached reporter causes the selection of drab, relatively colorless words. The paragraph shows the relationship of these words to the horror and surprise in the story.

# CHAPTER
# 6

# *The Theme About Setting*

SETTING refers to the natural and artificial scenery or environment in which characters in literature live and move. Setting also includes what in the theater would be called props or properties — the implements employed by the characters in various activities. Such things as the time of day and the consequent amount of light at which an event occurs, the flora and fauna, the sounds described, the smells, and the weather are also part of the setting. Paintbrushes, apples, pitchforks, rafts, six-shooters, watches, automobiles, horses and buggies, and innumerable other items belong to the setting. References to clothing, descriptions of physical appearance, and spatial relationships among the characters are also part of setting. In short, the setting of a work is the sum total of references to physical and temporal objects and artifacts.

The setting of a story or novel is much like the sets and properties of the stage, or the location for a motion picture. Dramatists writing for the stage are physically limited by what can be constructed and moved. Writers of nondramatic works, however, are limited only by their imagination. It is possible for them to include details of many places without the slightest external restraint. For our purposes, the references to setting will be to stories, novels, and those poems that establish a setting either in nature or in manufactured things.

It goes virtually without saying that the action of a story may occur in more than one place. In a novel, the locale may shift constantly. Although there may be several settings in a work, the term *setting* refers generally to all the places mentioned. If a story is short, all the scenes may be in one city or countryside, and so a theme about setting could include a discussion of all the locations within the story. If your assignment is on a novel, it is best to devote your discussion to the setting of only one major scene; otherwise you would be forced beyond the limits of a single theme.

## Types of Settings

### NATURAL SETTINGS

The setting for a great deal of literature is the out-of-doors, and, naturally enough, Nature itself is seen as a force that shapes character and action. The progress of civilization has been largely a process of overcoming and taming natural forces. Furthermore, Nature has not been, and is not now, completely understood. As a result, writers have often seen the land, the wind, and the sea as forces that are wild, indifferent, unpredictable, and mysterious. Destructive storms, blistering sun, drought, numbing cold; precipitous cliffs, burning deserts, quicksand; wolves, snakes, vultures—all these in the setting of a work are often presented as manifestations of Nature's hostility to human beings.

This is not to say that no writers show Nature as a friendly force, to be enjoyed and protected. Nature may inspire joy in many ways. Even the wild and dangerous places of the earth may become the setting of quests for identity, and for comparisons between the vastness of God and the smallness of people. If Nature is seen as a positive benefit, it is also seen as something to be protected. Coleridge's Ancient Mariner violated Nature by shooting an albatross, and as a result he was destined to an eternity of expiation. James Fenimore Cooper described the wholesale slaughter of passenger pigeons and was affronted and depressed by such a wanton destruction of Nature. Today, many writers have perceived that Nature as we know it is threatened by pollution, as are human beings. We may expect future literature in which many aspects of natural setting will emphasize the precarious state of the natural world and the need for protecting it.

### MANUFACTURED SETTINGS

Artificial scenery always reflects the societies that created it. Hence a building or a room bespeaks the character of those who build and inhabit it, and ultimately it reveals the social and political orders that maintain the condition. A sumptuous artificial setting emphasizes the sumptuous taste of the characters living in it, and also their financial and political resources. With a few cracks in the plaster and some chips in the paint, the same setting may reflect the same persons undergoing a decline in fortune and power. Recently development of the idea that environment has a vital influence on human character has produced a number of stories that emphasize the deleterious effect of dirty drab rooms. D. H. Lawrence, who wrote many works in which environment is shown to have a shaping influence on character, wrote vehemently that ugliness hurts human beings — an idea that underlies much *realistic*, or *naturalistic*, fiction:

> Now though perhaps nobody knew it, it was ugliness which really betrayed the spirit of man, in the nineteenth century. The great crime which the moneyed classes and promoters of industry committed in the palmy Victorian days was the condemning of the workers to ugliness, ugliness, ugliness: meanness and formless and ugly surroundings, ugly ideals, ugly religion, ugly hope, ugly love, ugly clothes, ugly furniture, ugly houses, ugly relationship between workers and employers.[1]

This is not to say that authors cannot describe slovenly conditions to show that their characters are also slovenly but they may often include such descriptions to show that an ugly environment has contributed to the weariness, insensitivity, negligence, or even hostility in their characters.

Setting refers not only to place but also to time and everything that time implies. Morning, for example, is a time of beginning, and perhaps of optimism, whereas twilight is close to evening and hence a less optimistic time. The spirits of the hero Werther in Goethe's novel *The Sorrows of Young Werther* are directly related to spring, summer, autumn, and winter; as the seasons change Werther becomes more depressed until the winter of his soul overwhelms him. A happier but also reflective mood is established by Wordsworth in "Lines Written in Early Spring," in which the title and the first two lines lead into a meditation on the discrepancy between the joyful season and the mismanagement of human beings by one another.

### Studying the Uses of Setting

On the very primary level, setting has served as a means of creating a semblance of realism in literature. A landscape setting in the High Sierras, or a street that actually exists in New Orleans, ties an imaginative work to the real world.

Realism in a broad sense may be extended to include what is described from philosophical or religious points of view; psychological and political viewpoints will also color what is seen and described yet still determine what is called "realistic."

As writers wish to stress character, plot, or action, they may emphasize or minimize setting. At times a setting will serve as a mere location for events, as in Henry James's short story "The Tree of Knowl-

---

[1]*The Portable D. H. Lawrence,* ed. Diana Trilling (New York: The Viking Press, 1947, reprinted 1950), p. 620.

edge." In this story the emphasis is on conversation and analysis of character. In other stories, the setting may become so significant that it virtually becomes an active participant in the action. A good example is the setting of Thomas Hardy's novel *The Return of the Native*. The desolate area known as Egdon Heath directly influences the characters who live there; it governs their lives and most of their activities. Although the Heath occasionally serves to bring characters together, more often it acts as a barrier, and it is even the active cause of the death of Mrs. Yeobright and Eustacia Vye.

In studying the setting of any work, your first concern should be to discover all details that conceivably form a part of setting and then to determine how the author has used these details. This concern is artistic. You might observe, for example, that the manipulation of setting may be a kind of direct language, a means by which authors make statements that they may or may not interpret. In the concluding scene of E. M. Forster's *A Passage to India*, a large rock divides the path along which the two major characters are riding. This rock is a direct barrier between them, and Forster is at pains to point out this fact.

Another way to use setting as a kind of statement is to describe a setting in lieu of describing events, in this sense placing the setting on the level of metaphor (this technique has become common in motion pictures). The language used by the author to describe the setting is an important clue for you to follow in interpreting his story. Allan Seager's "This Town and Salamanca" provides such an example: the narrator describes the adventures of a childhood friend who spent his early manhood as a world traveler. The narrator dwells longingly and lovingly on the places visited by the friend, using language that gives them a romantic, heroic glow. At the same time, he describes his home town in matter-of-fact, flat language. As a result of this technique, Seager makes the assumptions and ideals of his narrator clear.

Authors might also manipulate setting as a means of organizing stories. It is often comic, for example, to move a character from one environment to another (provided that no harm is done in the process). Thus, Stephen Crane provokes smiles in the first part of "The Bride Comes to Yellow Sky" by shifting a provincial town marshal into the plush setting of a Pullman car. Crane's description of the awkwardness of the marshal and the patronizing airs of the other characters is humorous. The same shifting of environment causes a bitterly comic and finally tragic effect in Aldous Huxley's *Brave New World*, in which the main character, John, leaves a primitive world for a hyper-modern, super-urbanized one.

Another structural manipulation of setting is the "framing" method: authors "frame" their stories by opening with a description of the setting and then return to the description at the end. Like a picture frame, the setting constantly influences the story. An outstanding example of the framing method is found in Hemingway's story "In Another Country," which is set in Milan in World War I. The opening picture is one of windy, autumnal chill, with dusky light illuminating dead animals hanging in a butcher's shop; the twilight casts a pall over a hospital courtyard. At the story's end, one of the principal characters receives news that his wife has died. He has been wounded in action and is in the hospital, and the news of his wife's death leaves him despondently looking out the windows. What he sees is obviously the same gloomy scene described at the opening of the story. By concluding in this way, Hemingway has framed the events in a setting of dusk, depression, and death.

A more full use of setting is the "enclosing" setting—a setting that serves as the place of the entire action and that is constant and prominent throughout the story. A notable example is the Usher mansion in Poe's "The Fall of the House of Usher." The house is approached, entered, and left by the narrator over a short period of time which comprises the entire action; all attention in the story is focused on the house and its owners. Details of the house itself are vital to the action, and the condition of the house is symbolic of the condition of its occupants. Few stories have had setting, character, action, and mood so skillfully integrated as this one.

To the degree that a setting can add metaphoric energy to its purely mechanical functions, the discussion of setting fuses with that of *imagery* (see Chapter 12). Setting is often a form of imagery, for the qualities of a setting, like anything else, can be abstracted; if these qualities are generally true, then the setting is metaphorical and may become symbolic. The ease with which the language itself becomes metaphoric assists this process. Thus, when Poe writes that the stones of the Usher mansion possess a "still perfect adaptation of parts and the crumbling condition of the individual stones," it is obvious that he speaks not only of the house but also of the deteriorating psyche of Roderick Usher. Robert Frost's poem "Mending Wall" describes the scene of two men mending a stone wall in the springtime. Frost makes it clear that the wall refers metaphorically to those barriers that prevent close relationships between human beings, those protections of silence and indifference that allow a person to refuse understanding and compassion to others. Once this metaphorical significance is established, it is possible to carry the meaning of the wall still further; it can refer to political or social boundaries or more generally to any barrier between individuals or groups.

The fact that setting merges into metaphor and symbol should make you constantly on the alert to determine when the two become one. You might note that the description of an action requires only a functional description of setting. An action set in a forest needs no more description than that the forest is there. But if writers describe the trees, the colors, the shapes, the light, the animal inhabitants, or the topography, you should try to determine the purpose. That is, descriptions of setting may vary from the purely functional and appropriate to the evocative and to the outrightly symbolic; but they are almost never purely accidental or gratuitous. A full, colorful description may be designed as an appropriate setting for a happy action; but it might just as easily be interpreted as an ironic backdrop for an unhappy one. As you read the story carefully, you can see when the setting becomes evocative and symbolic. In *Bleak House*, for example, Dickens describes a district called "Tom All Alone's" as a shadowy, dark, unhealthy, hopeless place. The district is symbolic of the bleak fate of all those human creatures doomed to live there. By contrast, Dickens creates a cheerful symbol in his constant references to the bubbling fountain toward the end of *David Copperfield*. The fountain suggests the upsurging fortunes of David and his growing love for Agnes.

### Setting and Atmosphere

Setting also affects the *atmosphere* or *mood* of stories and poems. The styles and shapes of things described, their colors, the language used to describe them — all have their own connotative life that authors may utilize to fulfill their aims. A description of happy colors (like reds, oranges, and yellows) may contribute to a mood of gaiety, whereas one of somber colors may suggest sobriety or gloom. References to smells and sounds bring the setting even more to life by asking additional sensory responses from the reader. The setting of a story on a farm or in a city apartment may evoke a response of these habitats that may contribute to a story's atmosphere.

The style with which things are described may have an effect on atmosphere: a writer may make the scene static with many linking and passive words for one mood, but evoke another mood in a lively scene through the use of active verbs. Sometimes a setting may speak for itself, but often the author will introduce comments designed to connect the setting with the characters or else to suggest the proper response to the reader. Here is a fragment from a lengthy description of a setting in Sir Walter Scott's *Kenilworth*, skillfully linking description to reader and character:

> . . . Formal walks and avenues, which, at different points, crossed this principal approach, were, in like manner, choked up and interrupted by piles of brushwood and billets, and in other places by underwood and brambles. Besides the general effect of desolation which is so strongly impressed, whenever we behold the contrivances of man wasted and obliterated by neglect, and witness the marks of social life effaced gradually

by the influence of vegetation, the size of the trees, and the outspreading extent of their boughs, diffused a gloom over the scene, even when the sun was at the highest, and made a proportional impression on the mind of those who visited it. This was felt even by Michael Lambourne, however alien his habits were to receiving any impressions, excepting from things which addressed themselves immediately to his passions.

Although the description of a setting may thus contribute to atmosphere in a number of ways, it is important to remember that atmosphere is a broad concept and is affected by everything in the story. Action, character, dialogue, idea, allusion, and style are all elements that contribute to atmosphere.

## Organizing Your Theme

The object of this theme should be to relate the setting to some aspect of the work being studied. Do not merely describe the setting; make your description a part of a point, such as "The author's description of setting reveals an eye for detail, spatial relationships, and color." Then, your discussion should take the shape required by your central idea. Your theme should move from a discussion of setting toward a discussion of its effects.

### INTRODUCTION

Here you limit that aspect of the setting you wish to discuss and relate it to your central idea and thesis sentence. Any special problems and qualifications should be mentioned here.

### BODY

Following are some ideas about what to include in the body of your theme. You may concentrate on one or more of these. Your principal aim should be to say as much as possible about the setting within the assigned length.

1. *The relationship of physical characteristics of the setting to some general observation about these characteristics.* If the author has been careful to mention many details of the setting, you could discuss them in an attempt to re-create what you think the author envisaged and to make observations about the qualities of the setting. The settings of Shirley Jackson's "The Lottery" or Franz Kafka's "In the Penal Colony" could be treated in this way. Among the questions you might attempt to answer are these: Can the setting be re-created and imagined by the reader? Are the details about the setting specific or vague? How great a bearing do the details have on the action of the story? Are they constantly used,

or are they put aside once the action has begun? What details are neglected that the author might possibly have mentioned? What-conclusions can you draw about the author's ability to paint a verbal picture (does the author describe shapes and distances better than colors, or vice versa)? Is the author perceptive to smells and sounds? Are new details introduced as the need seems to arise, or does the author rely on the first descriptions?

2. *The relationship of the setting to character.* In many instances the author emphasizes the effect of environment on character, as in O. E. Rölvaag's novel *Giants in the Earth,* Melville's story "Bartleby the Scrivener," or Theodore Roethke's poem "Dolor." Your aim here is to select those details that have the most bearing on character and to speak about their effects. Questions that would lead you into the topic might be the following: What tasks do the characters perform that involve them in the setting? What particular physical and moral strengths do these tasks require? What weaknesses do they bring out? What traits enable a person to cope with these conditions? What attitudes do the characters have that may be traced specifically to their environment? Are the views justified in terms of the life envisaged in the story, or do some characters receive false impressions? Do they ignore aspects of their environment? What other character traits may be traced to their particular way of life? Emphasize constantly the interaction of setting and character.

3. *The relationship of setting and (a) atmosphere, (b) structure and action, and (c) ideas.* This theme deals with artistic relationships and effects. A theme on atmosphere and setting should establish the prevailing atmosphere or mood of the work and then fit the setting into this whole. Colors, shapes, time of year (or day), and the effects that these things generally produce are relevant here. If the atmosphere is at variance with the general effect of the story, you should emphasize this variance and attempt to determine why it exists.

A theme about the relation of setting to structure and action should attempt to show how significant the setting is in the form and principal actions of the story. Is the setting a frame, an enclosure? Is it mentioned at various divisions or shifts in the action? Is it brought in as a natural place for the characters, or does it become significant accidentally? That is, do characters move naturally from, say, a park to a pastry shop to home, or do they move from the park and then accidentally walk down an unfamiliar street, where the main action takes place? How important a role does the setting play in the action? Do the characteristics of a room seem appropriate for what takes place there? Do the characteristics of a natural scene enter directly into the action as land that is to be plowed or great distances to be traversed? Does the setting afford any natural pleasures to the characters? Does it afford natural dangers that affect the action?

A theme about setting and ideas should emphasize the setting as statement and metaphor. A writer, for example, may establish that a ship where the action occurs is similar to the world at large, and therefore the ideas about life aboard ship are also true of life in general. A natural setting that is clear and bright, with precisely defined relationships, might be a way of saying that truth in the universe can be readily grasped; a setting that emphasizes haziness or vastness might be construed to mean that truth is not easily found and that much of life is mysterious. Similarly, the conditions of buildings or even tools might be interpreted as statements about the conditions of life. When settings become symbolic, then the value of the symbols should be described. In this theme you should stress not only the ideas represented by the setting but also the means by which the setting lends itself to statement. Before attempting a theme about setting and symbol, you would do well to read the chapter on imagery (Chapter 12).

**CONCLUSION**

In your conclusion you may consider briefly those aspects that you might have neglected in the body of your theme. Thus, you might have been treating the physical details of setting, and may wish to conclude with a reference to the relationship of the setting to character, or with a brief consideration of the contribution the setting makes to the atmosphere of the work. As long as your new material is connected to your central idea, it is relevant in your conclusion.

SAMPLE THEME

### The Setting of Joseph Conrad's Story "The Secret Sharer"

[1]     *In "The Secret Sharer" Conrad makes his setting an inseparable part of his action and ideas.** The story is a sea story, which could not exist without the many details about ocean, ships, currents, cabins, and the men who sail. While some of Conrad's ideas about guilt, human sympathies, and the connection of divinity to human beings may be vague, the physical details about the setting are completely realized. *The integration of setting and story may be followed in details about the Captain's cabin and the ocean itself, and also in Conrad's suggestions that large, cosmic forces are at work in human affairs.*†

In *The Portable Conrad*, ed. Morton Dauwen Zabel (New York: The Viking Press, 1950), pp. 648–699. All page numbers in the theme refer to this edition.

*Central idea.     †Thesis sentence.

[2]     *The Captain's cabin is essential as a place of action for the story, be-cause it enables the Captain successfully to conceal Leggatt.* The tension resulting from the near-discoveries by the steward depends on Conrad's detailed descriptions of the cabin (see, for example, pp. 685–687). It is described as having the shape of an *L*, with the door on the "short part of the letter" (p. 661). Because the "vertical" part is hidden from anyone entering, and because the coats, the curtained bunk, and the bathroom all furnish concealment, Leggatt is able to avoid the steward's searching eyes. Further, the noise made by sailors walking on the deck above the cabin permits the Captain and Leggatt to speak together without being overheard, and therefore the plans for Leggatt's escape can be safely communicated.

[3]     *The ocean is just as essential as the cabin.* It was during a severe storm that Leggatt decided to reef the sail that saved his ship, the *Sephora*. It was the disobedient sailor's insults, probably brought about by fear of the storm, that enraged Leggatt and made him strangle the sailor. Thus the ocean itself produces both a good and bad result, and it is the bad result that causes Leggatt to flee from the *Sephora*. When he escapes he swims to the Captain's ship at night, thus connecting the two men, who otherwise would never have met. When Leggatt leaves the Captain's ship at the end of the story, he does so by going into the sea from a rope hung from the sail locker, and because the Captain wishes to keep Leggatt as safe as possible, he steers too close to shore. Therefore the potential shallowness of the ocean becomes an immediate threat to the Captain, who risks his future (which could go "irretrievably to pieces") on the chance that he will not run aground (p. 691).

[4]     *While both the cabin and the ocean help in the adventure and tension of the story, Conrad also suggests a larger, philosophic setting against which his adventure is played.* At the beginning, for example, we read the Captain's words:

> In this breathless pause at the threshold of a long passage we seemed to be measuring our fitness for a long and arduous enterprise, the appointed task . . . to be carried out, far from all human eyes, with only sky and sea for spectators and for judges.
>
> —p. 649

When the Captain of the *Sephora* agrees that Leggatt's reefing of the sail saved his ship, he asserts that "God's own hand" was "in it. . . . Nothing less could have done it" (p. 675). In reflecting on Leggatt's both saving the *Sephora* and strangling the sailor, the Captain draws the following paradoxical conclusion:

> The same strung-up force which had given twenty-four men a chance, at least, for their lives, had, in a sort of recoil, crushed an unworthy mutinous existence.
>
> —p. 681

At the end of the story, when the hat on the water enables the Captain to save his ship by turning around (pp. 698–699), it is clear that the setting, through the currents of water, is intended to suggest cosmic approval of the Captain's decision to help Leggatt.

[5]      *An additional merging of setting and story should be mentioned in conclusion.* This concerns the character of the Captain. In his role as narrator, the observations he makes about the sea, the sky, and the things the ship will encounter on the way back to England (p. 653) all show him as a clear-sighted man who understands the sea and the forces that control it. It is his knowledge of the danger of the sea during storms that makes possible his own personal "verdict" acquitting Leggatt for having strangled the mutinous sailor. Setting in this instance is so important to Conrad's story that it has become the very material of the Captain's morality, and it is this morality that causes the central decision around which all the events in the story turn. Because of this and all the other details, it is no exaggeration to say that Conrad's setting and his story are inseparable.

### ★COMMENTARY ON THE THEME

This theme focuses on the connection between Conrad's setting and the action and ideas of the story. In its emphasis on action and setting, the theme illustrates some aspects of the first approach described in the section on Organizing Your Theme. In showing the connection between setting, character, and ideas, it illustrates approaches described in 2 and 3 of that section.

The introductory paragraph indicates the closeness of setting and story, and lays out the areas to be developed in the theme. Paragraph 2 in the body is developed with details about the importance of the Captain's cabin. Paragraph 3 presents details about the relationship of the ocean to the story: in storm as a cause of Leggatt's good and bad actions, in calm and night as a link between the Captain and Leggatt, and in shallow as a means of safety for Leggatt but as a threat to the Captain. Paragraph 4 presents details about the larger, cosmic aspects of the setting, for Conrad's story is not only about physical details but about the unseen forces that control human beings. The concluding paragraph illustrates the significance that knowledge of the ocean plays in the moral decision — and hence in the character — of the Captain.

# *The Theme*
# *Discussing Ideas*

AN IDEA, narrowly defined, is a concept, thought, opinion, or belief, but broadly speaking it is the product of any process of thinking. There are few words that resist strict definition so tenaciously, for when you engage in any discourse it is often difficult to know when you stop talking about *things* and begin talking about ideas. In literary study it is virtually impossible to separate ideas from the values, or the "value system," of an author. Unless an idea is abstract, say the idea of a geometric form, it usually carries with it some value judgment. Thus, authors may write poems in which they embody the idea that warfare both capitalizes upon human gullibility and destroys human life. Here is a fragment from such a poem, Stephen Crane's "Do Not Weep, Maiden, for War Is Kind":

> Do not weep, maiden, for war is kind.
> Because your lover threw wild hands toward the sky
> And the affrighted steed ran on alone,
> Do not weep,
> War is kind.
>
> —lines 1–5

Implicit in Crane's poem are the value judgments that life is a gift that should be treasured and not needlessly destroyed, and also that the power of persuasion—particularly the political persuasion in times of war that requires people to fight and be killed—can be destructive and therefore bad. If you were to talk about Crane's ideas in this poem, you would inevitably discuss his values as well.

Most general discussions about literature are about what is loosely defined as the *meaning* of the work. When you treat such questions as, "What was on the author's mind?" or "What is the implication of the work?" or "What is this work about?" you are in fact considering ideas, and are therefore almost automatically considering the author's assumptions about life also. The word *idea* is therefore a way of referring not only to ideas themselves, but also to the thought processes that go with them. In this chapter, whenever the word *idea* is used, you may assume that such a broad definition is intended.

## The Place of Ideas

In expository literature there are few special obstacles to understanding the principal idea or ideas, because a major purpose of exposition is to present ideas. In imaginative literature, however, which tells stories, dramatizes human conflicts, idealizes or attacks various attitudes, and deliberates generally on the human condition, perceiving ideas is more difficult. The ideas are usually presented indirectly, and often they are couched in metaphorical language. They are therefore subject to interpretation. In most stories, poems, and dramas, ideas are subordinate to the situations and actions. Although such works are often enjoyed without reference to ideas, it is true that ideas are important reasons for which the author originally took pen in hand. Authors are above all people with something to say. An idea may cause them to shape their story in a certain way, or to create characters with certain traits. Suppose writers have an idea that a particular custom or institution of society is wrong. They may then write stories or novels to make this idea apparent. Suppose they believe that human beings in the twentieth century have lost their intolerance of cruelty; might such a thought have prompted W. B. Yeats to write these lines that conclude his poem "The Second Coming":

> And what rough beast, its hour come round at last,
> Slouches towards Bethlehem to be born?

If you were to discuss the meaning of these lines you might consider warfare, genocide, displacement of peoples, and other examples of cruelty and insensitivity that have characterized warfare not only in the twentieth century but throughout the ages.

Many works similarly exemplify or dramatize political, psychological, or social ideas. Sometimes a writer may introduce the same idea into different works, perhaps to test the idea by varying it and seeing how far it can be pursued. Ideas, in short, are vital in the content and form of literature, and an analysis of ideas necessarily implies a consideration of their artistic effect.

**How to Find Ideas**

Authors can express ideas both directly and indirectly. The following descriptions are for convenient analysis only, because in a literary work the methods described may all occur simultaneously.

DIRECT STATEMENTS BY THE AUTHOR. Often authors make direct statements of ideas in order to guide or deepen your understanding of their stories. George Eliot, for example, is noted for the many discussions about human character and motivation interspersed throughout her novels. Also, authors manipulate literary devices such as metaphors, similes, settings, and physical descriptions so that they state their ideas. In the stories of J. D. Ṣalinger the introduction of a bright, intuitive child has the importance of a symbol, for the child always suggests Salinger's idea that the insights of children, who are close to God in time, serve as evidence of God's being and for this reason are spiritual and emotional stimuli to jaded adults.

When authors state ideas, you should consider these at face value. It is reasonable, in your discussion, to attribute them to the authors. Remember, however, that your attribution should not have the weight of absolute biographical fact. You are reading an authors' works, not their minds, and authors may well exercise their right to express ideas of the moment or ideas with which they do not agree. When in writing a theme you say "George Eliot believes. . . ." or "It is Faulkner's idea that. . . ." you must always realize that you are not talking absolutely about the *authors,* but about their *works.* With this reservation, your remarks about an author's ideas should usually be acceptable.

IMAGERY AND SYMBOLISM. Authors often embody their thoughts in figurative langauge or in symbolism (see also Chapter 12). Yeats's "rough beast" from "The Second Coming" is a symbol of Yeats's idea that the twentieth century is a period in which people are becoming increasingly brutalized. As an example of figurative language, here is an image from Chaucer's long poem *Troilus and Criseyde,* where Criseyde considers the effects upon herself that her physical love with Troilus will bring about:

> How that an eagle, feathered white as bone,
> Under her breast his long claws set
> And out her heart he rent [tore].

—II. 926-8

This image could prompt an extensive discussion about the nature of physical love as Criseyde sees it, for a great number of ideas about the relationship of men and women, the economic and social power possessed by the sexes, and the degree of emotional involvement of people in love are embodied here. Whenever you find figurative language of any sort, you will find a similarly broad area for the discussion of ideas.

DIRECT STATEMENTS BY THE AUTHOR'S PERSONA. Frequently, authors will write from the point of view of a character in the work (for example, Frederick Henry in *A Farewell to Arms* and Gulliver in *Gulliver's Travels*). Such characters are called *personae* with lives of their own and the freedom to state ideas peculiar to themselves. Whereas the author unquestionably might agree with the ideas of the persona, you can never know exactly when this agreement takes place. Although the statements of a persona may be direct, you must use your ingenuity and intuition in deciding how closely the persona's ideas correspond with the author's.

DRAMATIC STATEMENTS MADE BY THE CHARACTERS IN THE WORK. In many works, different characters will state ideas that are in conflict; authors may present thirteen ways of looking at a blackbird and leave the choice up to you. They may provide you with guides for your choice, however. For instance, they may create admirable characters whose ideas presumably coincide with their own. The reverse would be true for bad characters, and so forth.

CHARACTERS WHO STAND FOR IDEAS. The characters themselves often represent ideas. In this case, interactions of the characters may represent the interweaving of ideas, and the conflicts between characters may represent conflicts between ideas. For example, in allegories like *The Faerie Queene* and *Pilgrim's Progress*, the characters stand for ideas in conflict. Aldous Huxley, in his novels, evolved a form called *the novel of ideas,* in which the various characters are made to represent ideas that in Huxley's opinion gave his novels intellectual life.

THE WORK ITSELF AS IT IMPLIES IDEAS. Perhaps the most important method by which authors embody ideas in a literary work is to manage carefully the total impression of the work. All the events and characters may add up to an idea that is made particularly powerful by the emotional impact of the story itself. Thus, although an idea may never be stated in the work, it will be apparent after you have finished reading it. In the novel *A Passage to India*, E. M. Forster shows that political institutions and racial and national barriers prevent human beings from realizing that they are all part of the human family. He does not use these words, but this idea is clearly embodied in the novel: the separation of the Indian and Anglo-Indian communities, even after the charges against Dr. Aziz are dropped, and the differences in customs between the English and the Indians, and even between the Hindus and the Moslems among the Indians themselves, all point toward this idea. Your reading would be incomplete if you did not see this implication. Similarly, Shakespeare's *Hamlet* illustrates the idea that evil breeds evil upon evil, sweeping both the innocent and guilty before it. You will recognize that interpreting the basic idea in a work of fiction is the same process as forming a central idea for any theme you write.

Obviously, it is easiest to determine ideas when the author speaks directly. In all the other cases you must interpret indirect and dramatic statements and be alert to the implications of each work that you read. Be certain that there is adequate justification *in the literary work* for the points that you are making about it.

## Two Critical Problems

Two critical problems are raised by the analysis of literature for ideas. The first is whether literature should be purely "instructive" or purely "pleasing" or both. The classical or "Horatian" view is that it should be both. Some writers have denied one or the other of these two aims (for example, Poe, who said that the writer should aim only at giving pleasure, and Shaw, who said that the only justification for writing was to instruct). The issue is not only how pleasing ideas themselves are, but also how relevant they are to literature. You are free to decide this issue for yourself, but you should realize that the Horatian view has been the most influential, historically, and that therefore many writers have written with both an instructive and a pleasure-giving intention.

The word *intention* brings up the second problem, for it is often difficult and sometimes almost impossible to claim that an author *intended* that you derive a certain idea from the work. For example, there has been a long controversy over Shakespeare's idea about Shylock in *The Merchant of Venice*. Did Shakespeare present Shylock as a farcical outsider in a Christian society or as a sympathetic outcast and a victim of religious prejudice? Similarly, in reference to Shakespeare's *Henry V*, many critics have thought that Henry is engaged in a righteous war that brings out the valor and strength of the English people and that he is one of England's great kings. But other critics have thought that Henry cynically embarks on a war of aggression and is responsible for many needless deaths. These differences of interpretation bring up the question of whether writers' intentions are even relevant, because authors seldom state intentions explicitly.[1] Many critics have asserted that great works have new meanings for each succeeding generation, in spite of the writer's intention. There is some validity to this claim,

---

[1]See W. K. Wimsatt, Jr., "The Intentional Fallacy," *The Verbal Icon* (New York: The Noonday Press, 1960), pp. 3–18.

and one must assent to it to the degree that the ideas in every work are to be regarded as having value for the present, unless their irrelevance can be proved. Still other critics, as a result of research into the intellectual milieus of the various literary periods, have claimed that authors' probable intentions can be discovered and thus their works are important pieces of evidence in determining their intentions. This kind of research is essential in the historical study of literature. As with the first problem, of course, you are free to weigh the relative merits of these views and to decide what your position will be.

**Expressing Ideas as Ideas**

It is important to recognize that talking about an idea is not the same as retelling the story or simply defining the literary type to which a work belongs. The phrasing of your central idea is crucial in this process, for if you go wrong here you might go wrong in the rest of your theme. For example, Jane Austen's novel *Northanger Abbey* (completed in 1803) is commonly recognized as a satire on the supernatural, "Gothic" novels popular at the end of the eighteenth century. If you were framing a central idea for this novel, you would go wrong if you said, "*Northanger Abbey* is a story about a girl who learns to recognize truth" (retelling the story) or "*Northanger Abbey* is a satire on Gothic novels" (defining the literary type). Instead, you should take some aspect of the story or of its satiric thrust that can be analyzed and discussed *as an idea*. Possibly your central idea might become, "Jane Austen's idea is that the true qualities of heroism are stability and common sense." This idea can be derived from the satire of *Northanger Abbey* and could be treated readily within theme limits. But if you tried to explain the satire of the work you would probably wind up explaining how certain events and attitudes in the novel parallel similar events and attitudes that are characteristic of Gothic novels. With this type of treatment, your discussion of ideas would become secondary, and you would no longer be writing a theme about ideas. Remember that an author's decision to employ a literary mode like satire stems from an idea like the one cited above.

**Selecting a Single Idea for Discussion**

An important step in writing on ideas is to select the *one* idea that will determine the form of your theme. The idea you select usually can be expressed in a few words (for example: "Fitzgerald's main idea in the novel *Tender is the Night* is that human energies are depleted and destroyed by wealth"). But in order to write a good theme about it you must, in addition to naming and describing it, show how and where it is exemplified; you must demonstrate its importance in the work as a whole. A theme on the idea about *Northanger Abbey*, for example, might demonstrate that the development of the heroine's character takes the pattern of increasing awareness of the truth that heroism is stability and common sense. Everything that happens to her in the novel may be seen as demonstrating this truth.

In forming your own theme, you might help yourself by answering questions like the following: What is the best statement of the idea that you can make? What has the author done with the idea? How can the actions of the major character or characters be related to the idea? What values and assumptions are implicit in your statement of the idea? Does the author seem to be proposing any particular cause? Is this cause personal, social, economic, political, scientific, ethical, aesthetic, or religious? Can the organization of the story be seen as a function of the idea? Does the setting have any relationship to the idea? Is there imagery or symbolism that develops or illustrates the idea? Does this imagery or symbolism recur? Are there any characters, or actions, who may be measured according to how they fail to live up to the idea? In short, develop your theme by interpreting the work in light of the major idea you have chosen for discussion.

You can easily see that your discussion will lead you into statements with which someone else might take issue. Remember, however, that your interpretation will usually be respected as long as you base your statements accurately on the story itself. If for some reason you happen to make errors, either because of faulty understanding or because of your own prejudgments, you will of course be subject to correction. Be sure that your reading is accurate and that your interpretation can be defended at each point by material within the work.

### Organizing Your Theme

Your teacher will look for the intelligence, skill, and accuracy with which you use the literary materials as a base for your discussion of ideas. The general form of your theme will probably be (1) statement of the idea, and (2) discussion of the relevance and place of the idea in the work.

#### INTRODUCTION

In the introduction, naming the idea will in fact be the central idea of your theme. You should state that the idea has interest and importance in order to arouse your reader's curiosity about your paper. You might also show how you arrived at your decision to write about that particular idea. Conclude your introduction with a thesis sentence.

### BODY

The body of your paper should show the ways in which the writer has brought out the idea in his work. You might wish to explore the importance of the idea in the organization of the work (e.g., "The writer's idea that no human being can hold himself above respect for life causes him, first, to have the main figure commit a horrible crime, and second, to show this figure enduring a long and painful expiation for the crime."). It might be that you would study the importance of the idea in certain characters (e.g., "Eliot's Prufrock is an embodiment of the idea that human beings in the twentieth century have been deprived of their identity and importance."), or in certain actions (e.g., "Wordsworth's having crossed the Alps is an action showing the idea that high moments of achievement are possible in human life."). Though you might wish to bring all these aspects into your theme, it would be difficult to discuss everything fully. Therefore you must be selective in what you choose to discuss. Use only those details that are essential and clearly relevant.

It is easy, when you illustrate your point, to let the detail become an end in itself rather than a means toward asserting the truth of your central idea. Remember, *your central idea must always be foremost in your reader's mind.* As you are writing, stop at various times and ask yourself: "Is this material relevant to my point so that my reader could immediately see its relevance, or is it just a retelling of a story?" If, after serious examination, you must answer negatively, then you should revise so that you keep referring to your central idea. Be sure, of course, to use somewhat different phrases for each reference (see pp. 20–21 for an example of such revision). It is necessary to revise in this way to remind your reader of your purpose in writing. You must remember that your readers are not likely to be as aware of your point as you are. Don't force them to do too much guessing, or they may stop reading your paper.

### CONCLUSION

In your conclusion you might wish to add your own commentary on the author's idea. Here, in effect, you are considering the validity or force of the idea. If you are convinced by the author, you might wish to say that he has expressed his thoughts forcefully and convincingly, or else you might wish to show the applicability of the idea to current conditions. If you are not convinced, it is never enough just to voice your disagreement; show that your own views are drawn from a more accurate assessment of conditions than the author has made.

---

### The Idea in D. H. Lawrence's "The Horse Dealer's Daughter" that Human Destiny Is To Love

[1]     There are many ideas in this story about the love between men and women. Some of these are: that love is a part of the uncontrollable side of human life — the emotions; that love cannot exist without a physical basis; that love transforms life into something new; that love gives security; that only love gives meaning to life; that love is not only something to live for but something to be feared. *The one idea that takes in all these is that loving is an essential part of human nature — that it is human destiny to love.*\* This idea controls the form of Lawrence's story, and the characters seem to be judged on the basis of how they live up to it. *The idea is embodied negatively in characters who are without love, and positively in characters who find love.*†

[2]     *In the first part of the story, Lawrence illustrates characters who have no love, and whose lives are therefore negative, incomplete, and without a destiny.* According to his idea, he shows that human beings without love are frustrated, sullen, argumentative, and even cruel. Their lives are similar to those of the great draft horses, which Lawrence describes as moving with "a massive, slumbrous strength, and a stupidity which held them in subjection" (p. 77). Time, Lawrence implies, is running out on people in this condition, and unless they find love they are doomed to misery. And it must be real love, for according to the main idea, anything short of real love is an evasion and will surely hasten this doom. Thus Joe, the eldest of the Pervin brothers, has arranged for an apparently loveless marriage to achieve economic security. With deliberate finality, Lawrence disposes of Joe, who thereby becomes an example of the main idea: "He would marry and go into harness. His life was over, he would be a subject animal" (p. 77).

[3]     *The thought that life is impossible without love is finally brought to bear on Mabel, Joe's sister.* She is the lone woman in the Pervin family, and also the figure for whom the story is named. Just as the death of her father is causing the family to separate, the breakup is about to produce a drastic action on her part. Here the operation of Lawrence's idea is brought out clearly: since it is human destiny to love, and since life without love is a kind of death, and since Mabel loves no living person but has only the love for her dead mother to remember, she chooses real death with dead love, which she prefers to earthly life without any love at all. In this sense

In Leonard Lief and James F. Light, eds., *The Modern Age: Literature*, 3rd ed. (New York: Holt, Rinehart and Winston, 1976), pp. 76–86. Parenthetical page numbers refer to this edition.

\*Central idea.    †Thesis sentence.

her attempted suicide is a positive act. She walks "toward the centre of the pond, very slowly, gradually moving deeper into the motionless water, and still moving forward as the water got up to her breast" (p. 82).

[4]      *Rather than ending Mabel's life, however, the pond really begins it, for her attempted suicide is the occasion of her love with Dr. Jack Fergusson, and therefore it also is the positive means by which she moves toward her destiny.* Dr. Fergusson, who rescues her, has previously been introduced as a person leading a life of quiet desperation. Perhaps his common cold, mentioned when he first appears at the Pervin home, may be interpreted as suggestive of the sickness of the soul without love. Therefore his need to be well, like Mabel's need to be rescued from the pond, may be seen as support for Lawrence's basic idea. Whether this interpretation is right or not, however, it is clear that Dr. Fergusson's rescue of Mabel is therapeutic not only for Mabel, but also for himself. The rescue thus suggests that once love is attained, it restores life.

[5]      But love is also complex, suggests Lawrence, and it creates new problems once it has been realized. *Therefore, Lawrence builds the idea that one's destiny in love is not only something to be sought but also something to be feared.* It brings out emotions that are new and strange; it violates natural human inertia; it upsets one's emotional equilibrium; it changes life so fundamentally that no person will ever be the same after having been touched by it. It is no wonder that Lawrence concludes his story in the following words:

> "No, I want you, I want you," was all he answered, blindly, with that terrible intonation which frightened her almost more than the horror lest he should *not* want her (p. 86).

[6]      *This realistic presentation of human emotions raises Lawrence's treatment of his idea above the level of the popular, romantic, "Hollywooden" conception of love, and answers all potential objections that love between Mabel and the doctor happens too easily.* Clearly, Lawrence suggests, love itself creates problems as great as those it solves, but it also builds a platform of emotional strength from which these new problems can be attacked. The idea is that this strength can be achieved only when men and women know love, because only then are they living life as it was designed. The problems facing them then, Lawrence suggests, are the real problems that men and women should face, since the problems are a natural result of their destiny. By contrast, men and women without love, like those at the beginning of the story, have never reached fulfillment and consequently they face problems that, though certainly severe and immediate, are really peripheral to life as it should be lived. The entire story of Mabel and Jack is an extensive example of Lawrence's dominating idea that it is the destiny of men and women to love.

★COMMENTARY ON THE THEME

The introductory paragraph first illustrates the many phases of Lawrence's ideas about love, and then produces a comprehensive statement of the idea, to be developed as it applies to characters without love and to those who find it. In the body of the theme, paragraphs 2 and 3 emphasize the emptiness of the lives of characters without love. The relationship of these two paragraphs to the main idea is that if the characters are not living in accord with human destiny, they are cut off from life. Thus Joe is dismissed by Lawrence as a "subject animal," and Mabel, his sister, attempts suicide. Paragraphs 4 and 5 treat the positive aspects of Lawrence's idea, focusing on the renewing effect of love on both Mabel and Dr. Fergusson, but also on the complexity of their emotional response to their new love. The final paragraph evaluates Lawrence's idea, concluding that it is realistic and well balanced.

# *The Theme on a Close Reading*

THE CLOSE-READING theme gives you a chance to exercise your perceptions and knowledge as a reader. It can be either very general or very technical, depending on your level of writing skills.

The theme can take the form of your abilities and interests. You may, for example, be concerned with the principal character in a novel and you might wish to concentrate on what a particular paragraph reveals about that person. Or you may have acquired some interest in political science and may wish to concentrate on the political implications of a passage in one of Shakespeare's historical plays. In short, the close-reading assignment can change as you change. It might be interesting to write such a theme early in the school year and then to write another one later, perhaps even about the same passage, after you have acquired more experience as a reader.

The assumptions behind the close-reading theme are these: if you can read a page, you can read the entire book of which the page is a part; if you can read a speech, you can read the entire play; if you can read one poem by a poet, you can read other poems by the same poet. Underlying these assumptions are others: in a good literary work, each part is absolutely essential; nothing could be eliminated without damage to the work. In the same way, all the writings of each author form a homogeneous unit, with each work contributing something to that unity. A close reading of an individual passage, therefore, or of an entire work, should indicate essential truths about the work or about the author being studied. Your reading of a passage or of a poem should indicate your ability to handle entire works. This is not to say that the writing of an analytical-reading theme automatically qualifies you to read every work by the same author. Few people would maintain that the reading of passages from Joyce's *Dubliners* makes it possible to read passages from *Finnegans Wake* immediately. What you are showing instead is a skill, an ability to bring your knowledge and understanding to bear on a specific passage and to develop a thematically conceived response and interpretation.

A close reading of a passage requires a certain awareness of *prosody* and *prose style* (see Chapters 14 and 15), but your focus in this theme will only touch on these elements indirectly. Instead, you are to focus attention on everything in the passage or work assigned. If the work is particularly rich in meaning, you will need to select from the super-abundance; if the work seems thin, you can cover everything. Works by good writers, however, generally offer a great deal for your study.

## Various Assignments

A close-reading theme will frequently be part of a drama or po-etry assignment, although it can be related to any literature study. You will find use for the general technique of analysis in other classes also. In social studies, for example, parts of political speeches can be subjected to analytical scrutiny. Scientific discourse may be closely analyzed for ideas and assumptions. No matter what the course, most works that you read can be closely analyzed, with great benefit to yourself.

## Preparing to Write

It should be obvious that your first task is to read the *entire* work, no matter what the assignment is to cover, so that you can understand the relationship of all the parts. If you do not do so, you may make in-excusable blunders. Read carefully. Then study the passage you are to write about. First, be sure to use the dictionary for all words that are even slightly obscure. Sometimes you may not be getting the sense of a passage on the first or second reading. Remember that even words that at first appear simple may offer difficulties. If you look up *all* the words in a passage that is giving you trouble, frequently you will dis-cover that your difficulty resulted from attaching the incorrect meaning to a word. Use the dictionary whenever you have the slightest question. In Shakespeare's Sonnet No. 73, for example, this famous line appears:

Bare ruined choirs, where late the sweet birds sang.

If you regard *choirs* as organized groups of singers (as you are likely to do at first), you simply will not understand the line. The dictionary will tell you that *choirs* may be an architectural term referring to the part of a church in which the singers usually are placed. Let us take another line, this time from John Donne's first Holy Sonnet:

> And thou like Adamant draw mine iron heart.

Unless you look up *Adamant* and realize that Donne uses it to mean a magnet, you are likely not to know the sense of *draw*, and you will thus miss the meaning of the entire line.

You also ought to use your imagination to find whether the words convey any consistent patterns, as a pattern of references to flowers, to water, or to political life. Do not hesitate to pick out such references in each line. Try to put them into categories, for you can frequently achieve an extremely good reading by setting up relationships according to topics, and even by making drawings or schemes.

Once you have understood the words, pay some attention to the sentence structures, particularly in poetry. If you read the line "Thy merit hath my duty strongly knit," be sure that you figure out the proper subject and object of the verb ("Thy merit hath strongly knit my duty"). Or, look at these lines:

> Let such teach others who themselves excell,
> And censure freely who have written well.
> —Pope, *Essay on Criticism,* lines 15–16

On first reading, these lines are difficult. A person might conclude that Pope is asking the critic to censure (for an assignment, look up *censure* in the O.E.D.) those writers who have written well, until the lines are unraveled thus:

> Let such who themselves excell teach others,
> And [let such] who have written well censure freely.

There is quite a difference here between the correct reading and the misreading. What you must keep in mind is that your failure to understand a sentence structure that is no longer common can prevent your full understanding of a passage. Therefore you must be absolutely sure, in your preparation, that you have untied all the syntactic knots.

## Organizing Your Theme

### INTRODUCTION

Your introduction should describe the particular circumstances of the passage or work. Who is talking? To whom? Under what circumstances? Why? What is the general subject matter of the passage or work? These questions are relevant to whole poems as well as to fragments from a drama, story, or essay.

When you have answered these questions, you should make plain your central idea. Never begin to write until you have developed a general reaction to the passage or work assigned; your description of this reaction will be your central idea. The first sample theme in this chapter argues that in the passage analyzed Hamlet is speaking about himself. The remainder of the theme develops this idea. In a theme involving a close reading it is sometimes difficult to arrive at a central idea, but if your theme is to be good, you must produce some guiding point that makes sense out of your reading. When you begin your theme, resist the impulse to carry out a general discussion, even if it is related to the work you are analyzing. Instead, come right to grips with the material in your passage. Notice that both sample themes begin right with the passages, and avoid general opening discussions.

### BODY

Your plan here is to combine the results of your close reading with the central idea you have asserted. You might be guided by the following:

SPECIAL CIRCUMSTANCES.   Observe the special circumstances of the passage or work to see how they influence the language, and therefore how they illustrate your point (e.g., suppose that the speaker is in a plane crashing to the ground or on the way to meet a sweetheart; either of these circumstances must be mentioned and kept in mind throughout your discussion). The first sample theme analyzes Hamlet's disturbed state of mind when he is addressing the ghost, who has just left the stage. The presence of the ghost is a special circumstance that accounts for Hamlet's shock and confusion. The second sample theme indicates that Langston Hughes's poem "Theme for English B" is supposedly an actual response to an English assignment.

DICTION.   Discuss the meaning of the words as related to the speaker's background and state of mind. In Browning's "Soliloquy of the Spanish Cloister," for example, the speaker is a jealous, worldly monk. His language is the kind a monk might use, but his interjections and schemes all show that he is a spiteful, petty person. The first sample theme demonstrates that Hamlet's diction is that of a student; therefore it is natural for him to use the references to *tables* in the academic sense.

In your theme you may make observations on both the direct statements and the implications. Also, you might describe any special problems you had with words, and show how their solution (by aid of the dictionary) assisted you in your reading.

OTHER ELEMENTS.   Discuss all other things that are relevant to your point. You might include either or both of the following:

1. Any noteworthy ideas. (See also Chapter 7.) Your emphasis, however, should not be on the ideas *as ideas,* but on the way they are related to the central idea of your theme. For example, the first sample theme briefly discusses the Renaissance theory of faculty psychology (paragraph 3) but is less concerned with explaining this theory than with relating it to the central idea of Hamlet's self-revelation.

2. The sentence patterns and rhythms of your passage. Because this analysis is fairly technical, it anticipates the prosodic analysis of poetry and the stylistic analysis of prose. In this theme, however, you need to show only those qualities of style and versification that are relevant to your point. The first sample theme demonstrates that at the end of the passage there are falling, trochaic rhythms that are sympathetic to the spirit and mood of Hamlet's speech. By emphasizing relationships of this sort, you can make your discussion of technique contribute to the thematic unity of your paper.

### CONCLUSION

If the passage you have analyzed is a paragraph in a story or a portion of a play, you should conclude by making statements about the relationship of the fragment to the rest of the work. You are in effect pointing out the organic nature of the entire work, because you are emphasizing that your passage is essential to the whole (for more detail on this topic see Chapter 11, on *Structure*). The first sample theme asserts that the passage being analyzed is the climax of the first act of *Hamlet* and that it anticipates much of what Hamlet does later.

With more independent works, such as complete poems, you might conclude either with a brief recapitulation of your central idea or with a brief reference to some aspect that you did not consider in the work. Remember that your topic is an analysis of the work. Hence, even in a conclusion you should always be referring to something in the work about which you are making some inference.

### A Note on Mechanics

If the passage you are studying is not numbered, number it, by lines or sentences, beginning with 1. If you are quoting a passage that is already numbered, you should use these numbers in your duplication. (The following fragment from *Hamlet,* for example, is numbered according to the edition in Alice Griffin's *Rebels and Lovers.*) Whenever you quote from your passage, indicate in parentheses the line numbers of your quotation.

FIRST SAMPLE THEME (PASSAGE FROM A LONG WORK)

## *Hamlet's Self-Revelation:*
## *A Reading of Hamlet, I. v, 95–109*

| | |
|---|---|
| Remember thee? | 95 |
| Ay thou poor ghost, whiles memory holds a seat | 96 |
| In this distracted globe. Remember thee? | 97 |
| Yea, from the table of my memory | 98 |
| I'll wipe away all trivial fond records, | 99 |
| All saws of books, all forms, all pressures past, | 100 |
| That youth and observation copied there, | 101 |
| And thy commandment all alone shall live | 102 |
| Within the book and volume of my brain, | 103 |
| Unmixed with baser matter, yes, yes, by heaven: | 104 |
| O most pernicious woman! | 105 |
| O villain, villain, smiling, damnèd villain! | 106 |
| My tables, meet it is I set it down | 107 |
| That one may smile, and smile, and be a villain, | 108 |
| At least I am sure it may be so in Denmark. | 109 |

[1]    In this passage from Act I of *Hamlet*, Hamlet is alone on stage immediately after the ghost has left, and so the character addressed is the ghost, at least at first. Actually, the speech is a soliloquy, because Hamlet almost immediately seems to be talking to himself or to the open air. Although he speaks about the ghost, about his mother (who is the "most pernicious woman"), and about his uncle (the "villain"), *the real subject of the speech is himself.\* His thoughts show his disturbed condition, his selection of words indicates his background as a student, and the rhythm in the concluding part of the speech shows his forthcoming preoccupation with the "ills that flesh is heir to."†*

[2]    *First of all the speech shows that Hamlet has been greatly disturbed by the Ghost's message that Claudius is a murderer.* Whereas previously the young prince has been melancholy, feeling the need to do something but with no reason for action, he is now promising the Ghost to remember him and his desire for revenge. If one assumes that Hamlet is a person of normal sensibility, thoughts of murderous vengeance would necessarily create confusion. Such disturbance, which Hamlet himself feels in his "distracted globe" (97), is shown by his resolution to wipe away "all trivial fond records" from the "table" of his memory (99, 98), and then by his ac-

---

*Rebels and Lovers: Shakespeare's Young Heroes and Heroines,* ed. Alice Griffin (New York University Press, 1976), p. 321.

*Central idea.        †Thesis sentence.

tion of writing in his "tables" that "one may smile, and smile, and be a villain" (108). Surely this contradiction between intention and action demonstrates his disordered state.

[3]    *Just as the contradiction reveals Hamlet's troubled mind, the diction reveals his background as a student and therefore it shows that Shakespeare has completely visualized and perfected Hamlet's character.* The words are those to be expected from a student whose mind is full of matters associated with school. *Table, records, saws of books, copied, book and volume of my brain, baser matters, tables, set it down* — all these smack of the classroom, where Hamlet has so recently been occupied. And in lines 96 through 104 there is a complicated but brief description of Renaissance psychology, a subject that Hamlet has just been learning, presumably, at Wittenberg. Briefly, he states that his mind, or his memory, is like a writing tablet, from which he can erase previous experience and literature (the "pressures past" of line 100), and which he can then fill with the message that the ghost of his father has just transmitted to him. Even in the distracted condition of this speech, Hamlet is capable of analyzing and classifying what is happening to him. This is the reflexive action of a scholar.

[4]    *An additional indication of Hamlet's mental condition, perhaps a subtle one but certainly in keeping with Shakespeare's poetic genius, is the rhythm of the speech.* The full impact of what Hamlet is saying is that by wiping away all previous experience from his memory, and by thinking only about death and vengeance, his mind is taking a morbid turn. The last part of the speech is rhythmically consistent with this condition. There are many trochaic rhythms, which would have been described in Shakespeare's day as having a *dying fall*. There are thus falling rhythms on

yes, by heaven

and

O villain, villain, smiling, damnèd villain!

The last two lines end with trochees *(villain, Denmark)*. This rhythm is unlike most of what went before, but will be like most of what follows, particularly the interjections in the "To be or not to be" soliloquy and the conclusions in that soliloquy (on the word *action*).

[5]    *Since this passage reveals Hamlet's character so clearly, it is relevant to the rest of the play.* From this point onward Hamlet will constantly be spurred by this promise to the ghost, that the ghost's "commandment all alone shall live / Within the book and volume of . . . [his] brain" (102, 103) and Hamlet will feel guilty and will be overwhelmed with self-doubt and the urge for self-destruction because he does not act on this promise. His attitude toward Claudius, which previously was scornful, will now be vengeful. His budding love for Ophelia will be blighted by his obsession with vengeance, and as a result Ophelia, a tender plant, will die. Truly, this passage can be regarded as the climax of the first act, and it points the way to the grim but inevitable outcome of the play.

★COMMENTARY ON THE THEME

The theme begins by relating the speech to the previous message of the Ghost. At the end of the theme (paragraph 5) the relationship of Hamlet's condition in the speech is related to actions later in the play. In the analysis of a passage from a long work, it is correct to stress these relationships.

Because the central idea is that the subject of the speech is Hamlet himself, the analysis of the ideas, speech, and rhythm is not an end in itself but instead is done to show how the character is illuminated. Thus the scholarly cast of the diction (paragraph 3) is used to show Hamlet's turn of mind as a student, and the trochaic rhythm (paragraph 4) complements a downcast, morbid turn of mind.

---

SECOND SAMPLE THEME (SHORT POEM)

### A Reading of "Theme for English B" by Langston Hughes

[1]    In "Theme for English B," Langston Hughes asserts that there is more reason for people to unite than to divide. The poem is a lyric, supposedly prompted by a theme assignment made by an English instructor in a class in "a college on the hill above Harlem" (line 9). The requirement for the theme, which Hughes quotes in the first five lines, was to "write / a page" that was "to come out of" the student (2–4). This unusual response, a poem rather than a prose essay, is therefore highly personal. It is a meditation based on the relationship of the speaker as a Black (the "only colored student in the class" [10]) to the white culture represented by the college and the instructor. *The movement of the poem, in keeping with the idea that people are basically similar, is from the physical detail about the speaker's home to the abstract concept that people are interdependent.\** *Hughes emphasizes his thoughts by using bare, simple diction and by referring to habits and likes common to all people.†*

[2]    *The language of the poem is simple and direct, the language used by all people, even if they have specialized or complex vocabularies themselves.* Most of the words describe either things or ordinary states of feeling, with no subtle shades of complexity. For example, the following passage, beginning a short section on the difficulty of determining the nature of the self, is commendably simple and is therefore accessible to everyone:

*Central idea.        †Thesis sentence.

It's not easy to know what is true for you or me
at twenty-two, my age. But I guess I'm what
I feel and see and hear.

—lines 16–18

Similar is the poet's statement about his likes:

Well, I like to eat, sleep, drink, and be in love

—line 21

This simplicity and directness are effective as Hughes leads up to his major personal and philosophical theme in the poem, the interdependence of human beings:

You are white—
Yet a part of me, as I am a part of you.

—lines 31–32

This important idea is expressed without qualification. Hughes does not provide a context in moral law or historical movements, which might furnish grounds for equivocation.

[3]    *The same community of interest is shown in Hughes's emphasis on habits and likes common to all people.* Early in the poem he points out the racial difference between the speaker, on the one hand, and the class and the instructor on the other. The speaker is different, having been born in a different state and going to a different local home after school. But he is really the same, despite these surface differences, and it is the sameness which Hughes emphasizes. The focus on common things like eating, sleeping, drinking, loving, working, reading, learning, understanding life, and liking "Bessie, bop, or Bach" (21–24) provides a basis for the identification of the speaker and the instructor. With common human interests and needs, goes Hughes's thinking, there is no reason for preserving those accidental cultural differences that result from differences in skin color.

[4]    *The poem therefore develops the idea that life itself unites people.* Hughes does not deny racial difference, but emphasizes instead the many similarities among people that should outweigh the difference. His attitude is one of quiet acceptance of the difference, and mild assertiveness about the similarities. If one seeks, there could be found a touch of bitterness over the statement that the instructor is "somewhat more free" than the speaker (40), but the word "somewhat" indicates too much understanding for hatred. In its simplicity, the poem is an eloquent plea for togetherness.

★COMMENTARY ON THE THEME

The first paragraph of this analysis shows the cause of the poem and briefly describes the poem's structure. Once the central idea has been expressed, the analysis is confined to diction (paragraph 2) and the poet's emphasis on the common characteristics of people (paragraph 3). Like a passage from a longer work, Hughes's poem is shown to have an external context — the English class — but the finished poem itself applies not just to a single context, as Hamlet's speech does, but to general human situations.

# CHAPTER
# 9

# *The Theme on a Specific Problem*

A SPECIFIC PROBLEM, perhaps one that has puzzled members of your class, is frequently assigned as the subject of a theme. The development of a problem theme requires persuasiveness if you are to convince your reader that you have indeed solved your problem. This technique of problem solving will prove useful to you in just about every course you might take. In science, for example, you might need to write a paper about the validity of a particular scientific experiment recently conducted. Or in social studies you may encounter a problem of how to improve the quality of urban life. The techniques described in this chapter are applicable to problem solving in any field.

The question-and-answer discussion, with which you have become familiar in your classes, is perhaps the best experience you have had with the method used in writing a specific-problem theme. To answer a question like "In *Heart of Darkness*, why does Conrad state that Kurtz has made a lengthy study aimed at improving the lot of the natives?" you would put facts and conclusions together just as you would in writing this type of theme. Only rarely can you answer such questions merely by retelling a story or identifying characters in the work.

Too frequently people take for granted everything that they read, only to discover when challenged that they have not really understood the material. Therefore, if the material they read can be seen as a problem, or as containing immediately unanswerable questions, they will search the material more deeply and develop more command over it. As they do so, they are also developing those skills and habits that characterize educated people.

Active readers are inquisitive. They constantly ask questions such as "What would this work be like without that?" and "What would this character do in other circumstances?" As they raise these questions, they learn about art and broaden their general ability to read and think. In attempting to find answers they must try out a number of provisional solutions; they must organize and structure their material convincingly and originally. They can solve some problems by simple exposition, but they can solve others only by presenting an argument or by making a certain major assertion seem valid or invalid.

In order to provide a convincing solution to the specific problem, you must perceive the most significant implications of the problem and decide on a suitable order in which to deal with them. Then you must judge the relevance of materials from your text. Choose only those that have an immediate bearing on the problem. Of course, both your sharpness as a reader and your close study of the text will bear fruit here, because much material seemingly irrelevant to a careless reader can be interpreted as vital by a keen, knowledgeable reader. As in all your assignments, your first objective is therefore to think carefully.

## The Nature of Literary Problems

Problems may be of any kind, and in this respect all writing about literature may be fitted into the problem category. For convenience, the problems may be classified as *artistic* (style, arrangement, and general content), *conceptual* (ideas), and *historical* (influences, background, and genre).

You should realize that a problem will often cause a fusion of these three classifications, because they are all interlocked in work and because the problem may be relevant to more than one classification. Your method of handling the theme will depend on the way in which the problem is put. For example, the question "What is the influence of the pastoral machinery on Milton's 'Lycidas'?" would require an expository treatment of how the pastoral elements figure in the poem. The aim of a theme on this problem would be mainly expository. But a related problem might be "Does the pastoral convention spoil 'Lycidas' by making it seem too artificial?" Writing a theme on this second topic would require argument rather than simple exposition. Naturally a certain amount of exposition would be necessary, but such exposition would be used only as it related to the argument.

### ARTISTIC PROBLEMS

Almost anything in a literary work can be dealt with in artistic terms, but you are concerned here with problems as they relate to style, structure, and — by extension — motivation and character. Suppose you were asked the question, "What meaning does the name 'Joe Christmas' have in the novel *Light in August* (by William Faulkner)?" If you interpret Christmas as a "reverse image of Jesus Christ" (as some critics have done), then it is necessary for him to be killed at the end, if your parallel is to be exact. Your consideration would therefore involve you in a discussion of *structure,* an artistic concern.

As another case, suppose you ask why Browning, in "The Pied Piper of Hamelin," created "such a rhythmic verse and such happily jingling rhymes." To solve this problem, you would need to decide how true the assumption about the verse is, and then relate the quality of the verse to Browning's subject and intended audience (the subtitle "A Child's Story" suggests that the poet had a certain audience in mind). Your method would not be simply to analyze and scan the verse, but to bring to bear the results of your analysis and scansion on your conclusion.

Dealing with a problem may also involve a consideration of motivation and, necessarily, of character. If your problem is to answer the question of "How does Hurstwood change in Dreiser's *Sister Carrie?*" or "Why do the Schlegel sisters feel obligated to befriend Leonard Bast in E. M. Forster's *Howards End?*" you are dealing with causes, effects, and relationships among characters.

### CONCEPTUAL PROBLEMS

Your intention in dealing with a problem about ideas is argumentative. For example, after reading Aldous Huxley's novel *Point Counter Point,* you might ask how valid his ideas are about the role of politics in modern life. This problem requires not only that you describe Huxley's ideas on the subject (perhaps as expressed through the character Mark Rampion), but also that you criticize these ideas, showing their validity and stating the degree of their applicability to modern society. And, if you conclude that they are not applicable, what other answers might be more applicable? You can see that solving a problem about ideas sometimes requires subjective responses; on many occasions you might dispute with your author, at other times you might agree with him.

### HISTORICAL PROBLEMS

Most problems of this sort require a certain amount of research. Suppose that you are dealing with the problem of Virgil's influence on Chaucer. You probably would have to consult secondary sources. (A *secondary source* is a book *about* the work or author you are reading; a *primary source* is the work itself.) If this problem were put in a different way, however—let us say, "The similarity of ideas in certain works by Virgil and certain works by Chaucer"—you could probably deal with the problem yourself by using a comparison-contrast method (see Chapter 10). Even in this inquiry, however, you would probably use a secondary source.

Problems of *background* and *milieu* also require varying degrees of research. Background information about the position of the Jewish people in medieval history would assist you in solving the problem, "How did Chaucer's audience interpret *The Prioress's Tale?*" Milieu refers to the intellectual and artistic currents prevailing at the time of a particular writer. If you were asked to solve the problem, "What was the milieu of Shaw's *Mrs. Warren's Profession?*" you would need to research in secondary sources.

A similar need to do research would occur in problems of *genre* or *type.* If you determine the genre of a work, you will know what to expect from it and can thereby make a reasoned evaluation. It would be folly for you to read a Greek tragedy and compare it unfavorably with *Hamlet* because "*Hamlet* has more action than the Greek tragedy, and besides, the Greek choruses are dull"; you must understand that the conventions of Greek tragedies were different from those in Shakespeare's plays. Or, you may fail to appreciate certain works of poets who wrote during the neoclassic period of English literary history. If you realized that these writers wrote according to rules of genre, you could recognize the requirements that they set for themselves (i.e., epic satire, Horatian satire, mock-epic satire, pastoral poetry, discursive poetry, heroic drama) and would be better able to recognize their merits. In this way, the study of genre brings a wider range of appreciation than you could gain without it.

In dealing with a problem of genre, then, you will need to learn the special conditions under which the work was composed and the type that the work was supposed to be. Some problems of genre would be: "*Hamlet* as a revenge play," "*Gulliver's Travels* as a travel book," "Dryden's *Annus Mirabilis* as a 'historical' poem," "*An American Tragedy* as a realistic novel," "*The Nun's Priest's Tale* as a beast epic," "*The Rape of the Lock* as a mock-heroic poem," and "Virginia Woolf's *Mrs. Dalloway* as a stream-of-consciousness novel." Your problem would be to set up an idea of what to expect from the work and then to show how it successfully lived up to these expectations.

Problems of genre can also require a treatment employing argument. For instance, "To what extent is *Gulliver's Travels* more than just a parody of contemporary travel books?" or "Did the revenge motif in *Hamlet* limit Shakespeare in treating Hamlet's responses to Claudius?" In dealing with questions like these, you would (1) examine the truth of the assumption about genre, and (2) deal with the relation of the genre to the problem at hand.

## Your Approach in Writing

As you may have concluded, it is impossible to predict all the various problems that will occur not only in your classes but also in your mind as you read literature. For your theme, however, remember that your job is to convince your reader that your solution to the problem is valid. Your theme will therefore most often require an argument designed to support your central idea (which is in fact a short statement of your solution to the problem). The various parts of your theme will be subpoints supported by evidence.

As you read your work, take notes on relevant details. Study your notes carefully after you have finished reading. From your notes you should arrive at a major conclusion, which you will make the central idea of your theme. The material in your notes may then be arranged in an order suitable to the logical steps of your argument. When you begin to write, you may suddenly realize the importance of other material that you did not include in your original notes. Work in this new material, but take care to illustrate its relevance to your central idea.

Depending on the degree of argument required by your topic, you will find a need to examine closely the key words in the statement of your problem. It is always wise to study these words carefully. If your teacher has phrased the problem for you, the phrase may contain words having implications with which you do not agree. You will also find it necessary to determine the limits within which you wish a certain word to operate. Or, if you object to the way a problem is phrased, you may wish to rephrase it. What would you do, for example, with problems phrased like these: "How much misanthropy does Swift show in *Gulliver's Travels?*" or "Show why Faulkner is the great American novelist." You can see that these are "loaded" questions. To answer the first you would need to determine the meaning of *"misanthropy,"* and if you admitted the word at all, you would need to limit its use to Swift's meaning. For the second question you would need to spend time on the meaning and admissibility of the phrase *"is the great"* before you could write a good theme. The sample theme considers the meaning of the term *"effective"* when applied to Robert Frost's poem "Desert Places." This theme sets up reasonable conditions for determining whether or not the poem is effective and proceeds to argue and demonstrate that the conditions are met. It thereby develops from the discussion of one of the major terms presented in the original statement of the problem. You might profit from employing a similar method whenever you are confronted with a similar literary problem.

As with most themes, you may assume that your reader is familiar with the work you have read. Your job is to arrange your materials convincingly around your main point. You should not use anything from the work that is not relevant to your central idea. You do not need to discuss things in their order of appearance in the work. You are in control and must make your decisions about order so that your solution to the problem may be brought out most effectively.

## Organizing Your Theme

### INTRODUCTION

If your problem requires an examination of any of its key words, the introduction is the proper place for this examination. Once that is done, you should describe the problem in terms of either its importance in the work or its general importance in life and literature. Thus, say you have the problem, "Is Moll Flanders's bad life justified by her economic circumstances?" You might wish to look first at the phrase "bad life" and may conclude that it is properly descriptive. Then you might wish to deal with the issue of justification in either or both of two ways: (1) whether, and to what degree, the immediate circumstances justify the sins of which Moll is guilty; (2) whether environment is generally a justification for human conduct. Ultimately, you might find yourself raising other perplexing moral and artistic questions that develop from these, for once you have raised the original problem, more problems usually follow, and they should be used to strengthen your argument. Although the original problem is particular, it raises general implications that should also be dealt with if a solution is really to be found.

In your introduction you should also briefly state your solution to the problem, which is your central idea. Your thesis sentence should conclude the introduction.

### BODY

The body should contain the main points of your argument, arranged to persuade your reader that your solution to the problem is sound. First, state the main reasons for which you have made your solution. Second, introduce a certain amount of representative material that supports these reasons. Your goal should be to cause your reader to agree with you that your answers are correct and well supported. Remember to use the literary material as evidence in your argument, not as descriptive examples with no rhetorical relationships to your arguments. Remember also that just to present the material is to do no more than retell the story, and that this theme is designed to discuss a problem, not to retell a story or summarize an argument.

## CONCLUSION

Your conclusion should affirm your belief in the validity of your solution in view of the supporting evidence. Of course, in nonscientific subjects like literature there are rarely absolute proofs, so your conclusions will not actually be *proved* in the way you can prove triangles congruent. But your conclusions, along with the evidence, should be *convincing*. Thus, if in the body of your theme you have neglected any arguments, you should raise them briefly here, not to develop them fully, but to show your reader that you have left no stones unturned in treating your problem. It is also a good rhetorical method to answer any objections or contrary claims that might be raised against your solution. Whether you state the objections fully or only make them implicit, you ought to answer them. This method of dealing in advance with claims against your argument is called *procatalepsis* (or *anticipation*) by rhetoricians. It is a strong tool of argument, and it makes an effective conclusion.

SAMPLE THEME

### The Problem of Frost's Use of the Term *"desert places"* in the Poem *"Desert Places"*

[1]          In the last line of "Desert Places," Frost changes the meaning of the phrase "desert places" to refer not only to the snowy field described in the first stanza, but also to a negative state of soul. Does this change occur too late to be effective? In dealing with this problem, a person would have to say that the shift of meaning does not work if it occurs abruptly, without any preparation in the earlier parts of the poem. But if this preparation is made—that is, if Frost does introduce material related to a negative state of being—then the shift would be natural and effective, even though it comes at the very end. *It is clear from a close reading of the poem that Frost does present such material, and that therefore the shift is successful.* *The preparation for the shift may be seen both in Frost's references to living things being overcome and in particular words in the third stanza, and as a result the concluding shift is an effective climax.*†

[2]          *In the first two stanzas Frost's references to living things being overcome by winter snow include not just Nature but the speaker too.* The scene first described is that of "weeds and stubble showing last" (line 4). Then the

Robert Frost, "Desert Places," in *Complete Poems of Robert Frost, 1949* (New York: Henry Holt and Co., 1949), p. 386.

*Central idea.       †Thesis sentence.

speaker refers to hibernating animals which are "smothered in their lairs" (6). Finally, in lines 7 and 8, he includes himself. He states that he is "too absent-spirited to count," and that the "loneliness" of the scene "includes" him "unawares." The aim of this movement — from vegetable, to animal, to human — is to show that everything alive is being changed by the falling snow. Obviously the speaker is not going to die like the grass or hibernate like the animals, but he indicates that the "loneliness" — that is, sadness or depression — overcomes him as he thinks about the bleak scene. While being sad or depressed is maybe not the same as the "negative state of soul" defined by the shift, these first eight lines do connect the loneliness with the speaker, and therefore they prepare the reader for Frost's concluding phrase.

[3]     *Particular words in the third stanza also prepare the reader to accept the concluding shift of meaning.* The words *lonely* and *loneliness* (line 9), *more lonely* (10), *blanker* and *benighted* (11), and *no expression, nothing to express* (12) all can easily refer to human as well as natural conditions. The word *benighted* is most important, because it refers not only to night, but also to intellectual or moral ignorance. From all these words it would seem that Frost is genuinely inviting the reader to think of negative mental and emotional states; he is providing a context in which the concluding shift of meaning will come naturally.

[4]     *Because of this preparation, the final stanza, concluding with the two words "desert places," is an effective climax.* All along, the speaker has been referring to the bleak, wintry field, but has increasingly been suggesting a bleak, wintry soul as well. The final lines make this suggestion absolutely clear:

> I have it in me so much nearer home
> To scare myself with my own desert places.
> —lines 15, 16

The last words therefore pull together and focus the developing thoughts of the poem, so that, instead of spoiling the poem with something out of context, they are a major cause of Frost's success, a climax of the poet's ideas. On close, sympathetic reading, the problem becomes no problem at all.

[5]     Despite these arguments, the shifts of meaning may still be open to the charge that Frost does not develop the idea of the negative state of the soul. He simply states it and ends the poem. It would be good to remember, however, that Frost is not writing a psychoanalytic study of bad aspects of personality, but is instead creating a short poem which ends in a moment of insight. To ask for more than this insight would be to expect more than a short lyric poem can provide. A better charge might be that the final meaning of "desert places" is trite and that it spoils the poem for this reason. If the phrase were removed from its poetic context, this criticism might be valid. But the phrase must be kept in the poem, right where Frost put it, and there it provides freshness and surprise. Frost has used "desert places" to suggest human coldness, blankness,

unconcern, callousness, and maybe even cruelty (he does not say exactly, but leaves each reader to supply appropriate interpretations). Thus the shift of meaning is a major element of success in a successful poem.


★COMMENTARY ON THE THEME

The introductory paragraph states the problem and provides a condition which would solve it. The central idea indicates that this condition is met in the poem, and the thesis sentence indicates three areas of development. In the body, paragraph 2 shows that Frost connects the natural loneliness of the field with the speaker's state of mind. This paragraph thus shows that there is preparation early in the poem for the concluding "shift" of meaning about which the problem was raised. Paragraph 3 continues this line of development, showing how certain words in the third stanza of Frost's poem can refer directly to a human state. The fourth paragraph indicates that the final words are in effect a climax of this development in the poem. The concluding paragraph (5) raises additional problems, and answers them. The theme thus succeeds by showing that the original problem was based on a lack of attention to the earlier parts of the poem. The idea of the theme is, in effect, that the problem was really no problem at all.

# 10

<br>

# *The Theme of Comparison-Contrast*

THE COMPARISON THEME may be used to compare and contrast different authors, two or more works by the same author, different drafts of the same work, or characters, incidents, and ideas within the same work or in different works. Not only is comparison-contrast popular in literature assignments, but it is one of the commonest approaches you will find in other studies, too. The ideas of two historians may be compared, or the approaches of two schools of politics, or two conflicting economic theories. The possibilities for using comparison-contrast are extensive.

## Comparison-Contrast as a
## Way to Knowledge

Comparison and contrast are important means to gaining understanding. For example, suppose that you are having trouble understanding separately the poems "War is Kind" by Stephen Crane and "The Fury of Aerial Bombardment" by Richard Eberhart. When you start comparing the two poems, however, you will immediately notice things that you may not have noticed at first. Both of them treat the horrors of war, but they do so differently. Crane is ironic, whereas Eberhart is quietly bitter. Though Eberhart's topic is the "fury" of bombardment, he does not describe explosions and anguished death, but rather draws attention to humanity's collective stupidity and to the regrettable deaths of people with great potential. Crane, on the other hand, achieves his ironic effect by speaking of "slaughter" and "corpses" at the same time he also speaks of war's being "kind." Both poems ultimately agree on the irrationality of war. Making a comparison and contrast in this way enables you to see each poem in perspective, and therefore more clearly. The comparison-contrast method is similarly rewarding whenever you apply it, for perhaps the quickest way to get at the essence of an artistic work is to compare it with another work. Similarities are brought out by comparison, and differences are shown by contrast.

The comparison-contrast method is closely related to the study of *definition*, because definition aims at the description of a particular thing by identifying its properties while also isolating it from everything else. Comparison-contrast is also closely allied with Plato's idea that we learn a thing best by reference to its opposite; that is, one way of finding out what a thing *is* is to find out what it is *not.*

## Clarify Your Intention

Do not begin to write this or any theme without a plan. Your first problem is to decide your objective. You ought to relate the material of the assignment to the purposes of the course, for the comparison-contrast method can be focused on a number of points. One focal point may simply be the equal and mutual illumination of both (or more) subjects of comparison; thus, where your purpose is to gain a general understanding of all the writers in your English course, a theme about Milton and Pope would serve to describe the methods of both poets without throwing primary attention on either. But suppose your unit focuses more on Milton—then your comparison-contrast theme could use Pope's methods as a means of highlighting Milton's your theme would finally be about Milton, and your discussion of Pope would be relevant only as it related to this purpose. Conversely, if your class is concentrating on eighteenth-century literature, you might use a discussion of Milton only as it illuminated Pope. Your first task is therefore to decide where to place your emphasis. The first sample theme illustrates the first type, namely the illumination of both works being considered. Unless you want to claim superiority for one particular work, you will find this type suitable for most comparisons.

## Find Common Grounds for Comparison

Your second problem is to select the proper material—the grounds of your discussion. It is useless to compare essentially dissimilar things, for then your basic conclusions will be of limited value. Therefore your task is to put the works or writers you are comparing onto common ground. Compare like with like: style with style, subject with subject, idea with idea, structure with structure, characterization with characterization. Nothing can be learned from a comparison of "Pope's style and Milton's philosophy." But a comparison of "the influence of philosophy on style in Milton and Pope" suggests common ground, with points of both comparison and divergence and with further implications about the ages in which the two poets lived.

In attempting to find common ground, seek possible similarities as you prepare yourself by reading and taking notes for the assignment. Here your generalizing powers will assist you, for apparently dissimilar materials may meet — if you are able to perceive the meeting place. Thus a comparison of *The House of Mirth* by Edith Wharton and *The Catcher in the Rye* by J. D. Salinger might put the works on the common ground of "The Treatment of the 'Outsider'" or "Corrosive Influences of an Affluent Society on the Individual" or "The Basis of Social Criticism," even though the works are about different characters living in different ages. As you can see, what appears at first dissimilar can often be put into a frame of reference that permits analytical comparison and contrast. Much of your success in writing will depend on your ingenuity in finding a suitable basis for comparison.

## Methods of Comparison

Let us assume that you have decided on your rhetorical purpose and on the basis or bases of your comparison: you have done your reading, taken your notes, and know what you want to say. The remaining problem is the treatment of your material. Here are two acceptable ways.

A common, but inferior, way is to make your points first about one work and then do the same for the other. This method makes your paper seem like two big lumps, and it also involves much repetition because you must repeat the same points as you treat your second subject. This first method is only satisfactory.

The superior method is to treat your main idea in its major aspects and to make references to the two (or more) writers as the reference illustrates and illuminates your main idea. Thus you would be constantly referring to both writers, sometimes within the same sentence, and would be reminding your reader of the point of your discussion. There are reasons for the superiority of the second method: (1) you do not need to repeat your points unnecessarily, for you can document them as you raise them; (2) by referring to the two writers in relatively close juxtaposition in relation to a clearly stated basis of comparison, you can avoid making a reader with a poor memory reread previous sections. Frequently such readers do not bother to reread, and as a result they are never really clear about what you have said. As a good example, here is a paragraph from a student theme on "Nature as a basis of comparison in William Wordsworth's 'The World Is Too Much with Us' and Gerard Manley Hopkins's 'God's Grandeur.'" The virtue of the paragraph is that it uses material from both poets as a means of development; the material is synthesized by the student (sentence numbers in brackets) as follows:

> [1] Hopkins's ideas are Christian, though not genuinely other-worldly. [2] God is a God of the world for Hopkins, and "broods with warm breast and with ah! bright wings" (line 14); Hopkins is convinced that God is here and everywhere, for his first line triumphantly proclaims this. [3] Wordsworth, by contrast, is able to perceive the beauty of Nature, but feels that God in the Christian sense has deserted him. [4] Wordsworth is to be defended here, though, because his wish to see Proteus or to hear Triton is not pagan. [5] He wants, instead, to have faith, to have the conviction that Hopkins so confidently claims. [6] Even if the faith is pagan, Wordsworth would like it just so he could have firm, unshakable faith. [7] As a matter of fact, however, Wordsworth's perception of Nature contradicts the lack of faith he claims. [8] His God is really Nature itself. [9] Hopkins's more abstract views of Nature make me feel that the Catholic believes that Nature is only a means to the worship of God. [10] For Hopkins, God is supreme; for Wordsworth, Nature is.

Letting $H$ stand for ideas about Hopkins, and $W$ for ideas about Wordsworth, the paragraph may be schematized as follows (numbers refer to sentences):

$$1 = H. \quad 2 = H. \quad 3 = W. \quad 4 = W. \quad 5 = W, H. \quad 6 = W.$$
$$7 = W. \quad 8 = W. \quad 9 = H. \quad 10 = H, W.$$

The interweaving of subject material gives the impression that the student has learned both works so well that he is able to think of them together. Mental "digestion" has taken place. When the student discusses Hopkins's idea of Nature, he is able to think of it immediately in relation to Wordsworth's, and brings out references to both poets as he writes. You can profit from his example. If you can develop your comparison-contrast theme in such an interlocking way, you will write it more economically and clearly than you would by the first method (this statement is true of tests as well as themes). Beyond that, if you have actually digested the material as successfully as this method would show, you will be demonstrating that you have fulfilled one of the primary goals of education — the assimilation and *use* of material. Too often education as presented in a course-by-course and writer-by-writer approach seems to be compartmentalized. But you should always be trying to synthesize the materials you acquire, to put them together through comparison and contrast so that you can accustom yourself to seeing things not as *fragments* but as parts of *wholes*.

## Avoid the "Tennis-Ball" Method

As you make your comparison, do not confuse an interlocking method with a "tennis-ball" method, in which you bounce your subject back and forth constantly and repetitively. The tennis-ball method is shown in the following example from a comparison of A. E. Housman's "On Wenlock Edge" and Theodore Roethke's "Dolor":

> Housman talks about the eternal nature of people's troubles whereas Roethke talks about the "dolor" of modern business life. Housman uses details of woods, gales, snow, leaves, and hills, whereas Roethke selects details of pencils, boxes, paper-weights, mucilage, and lava-tories. Housman's focus is therefore on the torments of people close to Nature; Roethke's on civilized, ordered, duplicated, gray-flanneled people. Housman states that the significance of human problems fades in the perspective of eternity; Roethke does not mention eternity but makes people's problems seem even smaller by showing that business life has virtually erased human emotion.

Imagine the effect of reading an entire theme presented in this fashion. Aside from its power to bore, the tennis-ball method does not give you the chance to develop your points. You should not feel so cramped that you cannot take several sentences to develop a point about one writer or subject before you bring in comparison with another. If you remember to interlock the two points of comparison, however, as in the example comparing Hopkins and Wordsworth, your method will be satisfactory.

## The Extended Comparison-Contrast

For a longer theme, such as a controlled research paper, the technique of comparison-contrast may be extended to the consideration of many works. The extended theme is also used to deal with comprehensive, general questions which may require the treatment of many authors. For themes of this larger scope, the requirement that you treat a common topic still applies, although with more works to account for you will need to modify the comparison-contrast method.

Let us assume that you have been asked to consider not just two literary works but five or six. You need first to determine a common ground among them which will give your theme a central, unifying idea. When you sketch your ideas and make your early draft, try to bring all the works together on your major points; here the longer form requires no modification. But when you make your comparisons you will find the need to classify your works into groups. Thus, if all your works express a common idea, there is no need to identify each work separately as being associated with the idea. You may wish to concentrate instead on the expression in one work, and then point out that the other works are in substantial agreement. In this way you provide the concreteness that the study of one work can furnish and also the comprehensiveness needed for the full treatment of all the works.

When you wish to make contrasts, you should try to group your works. Three or four works may treat a topic in one way while one or two do it in another. Here you will in effect treat the topic itself in a straightforward contrast method, but may wish to use details from the works on each side of the issue to support your contrasts. Again, it is desirable to use the analysis of the particular point from one work so that you can provide the vividness your reader will need to grasp your ideas. Once you have thus exemplified your point there is no need to go into detail from the other works; just describe briefly the fact of agreement. For variety, interest, and comprehensiveness, you ought to include some detail from each of the works. You can keep within a reasonable length, however, if you remember to group your works on points of similarity so that you do not go into unproductive detail.

For this longer comparison-contrast theme you will encounter a problem of documentation. If your list of works becomes extensive, you will need to use footnotes to locate the materials you are citing. (See Appendix B for a description of footnoting.) While it is always advantageous to use informal, parenthetical page numbers when you refer to a single work many times, you may need to refer to a number of works within a short passage in your theme. When this occurs you must use footnotes to avoid the confusion that parenthetical page numbers might cause. If you set up an exact system of abbreviation-style references, however, the parenthetical system would still work. Again, see Appendix B for this system.

## Organizing Your Theme

First you must narrow your subject into a topic you can handle conveniently within the limits of the assignment. For example, if you have been assigned a comparison of Tennyson and Pope, pick out one or two poems of each poet and write your theme about them. You must be wary, however, of the limitations of this selection: generalizations made from one or two works may not apply to the broad subject originally proposed.

### INTRODUCTION

State what works, authors, characters, and ideas are under consideration, then show how you have narrowed the basis of your comparison. Your central idea will be a brief statement of what can be learned from your paper: the general similarities and differences that you have observed from your comparison and/or the superiority of one work or author over another. Your thesis sentence should anticipate the body of your theme.

### BODY

The body of your theme depends on the points you have chosen for comparison. You might be comparing two works on the basis of *structure, tone, style,* two authors on *ideas,* or two characters on *character traits.* In your discussion you would necessarily use the same methods that you would use in writing about a single work, except that here (1) you are exemplifying your points by reference to more subjects than one, and (2) your ultimate rhetorical purpose is to illuminate the subjects on which your comparison is based. In this sense, the methods you use in talking about *structure* or *style* are not "pure" but are instead subordinate to your aims of comparison-contrast. Let us say that you are comparing the ideas in two different works. The first part of your theme might be devoted to analyzing and describing the similarities and dissimilarities of the ideas *as* ideas. Your interest here is not so much to explain the ideas of either work separately as to explain the ideas of both works in order to show points of agreement and disagreement. A second part might be given over to the influences of the ideas on the *structure* and *style* of the particular works; that is, how the ideas help make the works similar or dissimilar. If you are comparing characters, your points might be to show similarities and dissimilarities of mental and spiritual qualities and of activities in which the characters engage.

### CONCLUSION

Here you are comparatively free to reflect on other ideas in the works you have compared, to make observations on comparative qualities, or to summarize briefly the basic grounds of your comparison. The conclusion of an extended comparison-contrast theme should represent a final bringing together of the materials. In the body of the theme you may not have referred to all the works in each paragraph; however, in the conclusion you should try to refer to them all, if possible.

If your writers belonged to any "period" or "school," you also might wish to show in your conclusion how they relate to these larger movements. References of this sort provide a natural common ground for comparison.

FIRST SAMPLE THEME (TWO WORKS)

*The Ambiguous Treatment of Formal Education*
*in Down These Mean Streets by Piri Thomas and*
*A Portrait of the Artist as a Young Man by James Joyce*

[1]         Because both *Down These Mean Streets* by Piri Thomas and *A Portrait of the Artist as a Young Man* by James Joyce are about the early years
and recollections of their heroes, they both necessarily include the subject
of formal education, and *they both are ambiguous on the subject.** Both authors seem to agree that formal education is a pawn in larger political or
religious games, and to the degree that education is used to impose na-
tionalistic, religious, or racist values, both heroes — Piri and Stephen —
react violently. If one separates the wheat from the chaff, however, education may be seen as a liberating influence. Stephen is free by the time he
is twenty, when the story closes, whereas Piri does not begin his liberation through education until long after he has left school and has almost
been crushed by the life he sought on the streets. *The ambivalence toward
education may be seen in the punishment it represents in both works, in the
rebellious attitudes of the heroes, and in their respective liberation.*†

[2]         The most negative quality of education in both works is punishment or the fear which punishment brings. To a large degree, both Joyce
and Thomas agree that the educational establishment is out of step with
the needs of those being educated, and it imposes punishment to make up
for this failure. To show how obtuse and irrational the people who operate the systems are, both authors show that major incidents of punishment are prompted by similarly innocent activities of the heroes. Steph-
en's loss of his glasses prevents him from doing an assignment, and Piri
must go to the lavatory. The reactions of the prefect of studies and the
teacher in both cases are unreasonable, and it is this unreasonableness
which both boys either consciously or unconsciously associate with education. Thus Stephen constantly fears the pandybat, which he negatively
associates with the soutanes of his priestly educators, while Piri remembers the pursuing principal and "dear Miss Shepard" (p. 72) as threatening forces. Because Stephen's education is inseparable from his religious
instruction, the sermon on hell in Chapter 3 becomes for him an even
greater and more threatening punishment.

[3]         Even though punishment often intimidates people and thus gets
them back in "line," both Piri and Stephen are portrayed as too rebellious
to be cowed into submission. Piri describes his favorite school activity as
the "game of sneaking out of the room" (p. 70). His rebellion is to leave

        Quotations and page numbers refer to Piri Thomas, *Down These Mean Streets* (New
York: New American Library, 1967), and James Joyce, *A Portrait of the Artist as a Young
Man: Text, Criticism, and Notes,* ed. Chester G. Anderson (New York: The Viking Press,
1968).
        *Central idea.        †Thesis sentence.

whenever possible because of his hatred for school and everything it represents to him. Stephen's rebellion is more intellectual, but it is rebellion nevertheless. Because of one of his compositions, he is accused of "heresy" by "Mr. Tate, the English master" (p. 79). He admits his fault and offers a "submission" consistent with received dogma, but his independent and rebellious spirit is not defeated by the incident. Unlike Piri, Stephen never runs away from school — after all, he was in residence and could not — but he does try to overturn the establishment by appealing against the injustice of Father Dolan's punishment. In addition, he carries out his rebellion by developing a fondness for Byron, certainly not a writer who was approved in a religious school for his ideas or morals (pp. 80–82). Piri is represented as being far less articulate and sophisticated than Stephen, and hence when he flees he carries nothing beneficial with him, while Stephen is really using his education to attain greater mental independence.

[4]     It is independence and liberation that both Stephen and Piri finally experience, and it is here that education produces its most positive results. Even though at the end of the *Portrait* Stephen is leaving home, country, and church, his education has been so successful that he now has the confidence in himself to create a new and free life. By contrast, Piri has been a failure and does not renew his experience with education until he is in prison. His trouble in understanding words like *psychology* and *introspectively* (p. 284) when he is about twenty-five stands in stark and sad contrast with Stephen's learned discourses on art at the age of twenty. Still, Piri becomes "thirsty for anything that had to do with understanding" (p. 285), and his increased awareness of himself, gained through his studies and introspection, enables him to overcome his own rebelliousness which under other circumstances might have kept him locked in prison for life. With all the shortcomings of their respective educational systems, education somehow exerts enough of a positive influence to enable both heroes to push themselves toward freedom.

[5]     One could go on to consider how both Joyce and Thomas by implication indict formal education. If the establishment were less geared to political and religious indoctrination, and more in tune with the needs of persons represented by Piri and Stephen, it would fulfill the ideal of liberating minds in an atmosphere of joy. There would then be no need for the pain, fear, and hatred that accompany the educations of Piri and Stephen. But until such a golden future is realized, the educational path will be rocky and precipitous, and the experiences of both heroes will be repeated. Freedom and independence may be found at the end of the path, but getting there will entail many detours and discouragements. Thus the attitude of love-hate that is present in both novels will not change.

## ★COMMENTARY ON THE THEME

Although there are many points on which the two novels could be compared, this theme treats only one of them — the ambiguous treatment of formal education. The method of development in the theme is to go from the negative (punishment) to the positive (mental independence).

In paragraph 2, the first in the body of the theme, both novels are constantly kept in the reader's thoughts. Each sentence except the last refers to both works or to characters present in both works.

Paragraph 3 begins with a reference to both works, and follows this with two sentences on Piri. The next sentence goes to Stephen, after a comparison with Piri, and then four sentences follow on Stephen with one comparative reference to Piri. The concluding sentence compares both heroes on the topic of the success of their rebelliousness. Paragraph 5 continues the same interlocking pattern of development.

Because the concluding paragraph is not a part of the outline, it is free to take up a new but related topic: namely, the way in which the ambiguity toward education is part of a general indictment of the educational structure. Even though the topic is different from those in the outline, however, it is closely connected with the central idea.

### SECOND SAMPLE THEME (EXTENDED COMPARISON-CONTRAST)

#### *Disease and Illness as a Literary Symbol*

[1]     In life, disease is common; otherwise we would need no hospitals or cemeteries. In much literature, therefore, disease naturally attacks many characters and groups. While disease itself is always bad for those experiencing it, it can often bring out good human traits. A person may act heroically even in the face of a debilitating or incurable disease, or a medical researcher may devote long hours to finding cures. Disease may therefore be manipulated in a literary work to indicate either good or bad things about people, or it may suggest political or theological conditions. It is to this last area—the cosmic or theological—that the works studied here have relationship. *Disease may be seen as a symbol** in John Keats's "Ode to a Nightingale" (1819), the Biblical Book of Job, Daniel Defoe's *Journal of the Plague Year* (1722), Ernest Hemingway's *The Sun Also Rises* (1926), and Henrik Ibsen's *Ghosts* (1881). *As a symbol, disease or permanently crippling conditions stand for bleak but inevitable reality, for evidence of God's power, and for human madness and folly.*†

[2]     The most bleak view about disease is that it is a simple and inescapable reality of life which human beings cannot understand and over which they have no control. Keats presents such a view in his "Ode to a Nightingale." In the third stanza of this poem Keats describes the condition of a world diseased:

> Here, where men sit and hear each other groan;
> Where palsy shakes a few, sad, last gray hairs,
>     Where Youth grows pale, and spectre-thin, and dies;

*Central idea.     †Thesis sentence.

and

>Where Beauty cannot keep her lustrous eyes,
>Or new Love pine at them beyond tomorrow.[1]

Here Keats refers realistically to consumption and the diseases of age, but in the context of the poem, the illnesses assume a larger proportion. They suggest a permanent condition of life on earth, a constant affliction that causes the poet to dream of some other location where existence may be better. Disease stands for the realistic termination of all these dreams, the world to which the dreamer must return, finally restored to his or her "sole self" which will inevitably encounter disease and death (line 72). Here the condition of existence symbolized by disease is somber and pessimistic.

[3]       A major symbolic use of disease, and one as somber as that of Keats though not always as pessimistic, highlights the point that human knowledge and power are extremely limited while the power of God is vast and unsearchable. If writers are making this point, they show that disease comes as mysteriously as it goes, and that human beings are powerless to prevent it or cure it, even with strong medicines. The theory here is that God alone—whether visualized with human attributes or as a vast, cosmic force—has the knowledge and the power to make sense out of human experience. Because this view holds that there is a purpose in human misery, even if human beings do not understand it, the theological view is more optimistic than the view represented by Keats.

[4]       The Biblical Book of Job, written shortly after 400 B.C.,[2] is a prime example of this view of disease. Job is a wealthy man who is allowed by God to be cursed with all the miseries that Satan can inflict upon him. Job's children are killed and his properties are destroyed. Finally he is allowed to suffer with "running sores from head to foot."[3] In the course of the Book of Job it becomes clear that Job's illnesses symbolize that total of adversities with which human beings, generally, must contend. Ignorance, injustice, inequality, poverty, misery, pain—all these are suggested by Job's afflictions, and all these are encountered by human beings for no apparent cause. Keats's view of disease is similar to this—that disease is an apparently purposeless misery. Whereas Keats seeks imaginative and almost realistic oblivion, however, the writer of Job brings out the theological idea that all things are in God's hands, certainly the bad, and by implication the good. Both the "Ode to a Nightingale" and the Book of Job, at a point, merge in despair. Job's early lamentations are similar to Keats's views of human misery. In the midst of his sorrows, Job exclaims:

[1]*The Complete Poetical Works of Keats*, ed. Horace E. Scudder (Boston: Houghton Mifflin, 1899), p. 145 (lines 24–26, 29–30).

[2]James Hastings, ed., *Dictionary of the Bible*, rev. by Frederick C. Grant and H.A. Rowley (New York: Charles Scribner's Sons, 1963), p. 502.

[3]*The New English Bible With the Apocrypha* (Oxford and Cambridge: Oxford U.P. and Cambridge U.P., 1970), p. 561 (Job, II.7).

Perish the day when I was born.   (III.3; p. 363)

and

The arrows of the Almighty find their mark in me and their poison soaks into my spirit. (VI.4; p. 365)

An obvious difference between the two works on the issue of disease is that Job finally receives an earthly reward after his misery — the implication being that God should be trusted no matter how miserable one's lot becomes — while Keats is left pondering the nature of his consciousness, without reward but only with questions:

Fled is that music: — do I wake or sleep?
—line 80 (p. 146)

In both works, disease has served as a symbol to cause the writers to explore quite different views on the nature of the human condition.

[5]        It is a view similar to that of the writer of Job that Daniel Defoe makes in his *Journal of the Plague Year*. In this extensive, composite work of realism and fiction, Defoe treats the bubonic plague (that struck England in 1665) as a symbol of human inadequacy and divine power. Like the writer of Job, Defoe throws his ultimate focus on the providence and mercy of God. Treating the topic of how the plague finally left England, he combines the elements of human inadequacy and divine power with great insight and feeling:

Nothing, but the immediate Finger of God, nothing, but omnipotent Power could have done it [i.e., cured the plague]; the Contagion despised all medicine, Death rag'd in every Corner; and had it gone on as it did then, a few Weeks more would have clear'd the Town of all, and every thing that had a Soul: Men every where began to despair, every Heart fail'd them for Fear, People were made desperate thro' the Anguish of their Souls, and the Terrors of Death sat in the very Faces and Countenances of the People.[4]

[6]        Like the writer of Job, who provides a reward for Job after his affliction, but unlike Keats, who sees a return from his dream as a return to worldly misery, Defoe decides that those who were fortunate enough to survive the plague have been deemed worthy of God's mercy. Of the three, the most precise analyst, or the one most sure of his theological ground, is the writer of Job, for this ancient writer clearly points out that the cause of Job's diseases was Satan, as permitted by God. Defoe is a little less positive about the cause except that he allows the plague to represent mysterious evidence of God's will. Keats is completely silent about divine intervention; to him, affliction is as much a part of life as life itself, whatever the cause.

[7]        When disease is separated from theology, as in Keats, it can show

[4]Daniel Defoe, *A Journal of the Plague Year*, in Geoffrey Tillotson, *et al.*, eds., *Eighteenth-Century English Literature* (New York: Harcourt Brace Jovanovich, 1969), p. 259.

cosmic despair, or it can be directed at more human causes, such as the destructiveness of war or the madness of human dissipations. The most effective way of attacking war is to show its victims. In Ernest Hemingway's novel *The Sun Also Rises*, for example, the hero, Jake Barnes, is not afflicted so much with a disease as with a disability. He has been made impotent by a wound received in World War I. On the realistic, personal level, Jake's condition is unfortunate. It prevents him from achieving happiness in the novel, as is shown when he and Brett Ashley reach frustration as they embrace but realize that their love cannot be consummated:

> "Don't you love me [asks Jake]?"
> "Love you? I simply turn all to jelly when you touch me [responds Brett]."
> "Isn't there anything we can do about it [she adds]?"
> She was sitting up now. My arm was around her and she was leaning back against me, and we were quite calm. She was looking into my eyes with that way she had of looking that made you wonder whether she really saw out of her own eyes. They would look on and on after every one else's eyes in the world would have stopped looking. She looked as though there were nothing on earth she would not look at like that, and really she was afraid of so many things.
> "And there's not a . . . thing we could do," I said.[5]

More importantly as a symbol, however, Jake's condition suggests that warfare cripples human beings. Not only does the fury of war disable those who are alive, but it cuts off the future. In effect, Jake's impotence is more effective as a symbol than his death could have been, for the condition is a continuous reminder of the horrors of war, and his inability to have a normal marital relationship and to reproduce is a poignant reminder of what might have been. While Keats's pessimism results from helplessness before a vast, impersonal force, there is a degree of rage underlying Hemingway's view because human beings have caused Jake's condition, and because human beings could stop war but do not choose to do so.

[8]     While human madness as shown in warfare is the cause of Hemingway's view of Jake Barnes's condition, human folly is the source of the illness in Henrik Ibsen's play *Ghosts*. In Ibsen, one generation has entailed destruction upon the next. Oswald Alving has been cursed with congenital syphilis as a result of his father's dissipations. Here the past rises up literally to destroy the present and the future, right in front of the audience's eyes, just as the destructiveness of the past war is a constant element in the life of Hemingway's Jake Barnes. While Hemingway's novel ends in cynicism, Ibsen's play ends in blind idiocy, as Oswald is smitten with apparently irreversible brain damage:

[5]Ernest Hemingway, *The Sun Also Rises* (New York: Charles Scribner's Sons, 1926, rpt. 1970), p. 26.

MRS. ALVING *(going to him).*
> Oswald, what is the matter with you?
> (Oswald *seems to shrink up in the chair; all his muscles relax; his face loses its expression, and his eyes stare stupidly.* Mrs. Alving *is trembling with terror.)*
> What is it? *(Screams).* Oswald! What is the matter with you!
> *(Throws herself on her knees beside him and shakes him.)*
> Oswald! Oswald! Look at me! Don't you know me!

OSWALD *(in an expressionless voice, as before).*
> The sun — the sun.[6]

[9]     In both Hemingway and Ibsen, the cause of the misery is human beings, perhaps acting out of viciousness, as in warfare, or out of boredom, as in the excesses of Oswald Alving's father.[7] Any divinity involved in these afflictions is remote. For this reason both Hemingway and Ibsen are unlike Defoe and the writer of Job, and more like Keats. One could move from both Hemingway and Ibsen into politics, and start proposing platforms to deal with human problems, but one could not easily do so in Job, *A Journal of the Plague Year,* or the "Ode to a Nightingale," however, for no human cause can be linked to illness in these works. All the writers included here can be put into agreement, however, if one assumes that human motivation may be as obscure as the precise details about the origin of the universe or the spirit that controls life and death. Then all the writers would concur in the general idea that disease and affliction are symbolic of a general situation in which human beings have only limited control and imperfect understanding. The final answer to the meaning of the symbol goes beyond ordinary human comprehension, because the answer either lies deep within the human psyche or else is hidden in the impenetrable mystery of the universe.


★COMMENTARY ON THE THEME

The theme treats one topic as expressed in five major works. Paragraph one presents the reasons for treating disease as a symbol and thus lays the groundwork for the theme. Paragraph 2 shows the most pessimistic way to look at disease and uses the poem by Keats as a representative of this view. The third paragraph shows an alternative view in which theological considerations play a major role, and paragraph 4 compares and contrasts Job and Keats in this regard. The fifth paragraph refers to Defoe's work and compares it with Job. The sixth paragraph compares and contrasts all three works.

Paragraph 7 takes a new direction, the idea in Hemingway's novel,

---

[6]Henrik Ibsen, *Ghosts,* in *Trio,* 2nd ed. edited by Harold Simonson (New York: Harper & Row, 1965), p. 410.

[7]Ibsen, p. 369

with references contrasting the idea with Keats's. In the eighth paragraph the material of Ibsen's *Ghosts* is introduced with a contrast from Hemingway's novel. The concluding paragraph contains references to all five writers, generally contrasting them but also showing a way to make them come into general agreement.

While the theme devotes much detail to the individual works as they are introduced in the various paragraphs (as in paragraph 7, where Hemingway is first discussed), it is important to observe that none of the paragraphs is lacking in comparison and contrast material. The purpose of an extended theme of this sort is to write *one* paper on one topic, not several separate studies of a related topic. The only way to succeed in this goal is to make each paragraph contain comparisons and contrasts.

# 11

# The Theme Analyzing Structure

STRUCTURE in literary study may be defined as the organization of a literary work as influenced by its plot (in fictional works) or main idea (in expository works). The word is also sometimes defined as the pattern of emotions in the literary work. Although these two definitions are distinct, they are closely connected and under most circumstances are virtually inseparable. The word *structure* is in fact a metaphor implying that a work of literature, both topically and emotionally, is as connected and unified as a building—a structure.

In imaginative works, structure refers to the chronological position of parts, scenes, episodes, chapters, and acts; it also refers to the logical or associational relationships among stanzas, ideas, images, or other divisions. In expository works, the word necessarily refers to the arrangement and development of ideas. Structure is a matter of the relationships among parts that are often described in terms of cause and effect, position in time, association, symmetry, and balance and proportion.

## The Importance of Structure

In a very real sense, all studies of literature are either directly or indirectly concerned with structure. If you talk about the happy or unhappy ending of a short story, for example, you in fact consider the conclusion in relation to what went before it; inevitably you mention whether the earlier parts of the story demonstrated that the characters earned or deserved what happened to them. This consideration must touch on the logic of the story's action, and hence it is a subject of structure. Similarly, in considering Shakespeare's Sonnet No. 73, you may observe that the first quatrain compares the speaker to dead trees, the second to twilight, and the third to a dying and self-extinguishing fire. When you determine that there is a logical or topical relationship among these quatrains, you are discussing structure.

Since structure is so closely tied to all phases of literary study, you might ask in what way structure is unique. How, for example, does a theme about ideas, or a summary theme, differ from a theme about structure? The difference is one of emphasis: in studying structure you emphasize the logic, or the causes, underlying the major divisions in the work being analyzed; in a summary theme you emphasize the events or ideas that you have cast in a reasonable plan of organization; in a theme about ideas you emphasize the ideas and their importance as they are made apparent in the work. In fact, no matter what topic you are writing about, your finished theme is usually related to the structure of the work; for the major parts of your theme can be conveniently dictated by the organization of the work and the causes for it are your primary concern. Ideas, events, and other things such as tone, point of view, and imagery are relevant only as substance for your discussion of structure.

## Types of Structures

1. LOGIC.   In a good work of literature, the parts are not introduced accidentally. One part demands another, sometimes by logical requirement. Elder Olsen's study of Pope's poem *Epistle to Dr. Arbuthnot*,[1] shows that in the first sixty-eight lines Pope illustrates a comic idea that constitutes a minor logical premise; namely, that a number of bad poets and other people have been waving ass's ears in his face. Then in the next ten lines Pope illustrates a major premise, namely that when people have ass's ears, you have to tell them about it. Finally, in four following lines, Pope draws a logical conclusion (which is also a defense of himself as a satirist); namely, that he had written a lengthy poem, *The Dunciad*, to tell the world that the people mentioned in the first sixty-eight lines had ass's ears. In short, the first eighty-two lines of the poem form a syllogism, not necessarily valid logically, but certainly valid comically and rhetorically.

2. CHRONOLOGY.   It is never enough simply to assert that events happen in time; time is important only as it permits human reactions to occur, and hence chronology in literature is primarily a convenient classification for the logic of human motivation. For example, in Robert Frost's poem "The Road Not Taken," the first three stanzas describe

[1]"Rhetoric and the Appreciation of Pope," *Modern Philology* XXXVII (1939), 13–55.

the speaker's taking one road at a fork in the road he was already traveling. As the stanzas progress it becomes clear that the road taken was actually the way of life chosen by the speaker. In the final, fourth stanza, the speaker observes that his choice was a major landmark in his life, affecting his present and future and making him different from what he would have been had he taken the other road. The structure of the poem is such that the stanzas move naturally from a brief account of events to their human effects and implications. The last stanza stems inevitably from the first three; it could not be transposed and still make the same sense.

3. CONFLICTS. The structure of a work may be seen in terms of oppositions or conflicts that continue throughout a work until the final resolution. Conflicts may be seen in all literary works. In the broadest forms, there may be a conflict between life and death, *yes* and *no*, or love and hate. The conflict may be of human beings against other human beings or against the forces of Nature. If the hero of the work is a young person, the major conflict may be between success and failure; such a conflict may involve a series of lesser conflicts within the work, such as learning in school as against ignoring school, making friends or alienating people, escaping one's surroundings or being overwhelmed by them, meeting a person of the opposite sex or being lonely, and so on. It would be difficult to discover a literary work that does not create a conflict or set of oppositions as a basic element in its structure.

4. VARIATIONS ON SITUATIONS AND TYPES OF LITERARY WORKS. The structure of a work might also be seen in terms of how the author varies a particular situation or type of work. In a male-female relationship, for example, there are a number of actions which might develop, such as (a) lifelong success, (b) temporary success, (c) intermittent success and failure, (d) progressive indifference, (e) mutual toleration, and (f) complete failure. One could study the structure of Shakespeare's *Much Ado About Nothing* by following the developing relationship between Beatrice and Benedick. The relationship begins in toleration or even failure, for the two constantly express hostility toward each other, but as the play goes on the insults change to concern and ultimately to love. One could argue that the two really love each other at the start, and that the incidents in the play progressively make them realize their love. Either way, the discussion would make a successful study of the structure of the play.

Many other human situations may similarly enter into your consideration. Suppose characters are old, or are children. What would one generally expect of such people, and how does the author bring out and vary the expected situations? Or suppose characters are criminals. Do they continue their criminal activities throughout the work or do they discontinue them? What other sorts of variations could be presumed for such a character?

The category of work you are writing about may be shown to govern its structure. In an adventure story, for example, one should consider the expected ingredients of adventure and compare these with the actual events in the story you have read. If the subject is a love poem, one should list what might be present and then show how the poet either does or does not include these elements and in what order. Your concern here should be to establish the characteristics of the type, or a set of ideal expectations, and then to show the specific elements of the type that are present in the work, being careful to show how these elements determine the form of the work.

Let us take an example of a work that tells about an act of revenge. It is not difficult to determine a set of ideal expectations for such a work. First, the characters must follow a code or idea of justice that places personal revenge above police action. Then there must be an affront and a clear recognition of the affront. Then a decision must be made to carry out revenge, and any obstacles that stand in the way of revenge must be overcome. Finally, if revenge is to be successful, the avengers must arrange their escape, but if the affront has been severe enough, they may be less concerned with escaping than with inflicting the fatal blow on the persons who offended them. In studying the structure of Shakespeare's *Hamlet* you would find that the play follows this pattern of revenge fairly closely, except that the original affront—the murder of Hamlet's father by his uncle—has taken place before the play opens, and that Hamlet has a difficult time in determining the fact that he has indeed been affronted. Much of the play therefore is preoccupied with Hamlet's attempting to discover the truth about his father's death and the uncle's guilt. All the other elements are present in the play and in approximately the order listed.

5. EMOTIONS.    Each work of literature may justly be regarded as a pattern capable of producing a complex set of emotions in a reader. The emotions that you feel while reading are the result of an interaction of involvement, time, and the structure of the work. To see that each of these elements is essential, let us regard an experience common to many readers. Often a reader may read the conclusion of a story or novel before beginning to read seriously at the start. If you have ever "peeked" in this way you may recall that you knew the facts of the ending, but had little if any feelings about them. When you read that same conclusion in proper sequence, however, you probably had an emotional response to it, even though you had seen it before. The difference in the two readings was that the entire structure of the work itself had no influence on your response the first time, but strongly influenced you the second time. Involvement, time, structure—all these make up the basis of emotional response.

For this reason, even when you focus attention on an emotion that you felt at a particular moment in response to a work, you must necessarily relate this emotion to the sense of involvement, expectation, and apprehension that were ongoing emotions as you approached this moment. Discussing one emotion entails the discussion of the ways in which a literary work organizes and brings out related emotions. For example, Shakespeare's Sonnet No. 73 builds feelings of regret, sadness, and resignation, but concludes on a note of affirmation. Any account of an emotional response to the conclusion of this poem must also deal with the fact that the impact of the last lines depends on the effect of the three preceding quatrains.

Each work of literature may thus be seen as a complex emotional structure. Emotional responses to even a relatively simple literary form like detective fiction, for example, are complex. Such fiction creates suspense by introducing inquisitiveness, doubt, and anxiety, with related emotions of various shades of horror, fear, and sympathy. Detective stories also create both properly and improperly directed hostility (at the true criminal and at the "red herring"), and finally produce satisfaction when the solution of the mystery ends all doubt and anxiety. It is not at all uncommon for such stories to end according to the age-old advice of the theater to "leave them laughing." A joke or a comic description thus may produce a smile that ensures the final defeat of anxiety — at least as far as that story was concerned.

The creation of a certain degree of anxiety is perhaps the principal means by which authors maintain interest. The author of a story about a pioneering trip across the American plains, for example, creates anxiety about whether the forces of Nature will permit the journey to be concluded successfully. If human agents such as outlaws are introduced as antagonists, then this anxiety can be related to hostility and fear, and if the principal characters are virtuous, they usually become objects of admiration.

Such emotions are also coextensive with the structure of drama. In the nineteenth century a German novelist and critic, Gustav Freytag, suggested that the rising and falling actions and conflicts in the typical five-act drama resemble a pyramid: emotions are incited with the exposition of the drama and are heightened as the plot complications develop until a climax is reached in the third act; after this point, the falling action begins until the final catastrophe, or denouement, is reached. The emotions preceding the climax are those that spring from uncertainty; those afterward spring from inevitability. One major idea in the Aristotelian idea of tragedy is that tragedy aims at the purgation — catharsis — of pity and fear. In the Freytag pyramid, fear is touched most heavily before the climax, whereas pity becomes predominant after it, although the two are intermingled throughout a tragedy. The point here is that Aristotle's description of the aims of tragedy presupposes a proper ar-

rangement of incidents and that this concern, like his other commentaries on plot in *The Poetics* (VI-XIV), was mainly structural.

If a literary work is an emotional structure, it should reach a satisfactory emotional conclusion — a relaxation of tension. In Greek tragedy,
the concluding action, the *exodos,* consists of choral speeches that ponder
the meaning of the action. This relatively intellectual section provides
the opportunity to relax after the emotional peak of the play. In John
Milton's "Lycidas," although anger and indignation are strongly
brought out in Milton's famous "digressions" (which are integral in
the poem), the conclusion permits relaxation and satisfaction.

### Aids in Studying Structure

In studying structure, be sure to take whatever assistance the
author has given you. Are there divisions in the work, such as
stanzas, parts, chapters, cantos, or spaces between groups of paragraphs? Try to relate the subjects of these various divisions and develop a rationale for the divisions. Is there a geographical location
that lends its own mood and color to the various parts of the story?
How can these be related to the events? Does the time of day or time
of year shift as the work progresses? Can the events be shown to
have a relationship to these various times? Does one event grow inevitably out of another  that is, do the events have logical as well as
chronological causation? Is a new topic introduced because it is similar to another topic? Such questions should assist you in your study.

You might also help yourself by following a suggestion made by
Aristotle in his *Poetics:*

> . . . the plot [of any work], being an imitation of an action, must imitate
> one action and that a whole, the structural union of the parts being such
> that, if any one of them is displaced or removed, the whole will be dis-
> jointed and disturbed. For a thing whose presence or absence make no
> visible difference, is not an organic part of the whole.[2]

As an exercise in applying Aristotle's ideas to the structure of a
work, you might imagine that a certain part of the work has been taken
away. You might then ask what is wrong with the work remaining. Does
it make sense? Does it seem truncated? Why should the missing part be
returned? As you answer these questions, you are really dealing with
the logical necessity of structural wholeness. For example, let us suppose that the second stanza of Frost's "The Road Not Taken" is missing.

---

[2]Ch. VIII. 4, in S. H. Butcher, *Aristotle's Theory of Poetry and Fine Art,* 4th ed. (New
York: Dover Publications, Inc., 1951), p. 35.

The poem immediately becomes illogical because it omits the chrono-logical event leading to the conclusion, and it also omits the logic of the speaker's choice of the road he selected. If you attempt similar imagina-tive exercises with other works, you can help yourself in determining whether these works are organic wholes.

You might also aid yourself by drawing a scheme or plan to ex-plain, graphically, the structure of the work. Not everyone can benefit from drawings, but if you are visually oriented, then making a drawing might help you to organize your thoughts and to improve your final theme. The story "Miss Brill," by Katherine Mansfield, for example, may be conveniently compared with a person running happily along a narrow path deep within a dark forest and making a turn only to plunge suddenly and unexpectedly off a steep cliff. You might graph this com-parison like this:

In writing a theme about the story, you could employ this scheme as a guide for your discussion. This is not to say that the structure of the story could not be profitably analyzed in another way but rather that the scheme would help to give your own study penetration, meaning, and form.

An effective illustration is one that encourages you to see the rela-tionships of the various parts of the work. You might use line drawings like the one for "Miss Brill," or you might use circles, lines, planes, or other geometric forms. One student effectively compared the structure of Donne's poem "The Canonization" to a person entering a building and going upstairs to the top floors. This comparison was effectively augmented with an explanatory drawing. Such a comparison might not readily occur to everyone, but if the scheme is effectively carried out and if the parts of the work are adequately accounted for, the purpose of structural analysis can be effectively served with visual aids of this sort.

## Problems

It is important to develop a central idea that is comprehensive enough to prevent any errors in your assessment of the work's structure. If your first judgment is that a part is not integral to the work, for example, be sure that you have not missed some essential idea that would make it relevant. Ernest Hemingway stated that the last section of *Huckleberry Finn* is "just cheating." It seems apparent that his judgment resulted from an inadequate idea about the meaning of the novel. If he had considered that the work contrasts common sense (Huck's idea of freeing Jim) with quixotism or faulty judgment (Tom's idea of freeing Jim with "style"), he might have modified his statement.

You also have the usual problem of selectivity. What you choose to discuss will be made on the basis of your initial analysis and the approach you wish to make. A mere description of what happens in the work and where it happens is not much more than a precis. Your teacher is of course interested in your ability to describe the organization of the work, but is much more interested in what you *make* out of your description. As always, your point is of primary importance and should be kept foremost.

## Organizing Your Theme

### INTRODUCTION

You should first describe the approach to structure that you plan to take in your theme. You might be studying Andrew Marvell's seventeenth-century poem "To His Coy Mistress," and might wish to analyze the logical form of Marvell's argument. Or you might be considering the structure of Milton's pastoral poem "Lycidas" as a funerary meditation. Your central idea should be about the structure, as in the sample theme, where the conflict in Thomas Hardy's story "The Three Strangers" is related to the contrast between the spirit and the letter of the law. If your aim is to show how your work is related to a general type, the introduction is the place to develop your description of the type. Conclude your introduction with your thesis sentence.

### BODY

Work from your introduction into a discussion of the way in which the idea influences the form of the work. If the work is arranged according to stanzas, cantos, books, scenes, acts, chapters, or sections, try to determine the logic of this arrangement. Your emphasis should be on the way in which each of the parts bears on the idea or statement you have accepted as the governing idea or plan of the work, and upon the relationship of part to part. You might talk about *movement* from one part to the next. Does one part end on a note of expectation? Does the next part present material that satisfies that expectation? Does the logic of one part require that other events follow? Does the author provide these events, or are the ordinary requirements of logic exceeded? Does the movement of the work depend on the mental functioning and consequent action of a certain character? Does the author demonstrate that such functioning and actions are truly part of this character? If you have made any graph or drawing that helps to explain the structure, you could use that as an aid in discussing the relationship of part to part.

If you are showing the structure of your work as it is related to a general type, you should use the technique of comparison-contrast in the body of your paper (see Chapter 10). Obviously your major problem will be to determine an ideal form for your type. This is not difficult to do if you concentrate on your topic. Begin where the story begins, or where the character is at a stage in his life, and then go from there. Thus, if your story begins with a young couple meeting, you could imagine a series of typical incidents which would include (1) early acquaintance, (2) growing love, (3) complications (that is, misunderstandings, parental objections, racial or religious differences, money troubles, etc.), (4) the resolution of the complications, and (5) marriage. If the couple is married when the story begins, you might consider whether your couple moves toward success or failure in the work. If success is achieved, then you might establish a form of (1) difficulties (financial, medical, personal, marital, etc.) leading to (2) a successful resolution. If failure is at the end of the road for the couple, then the pattern might be (1) difficulties, leading to (2) defeat. In either case, you would need to establish a form also for the particular nature of the difficulty. Thus, personal difficulties can take the form of conflicts with others, unfair treatment, psychological disturbances, and so on. Your concern would be to show where the author places the emphasis.

### CONCLUSION

You might conclude your theme with an evaluation of the author's success as far as structure is concerned. Are all the parts of the work equally necessary? Do they occur in the best order? Would the work be damaged if any parts were left out or transposed? Often a work has smaller internal structures that are related to the major one. Thus the story may have been about persons going through a typical day on their way to success, but the story might also contain shorter accounts of other characters either succeeding or failing. Also, major characters may be engaged in an important meeting while minor characters may be meeting on a matter of lesser importance. If you can show how these minor events are related to the major ones, as in the concluding paragraph of the sample theme, you will be stressing your central idea and strengthening your theme.

_____

SAMPLE THEME

_____

### Conflict and Suspense in the Structure of Thomas Hardy's Story "The Three Strangers"

[1]    "The Three Strangers" is an intricately woven story of suspense and conflict. The suspense is essential to the conflict, which is an opposition of right and wrong when applied to criminal justice. *Hardy's contrasting idea is in keeping with the Apostle Paul's idea that "the letter killeth, but the spirit giveth life" (2 Corinthians, III.6).** Legality in Hardy's story is wrong, while illegality is shown to be right. As specific material for this idea, Hardy creates a major incident which presents a conflict for his Wessex shepherds between (1) duty toward law, and (2) duty toward a human being who has been legally condemned but whose crime has in their eyes been extenuated. *Hardy develops his conflict and brings out his idea by showing the lives of his natives positively, by portraying his hangman negatively, and by creating suspense about his first stranger, who is the legally condemned "criminal."*†

[2]    Although readers may not be aware of it during the early part of the story, they are being emotionally manipulated to accept Hardy's view of right and wrong. The first one-sixth of the story is pure description of the way of life of the natives of Higher Crowstairs, who are shown to be warm and human. But in the service of his idea, Hardy is really building up one "side" of the conflict by demonstrating that his natives are such nice, ordinary peasant folk that their judgment on matters of life and death is to be trusted. This is the positive side of Hardy's conflict.

[3]    When Hardy does engage both sides of the conflict, at about midpoint in the story, by introducing the second stranger (the hangman), he has already won his case, but he makes sure by negatively presenting this grisly figure as brash, selfish, and obnoxious. When the natives learn of the second stranger's identity as the hangman, they are startled "with suppressed explanations" (p. 406). The explanations apparently take the form that if men like the hangman are associated with the letter of the law, the natives—along with the reader—will prefer the spirit even though the spirit may at times be branded as illegal. This reaction could of course not be sustained if the crime of the escaped criminal had been one of violence, but the "crime" was really the theft of a sheep to feed his starving family (p. 407). One may grant that Hardy is rigging the case here, but the con-

_____

In James H. Pickering, ed., *Fiction 100* (New York: Macmillan Company, 1974), pp. 400–411. Parenthetical page numbers refer to this edition.

*Central idea.        †Thesis sentence.

flict is not between right when it is right and wrong when it is wrong, but rather between *legality* when it is *wrong* and *illegality* when it is *right*. It is therefore impossible to disagree with the judgment of the natives at the end that the intended hanging of the sheep thief "was cruelly disproportioned to the transgression" (p. 411), for even if a person were inclined to disagree on abstract legal principles, the emotional thrust of the story is toward extenuation.

[4]     Critical to this extenuation is Hardy's creation of suspense about the identity of the first stranger as Timothy Summers, the escaped thief. In winning the assent of his readers to the values of right and wrong in the story, Hardy avoids a purely legalist reaction against Summers by keeping his identity hidden until the end. In this way, Hardy puts Summers before the eyes of the readers, though unidentified, and develops him as a brave and witty human being. The revelation at the end therefore causes the reader to take a second view of Summers. In retrospect, readers must admire, with the natives, his "marvellous coolness and daring in hob-and-nobbing with the hangman" (p. 411), and would be outraged if such a person were to be hanged. It is perhaps difficult for readers to take any law seriously that proposes to hang a person for petty theft, but if the issue is seen as one between the letter and the spirit of the law, then Hardy's values are still relevant and his story still possesses great vitality.

[5]     Related to the major conflict are a number of lesser conflicts which are constantly appearing in the story. There is an undertone of fear of the law, for example, among the natives, who live marginally in the "country about Higher Crowstairs" (p. 411) and who therefore perceive the conviction of a person like Summers as a threat to themselves also. There is also a contrast between the law itself, which as an abstract force should be admirable, and the conceited, obnoxious hangman who carries out sentences of the law. In a comic vein, Hardy creates a contrast between the law and the ineptness of the shepherds who are called upon to enforce it; when they make an arrest they use words more appropriate to criminals or to priests. Also, the shepherds are diligent in searching for Summers everywhere but where they know he can be found, to good comic effect.

[6]     In addition there are other little but human contrasts in the story. The Fennels are giving a party for twenty people, but Mrs. Fennel is alarmed about giving away too much food and drink to her guests, and she is disturbed by the self-indulgence of the hangman. There is a small family conflict on this score. Another small conflict occurs on the issue of the musicians whom Mrs. Fennel asks to stop playing but who continue because they have been bribed by an amorous shepherd, Oliver Giles. There are also some noticeable contrasts in age among couples. Oliver is seventeen, but is in love with a woman of thirty-three (p. 401), and a young woman is engaged to a man of fifty (p. 406). Beyond all these contrasts or opposites which make up the texture of the story, the technique of suspense is a contrast in itself, for it forces a reconsideration of events already considered, and creates the need to redefine these events. These are all conflicts which Hardy employs in developing his major conflict between the right of the spirit and the wrong of the letter in "The Three Strangers."

★COMMENTARY ON THE THEME

The major aspect of structure discussed in the sample theme is conflict. The conflict is between the natives and a positive view of the spirit of the law, on the one hand, and the hangman and a negative view of the law, on the other.

A second aspect of the structure is the use of suspense, which is shown to be related to the positive aspect of the conflict. The emotional aspect of the structure is emphasized throughout the theme, but particularly in paragraph 2, where the positive view of the spirit of the law is shown to be connected to the reader's emotional assent to the natives. The concluding two paragraphs show that a number of lesser conflicts are related to the major conflict of the story.

# The Theme on
# Imagery or Symbolism

IMAGERY is a broad term referring to the verbal comparison of one or many objects, ideas, or emotional states with something else. Authors use imagery to evoke responses out of the reader's own experience and imagination. This is accomplished by means of *analogy*. At the heart of communication through imagery is this assumption: "I cannot describe this idea for you, nor can I tell you how this character felt, but I can provide you with an analogy—an image—which by its similarity to your own experience or by its ability to touch your imagination will make you understand the idea or re-create the character's emotional state." Thus, a writer wishing to express characters' joy may say not simply "They were happy" but rather "They felt as though they had just received a million-dollar check." It is unlikely that any of the author's readers have had such an experience themselves, but they can easily *imagine* how elated such an experience would make them feel, and therefore they can re-create the joy experienced by the literary characters. The author has illustrated one thing—joy—in terms of another—the receipt of a large sum of money.

As a literary example, let us examine Keats's poem "On First Looking Into Chapman's Homer." Keats wrote the poem after he first read Chapman's translation of Homer, and his main idea is that Chapman not only translated Homer's words but also transmitted his greatness. A fair expository restatement of the poem might be the following:

> I have read much European literature and have been told that Homer is the best writer of all, but not knowing Greek, I couldn't appreciate his works until I read them in Chapman's translation. To me, this experience was an exciting and awe-inspiring discovery with extensive implications that I only dimly realized.

It is also fair to say that this paraphrase destroys Keats's poetry. Contrast the second sentence of the paraphrase with the last six lines of the sonnet as Keats wrote them:

> Then felt I like some watcher of the skies
> When a new planet swims into his ken;
> Or like stout Cortez when with eagle eyes
> He stared at the Pacific — and all his men
> Looked at each other with a wild surmise —
> Silent, upon a peak in Darien.

If Keats had said only "I felt excited," his poem would probably not cause anything but skepticism or boredom in us, because we would find no descriptions of objects from which we could reconstruct the precise degree of his emotion. But we certainly can respond to the situation that Keats's imagery causes us to visualize. Imagery, in other words, conveys a close approximation of experience itself, and it calls forth the most strenuous imaginative responses from the reader.

## Some Definitions

The word *image* refers to single literary comparisons. Keats's reference to the "watcher of the skies," for example, is an image. *Imagery* is a broader term referring to all the images within a passage ("the imagery of line 5, or of stanza 6"), an entire work ("the imagery of Eliot's 'Prufrock'"), a group of works ("the imagery of Shakespeare's Roman plays"), or an entire body of works ("the development of Shakespeare's imagery").

To describe the relationship between writers' ideas and the images, particularly the metaphors, that they choose to objectify them, two useful terms have been coined by I. A. Richards (in *The Philosophy of Rhetoric*). First is the *tenor*, which is the sum total of ideas and attitudes not only of the literary speaker but also of the author. Thus, the *tenor* of the million-dollar check image is joy or elation. Second is the *vehicle*, or the details that carry the tenor; the vehicle of the check image is the description of the receipt of the check. Similarly, the tenor of the sestet of Keats's sonnet on Chapman's Homer is awe and wonder; the vehicle is the reference to astronomical and geographical discovery.

## Characteristics of Literary Imagery

Imagery is important in both expository and imaginative writing. In fact, it would be difficult to find any good piece of writing that does not employ imagery to some extent. But imagery is most vital in imaginative writing, where it promotes immediate understanding and makes suggestions and implications—nonlogical processes that are not central to expository writing.

Usually, imagery is embodied in words or descriptions denoting sense experience that leads to many associations. A single word naming a flower, say *rose*, evokes a definite response in most readers: a person might visualize a rose, recall its smell, associate it with the summer sun and pleasant days, and recall the love and respect that a bouquet of roses represents as a gift. But the word *rose* is not an image until its associations are called into play by a writer, as in these famous lines by Robert Burns:

> O, my luve's like a red, red rose
> That's newly sprung in June . . .

Once the comparison has been drawn, all the pleasant connotations of the word *rose* are evoked; these connotations become the *tenor* of the image. That a rose may have unpleasant associations, however, perhaps because of its thorns, should probably not be considered. Such an extension of meaning, although truthful, would likely represent a misreading of the lines.

It would, that is, unless the writer deliberately calls some of these less happy ideas to mind. In one of the most famous poems about a rose, by Edmund Waller ("Go Lovely Rose," in which the speaker addresses a rose that he is about to send to his reluctant sweetheart), the speaker draws attention to the fact that roses, when cut, die:

> Then die—that she
> The common fate of all things rare
>    May read in thee:
> How small a part of time they share
> That are so wondrous sweet and fair.

Here the poet is directing the reader's responses to the speaker's original comparison of the rose with his sweetheart, and the structure of the poem is coextensive with the development of the image. In this poem, the tenor is an awareness that life is both lovely and fragile.

Imagery is obviously most vivid when it appeals directly to sensuous experience; references to senses like sight and touch will produce an immediate imaginative response. More complex and intellectualized images will require greater effort in reconstruction. Matthew Arnold stated in "Dover Beach" that the world seemed "to lie before us like a land of dreams," a figurative image that has prompted considerable intellectual speculation. Shakespeare's line "And summer's lease hath all too short a date" from Sonnet 18 makes the reader consider the situation of renting and leasing property. Despite such variety in the materials from which imagery can be drawn, the common element is always the attempt by writers to communicate their ideas by referring to sense impressions, objects, and situations which readers can imaginatively reconstruct and to which they can emotionally and intellectually respond.

Imagery may become extensive in the service of moral, political, or religious argumentation. Aristotle, in describing methods of argumentation in his *Rhetoric*, states that writers often use *inductions* or *examples* to advance their ideas (Book II, Ch. 20). An induction is actually an image that embodies the argument—it is an integral part of argument. In this respect, certain literary forms may be considered as extended images. The ancient Aesop composed *fables*, which were little pointed stories to which later editors have attached morals, or explanations of Aesop's arguments. Jesus Christ spoke constantly in *parables*, which are short narratives embodying profound religious insights. These parables, like those of the Good Samaritan and the Prodigal Son, are being interpreted today in sermons and church-school classes throughout the world. Medieval preachers utilized the *exemplum*, a little story that served as the illustrative springboard for a sermon.

### Imagery and Rhetorical Devices

The vehicles of imagery have been classified rhetorically; the fable and the parable, for example, are distinctive enough to be classified as rhetorical types. The most important types you can look for are these:

#### SHORTER RHETORICAL FORMS

SIMILE.   A simile is a comparison using "like" or "as." The second of these two lines is a simile:

> It glows and glitters in my cloudy breast
> Like stars upon some gloomy grove.

In the six lines from the Keats sonnet quoted on p. 144 there are two similes, each conveying the excitement of discovery.

METAPHOR.   A metaphor is a comparison that does not use "like" or "as." The tenor is *implied* in the vehicle and is not introduced by a preposition or a clause marker. A metaphor may consist of a single word, as in Keats's poem "To My Brothers."

> Small, busy flames *play* through the fresh-laid coals.

It may also be more extensive, as in Shakespeare's Sonnet No. 146, when the speaker compares his body to a house and his soul to a tenant in the house.

> Why so large cost, having so short a lease,
> Dost thou upon thy fading mansion spend?

CONCEIT. A conceit, specifically a "metaphysical conceit," is a fairly long simile or metaphor that introduces an unusual or witty image. Frequently the development of the concept controls the structure of the poem. Perhaps the most famous metaphysical conceit is Donne's comparison of lovers and compasses in "A Valediction: Forbidding Mourning."

SYNECDOCHE. In a synecdoche, which is a special kind of metaphor, a small part stands for a large part, as in the nautical phrase "All hands on deck" in which the word *hands* signifies all the sailors, presumably because their hands are so vital in the management of the ship.

METONYMY. A metonym, also a metaphor, is a term that stands for something with which it is closely associated. The President, for example, is closely associated with the White House, so that "news from the White House" is in effect news of actions and policies of the President. Similar to this are "the Pentagon," "Ivy League," "Broadway," and so on.

PERSONIFICATION. In personification, something abstract, like a season of the year, is given human attributes, as in this famous example from Tennyson's "In Memoriam":

> . . . Nature, red in tooth and claw,
> With ravine, shriek'd against his creeds.

### LONGER RHETORICAL FORMS

SYMBOL, SYMBOLISM. A symbol is a thing, place, activity, person, or concept that stands for something else. In a story or poem it has its own objective reality—unless it had this inward validity it would be weak—but it is constantly being pressed by the author outwardly into areas of greater and greater meaning. In Shirley Jackson's story "The Lottery," for example (see Chapter 5), the custom of holding the lottery stands for a quality in human beings which causes them (1) to perpetuate certain institutions long after they have outlived their usefulness, (2) to throw the blame for individual faults on others (the "scapegoat") and thus avoid personal recognition of individual responsibility, and (3) to be cruel and insensitive to individual suffering. Thus the vehicle— the lottery itself—has a fairly extensive meaning, or tenor. It would perhaps sound like preaching if Shirley Jackson had explained her meaning in direct prose; her work would then change to an essay, and the reader might take exception to some of her statements. But by using the lottery as a symbol for these negative human traits, she renders her idea dramatically and forcefully. She affects the reader's emotions directly and creates the sort of self-analysis that helps to make human beings more human.

The use of symbolism has characterized a great deal of modern literature. James Joyce, in his fiction, developed a theory of symbolism that he employed in his works—the idea of "epiphany" or radiance. Joyce thought that certain objects, statements, actions, and details crystallized or summarized everything he wanted to say about a character or group of characters. Thus, in the story "Counterparts" from *Dubliners,* a man beats his young son after a day during which he himself has been browbeaten. His action symbolizes a human tendency to take frustrations out on others, even those who are loved most dearly.

CONTROLLING IMAGE.    Closely connected with symbolism is the term *controlling image*—an image developed so thoroughly throughout a work or so vital and pervasive that one may interpret the work in the light of the image. The difference between a symbol and a controlling image is that the thrust of the controlling image is internal, while the symbol moves outwardly as well to general concepts and values. Joyce's man beating his son is a symbol, but cannot be a controlling image because it comes at the very end of the story. By contrast, at the beginning of John of Gaunt's speech in Shakespeare's *Richard II* (II.i.33-70), there is a controlling image when Gaunt compares himself to a "prophet." The entire speech is colored by the idea that the speaker giving it, being close to death and therefore closer to God and the riddles of the universe, is presenting an absolutely accurate forecast of the future.

VIVID WRITING.    Also merging with symbol and metaphor is intensely vivid descriptive writing. Such writing, of course, is every author's goal, and it is usually not regarded as imagery. To the degree that an accurate and vivid description can evoke an impression that the author wishes to control, however, the effect of vivid writing is the same as that of imagery and specifically symbolism. John Masefield's poem "Cargoes" is a three-stanza poem describing three ships from three periods of history. Although Masefield does not make any comparisons, his views of the different periods are made explicitly clear by his descriptions. His "Quinquireme of Nineveh" symbolizes the majesty and romance of the past, while his mad cutter butting through the channel suggests the cheapness, dirt, and tawdriness that Masefield clearly associates with modern life and commerce.

ALLEGORY.    An allegory is to a symbol as a motion picture is to a still picture. The allegory puts the symbol into action. In form the allegory is a complete and self-sufficient narrative, but it also signifies another series of events or a condition of life as expressed in a religion or philosophy. The most widely read allegory in our language has been Bunyan's *Pilgrim's Progress,* which at one time was almost as important as the Bible. Spenser's *The Faerie Queene* is a series of allegorical narrative poems, each one referring to separate concepts of Christian goodness. The parable and the fable without the moral attached are in effect short allegories. Ancient *myths* were also allegorical in nature.

### Imagery and Attitudes

Imagery is effective in rendering attitudes. It can elevate the subject matter or reduce it in size or ridicule it. Furthermore, it can produce these same effects on the speaker, if the author so wishes. To see some of these effects operating in a short space, the following passage from Shakespeare's *Antony and Cleopatra* (IV.xii.20–24) is instructive:

> The hearts
> That [spaniel'd] me at heels, to whom I gave
> Their wishes, do discandy, melt their sweets
> On blossoming Caesar; and this pine is bark'd,
> That overtopp'd them all.

The word *hearts* in the first line is a synecdoche: "hearts" refers to Antony's followers. The image implies (1) that his followers seemed to be fully committed to him ("with all their hearts"), and (2) that they stayed with him through emotion and not principle, and therefore they found it easy to leave him when their emotions had shifted.[1] The images of *discandying* and *blossoming* both connote a strong attitude of disparagement on Antony's part, particularly when they are compared with the final metaphor, which is drawn from the experience of woodsmen. Antony is tall and firm as a pine, and like a pine he "overtopp'd" everyone and everything around him. But now his strength is gone, as is the strength of a tree when its bark is removed; even though he has not yet crashed to the ground and is as tall as ever, he will inevitably die. His imagery indicates that he knows the political fate of a leader without followers, and it also suggests his belief that he still is superior to those who will replace him in power and prestige. As you can see, these images convey a completeness of statement and implication that literal language could approximate only with many more words and then not as well.

Imagery can serve the interests of both praise and blame. Both concerns may be seen in a satiric work entitled *The Battle of the Books* by Jonathan Swift. Swift was adept at employing images in his prose. At one point he introduces a short account of a bee, who by going from flower to flower to gather pollen, produces honey and bees-

---

[1]The word *spaniel'd* in line 21 is a conjectural emendation by one of Shakespeare's editors, but it is a powerful comparison of dogs and Antony's followers that would be worthy of Shakespeare's imaginative genius, and it is very likely the word that Shakespeare used.

wax. These in turn stand for "sweetness" (through honey) and "light" (through candles), and they refer to ideas that are both pleasing and instructive. In contrast to this positive imagery, Swift introduces the image of a spider, who spins its web out of itself and locates its home in useless, uncleaned corners of rooms. The spider thus stands for writers whose works, being nothing much more than excrement, are foul and useless and deserve to be thrown away. In other works Swift used many other negative images to attack various customs and institutions.

## Imagery and Allusions

Imagery is often complicated by the *allusion* to other works, such as the classics or the Bible. The image in the original source, having been used in this way, then becomes a vital part of the writer's context. In Donne's sonnet "I Am a Little World Made Cunningly," for example, the concluding lines are:

> . . . burn me, O Lord, with a fiery zeal
> Of Thee and Thy house, which doth in eating heal.

The problem raised by the paradox in the last line is partially solved when you realize that the image in the metaphor is from *Psalms* 69, 9: "For the zeal of thine house hath eaten me up." Until the Biblical image is known, however, the line will be difficult to visualize and understand completely.

This example brings up the problem of the amount of definition necessary for the comprehension of imagery. For the most part your attempt to visualize, smell, taste, touch, and hear the experience described or suggested will suffice to convey the meaning of the imagery to you. In these cases a dictionary is superfluous. But an allusive image, like the Biblical one in Donne's poem, or an archaic image, may require a dictionary in addition to any explanatory notes supplied by the editor of the work you are reading. As an example, let us look briefly at these lines from Pope's *Essay on Criticism*:

> Some, to whom Heav'n in Wit has been profuse,
> Want as much more, to turn it to its use;
> For *Wit* and *Judgment* often are at strife,
> Tho' meant each other's Aid, like *Man* and *Wife*.
> 'Tis more to *guide* than *spur* the Muse's Steed;
> Restrain his Fury, than provoke his Speed;
> The winged Courser, like a gen'rous Horse,
> Shows most true Mettle when you *check* his Course.
> —lines 80–87

Pope has sometimes been dispraised by the assertion that he was not an imaginative poet, but instead was ratiocinative or "discursive." A close look at a passage like this one renders this assertion absurd. Pope is talking about the relationship of reason to imagination, and is stating, briefly, that judgment (the perceptive, critical, discriminating faculty) must always be in control of imagination (or *fancy*, the other common word for the faculty, which is related to the words *fanciful* and *fantastic*). Pope compares judgment to a rider on a race horse. All the strength and speed of a thoroughbred ("gen'rous Horse") are of no value, he says, unless a good jockey rides and paces it well. In line 86 Pope mentions "The winged Courser" (a flying horse) and opens the door to allusion. By referring to a classical dictionary, you can learn that the flying horse of antiquity was Pegasus, who was ridden by Bellerophon in his fight against the monster Chimaera. Bellerophon was assisted in his fight by the gods, particularly by Athena, who was the goddess of wisdom. Other references may also apply. A dictionary tells you that the word *chimerical* (fantastically unreal) is derived from the name of the monster. The editor may tell you that in the seventeenth and eighteenth centuries pure fantasy was regarded as being akin to madness. In the context of the time when Pope wrote, this allusion to the winged horse seems to be saying: "If you wish to avoid madness or just foolishness in your writing, and if you wish to be favored by the goddess of wisdom, you must guide your imagination by judgment." Thus Pope's imagery works in two ways, literal and allusive, to strengthen his point that judgment is necessary in works of imagination and criticism.

You can see that reference books and annotated editions can be indispensable in guiding you to an understanding of at least some of the implications of an author's imagery. The scope of your Collegiate dictionary will surprise you. If you cannot find a reference in your dictionary, however, try an encyclopedia, or ask your reference librarian about standard reference guides such as *The Oxford Companion to English Literature*, *The Oxford Companion to Classical Literature*, or William Rose Benét's *The Reader's Encyclopaedia*. If you continue to have difficulties after using sources like these, see your teacher.

### Preparing Your Theme

Your job in preparing this theme, as always, is to be alert and to employ all facilities that can aid your understanding and appreciation. You must study your poem or passage word by word. Savor each word and set up a classification of what sorts of responses the words elicit. You might set up a series of lists headed by the words *Sight, Smell, Taste, Hearing, Touch,* and *Combinations* (how could you classify the image

"embalmed darkness" except by this latter category?). Then check yourself: Can you visualize a word or description? Can you recall a touch or
taste similar to that which the words describe?

With images that cause visual responses you might aid your imagination by drawing sketches. Some people might object to sketching
images on the grounds that it tends to limit your responses too narrowly,
but if it aids you in responding to a work, there is nothing wrong with
it. In Shakespeare's Sonnet No. 146, for example, line 13 offers an interesting challenge to the imagination that might be aided by a sketch:

> So shalt thou [the speaker's Soul] feed on
> Death that feeds on men, . . .

Just how far does the image invite complete visualization? That is one
problem faced by the student with a theme to write about this poem. Do
the metaphors *feed* and *feeds* invite a response visualizing an eater,
while eating, being eaten, or should the words be read without the
reader's attempting to imagine specific feeders? One student responded
to these lines with the following drawing:

This drawing vividly shows the relationships involved, though it tends
to demean Soul, Death, and Men (perhaps the student was thinking that
men, in this case, are "poor fish"). Whether or not you carry your visualization this far, it is clear that Shakespeare's speaker is calling Death
voracious because it seizes men for prey. But he is also asserting that
the Soul can be equally voracious and more powerful than Death, even
though it is also dependent on Death for its sustenance.

Whether you make a drawing or use your ability to visualize the
impressions suggested by the words, you are concerned in your analysis
with seeing the effect of imagery in the work. How does the imagery
convey meaning? What particular attitudes does it communicate or suggest? (That is, how do you feel about Death and the Soul after reading
the line from Shakespeare? Or how do you feel about Keats's excitement presented in "On First Looking into Chapman's Homer"?) How
fully developed are the images? Do they stem from single words, or are
they developed at greater length throughout a line or several lines, or
perhaps even throughout the entire work? Is there a controlling image,
and what is its effect? Are there many images or few? Do the images

make the work particularly powerful, feeble? Why? Are there symbols? Is the story allegorical? Does the imagery at one point in the work create any special effect on other parts of the work? Does the imagery seem to develop in any special pattern? (For example, Robert Frost's poem "Out, Out —" develops a pattern of sound beginning with the noisy, snarling buzz saw and ending with the feeble heartbeat of the dying boy; after the boy's death, Frost's description of the people turning away contains no words describing sound. The references to sound and silence within the poem therefore create an image suggesting what happens to the boy's heart.) These are the questions that you should try to answer in your theme.

### Organizing Your Theme

#### INTRODUCTION

In your introduction you should make a brief statement about the nature of the work you are analyzing. Related to this will be your central idea, which is the statement of the main point you wish to illustrate about the imagery (i.e., that it is mainly visual, or that it makes the poem powerful, or that it is ineffective, or some other point that your analysis has uncovered). If you are discussing symbolism or allegory, show here the grounds on which you have determined that this approach is justifiable. For example, in John Cheever's story "The Swimmer," there are many swimming pools that figure prominently in the action of the story. It would not be proper to treat these as symbols unless the writer clearly suggests that pools are vital in the social lives of the characters in the story. In fact, he does connect the pools to the society, so that a symbolic treatment is justifiable. An introduction is the proper place for establishing this sort of justification.

#### BODY

There are a number of approaches to discussing imagery, and you may choose whatever method, or combination of methods, you wish. Here are some possible choices:

1. *The meaning and effect of the imagery.*   Here you explain your interpretation of the various images. In Eve Merriam's poem "Robin Hood," for example, Robin Hood comes back to Sherwood Forest to establish the forest as a preserve next to the "Hood enterprises / for Sherwood Homesites." In explaining this action as a metaphor, you would say that modern commercialism has preempted the sense of adventure, romance, and justice that may have existed in earlier times. In

determining the effect of the metaphor you would probably draw attention to its combination of cynicism, derision, and amusement.

2. *Symbolism.*   You might select from two approaches here. First, you might wish to study the meaning of one particular symbol and its relationship to the entire work you have studied. What does the symbol mean? How is this meaning made clear by the details of the work? How often is the symbol introduced in the work? Does the meaning of the symbol change as it reappears, or does the author achieve any ironies by reintroducing the symbol into different contexts? A second approach is to speak about a number of symbols that may be used in the work. How are the symbols used? How are they related in the work, structurally? How are their meanings related? Does one symbol predominate at the beginning whereas another might become more important at the end? What does such a change indicate about the author's idea?

3. *The frequency and the types of images.*   Does the writer characteristically use expressions of imagery? How many images are there? How often do they occur? Does the writer use images appealing to one sense (sight, hearing, smell, taste, touch) rather than to another? Are colors, sounds, and shapes recorded? Do the images function integrally in the ideas of the work, or in the type of work (i.e., a poet might refer to all the senses, while a novelist may emphasize images of sight, or vice versa)? How fully does the author rely on the associations of sensuous imagery (do references to green plants and trees, for example, suggest that life may be rich and full, or do references to touch suggest amorous warmth)? What conclusions can you draw about the author's—or the persona's—taste or sensibility as a result of your study?

4. *The frames of reference of the imagery, and the appropriateness of the imagery to the subject matter.*   Here you might show the locations from which the images are derived. Does the writer favor images from Nature, science, warfare, politics, reading, and so on? Are these images appropriate to the subject matter? If the subject is the dreariness of a 9 to 5 office routine, for example, would an image of paper clips and commas be appropriate (see Theodore Roethke's poem "Dolor")? Similarly, in a tragedy, would it be appropriate or not to draw images from joyous rituals of springtime? What other conclusions can you draw?

5. *The effect of one image, or series of images, on the other images and ideas in the poem.*   Usually you would pick an image that occurs early in the work and ask if this image acts as a controlling image over the

ideas or mood (tone) of the work. Thus, the first paragraph of Swift's *Battle of the Books* (a prose work) contains an uncomplimentary image pertaining to the behavior of hungry dogs; in this way Swift conveys the impression that the whole battle between the "Ancients" and "Moderns" has a physiological origin that is anything but flattering. In an analysis of this sort, you would try to show the importance of the controlling image throughout the work.

6. *The extent to which the imagery points a work outward, toward those virtually indefinable areas of implication and suggestion that make literature an enduring art.* For example, in a poem entitled "All Watched Over by Machines of Loving Grace," Richard Brautigan describes a vision in which "deer stroll peacefully / past computers." This symbol pushes the imagination through a cynical exposé of mindless naiveté into a region of general hope, but the mind is never quite freed from Brautigan's gentle smile at both his speaker and reader. As for most symbols, the vehicle is not complex; it associates Nature and machine. But the tenor becomes exceedingly complex and suggestive. In carrying on a discussion of imagery along such lines, you would be in fact refining the type of discussion suggested in types 1 and 4. Your emphasis here, however, is not so much on explanation as on the richness and suggestiveness of the writer's images. Your procedure might be an *ad hoc* one, for your point would be to let your imagination go as far as the images will take you, and you may wish to apply the images to other works and situations. Thus you might settle on pursuing the meaning of one image, or you might select two or more. Although the idea in this approach is to be free, remember always to keep referring to your work.

### CONCLUSION

In your conclusion you should describe your general impressions. You might briefly refer to images that you did not discuss in the body of your theme, with the idea of showing that there is much that could still be uncovered. Or you might try to describe the general relationship of the imagery to some of the various ideas made in the work you have been discussing. You might also state how the imagery deepened your experience of the work or your insight into the nature of literature itself (if you have been working with type 6 exclusively, however, you will have concentrated on this aspect of imagery in the body of your theme). In a more comprehensive analysis you might compare the imagery in the work you have analyzed with imagery employed by the same writer in earlier or later works. Conclusions of this kind can reveal a great deal about a writer's development.

### A Study of Shakespeare's Imagery in Sonnet XXX

| | |
|---|---|
| When to the sessions of sweet silent thought, | 1 |
| I summon up remembrance of things past, | 2 |
| I sigh the lack of many a thing I sought, | 3 |
| And with old woes new wail my dear time's waste: | 4 |
| Then can I drown an eye (un-used to flow) | 5 |
| For precious friends hid in death's dateless night, | 6 |
| And weep afresh love's long since cancelled woe, | 7 |
| And moan th'expense of many a vanished sight. | 8 |
| Then can I grieve at grievances foregone, | 9 |
| And heavily from woe to woe tell o'er | 10 |
| The sad account of fore-bemoaned moan, | 11 |
| Which I new pay, as if not paid before. | 12 |
| But if the while I think on thee (dear friend) | 13 |
| All losses are restored, and sorrows end. | 14 |

[1]     In this sonnet Shakespeare emphasizes the sadness and regret that one's memories bring, but he asserts that these emotions are overcome by the thought of present friendship. The poem is a short, fourteen-line sonnet, but *Shakespeare's striking and ingenious imagery expands the thought far beyond these bounds.** One might say that the imagery almost "teases us out of thought," to borrow a phrase from Keats's "Ode on a Grecian Urn." *Shakespeare first presents images drawn from the courtroom, and then adds images from banking and business.*†

[2]     He introduces his legal image in the first four lines, where the speaker compares thinking about his past to a session of court, suggesting that his reverie is similar to a courtroom hearing. Like a judge, the speaker summons his past experience to appear before him to go on trial. This image is appropriate to the introspection and self-evaluation that are a part at least of each person's life. Shakespeare suggests that people themselves are their own judges, using their ideals and morals as laws by which to measure their own conduct. The speaker finds himself guilty of wasting his time in the past. Perhaps removing himself, however, from the strict application of the image, he becomes a sympathetic judge, and thus he does not condemn himself for his "dear time's waste," but instead laments it (line 4).

[3]     The thought of wastefulness and a sense of loss brings up the second pattern of imagery in the sonnet, namely the comparison of his past experience and dead friends to the spending of money. Continuing the legal hearing suggested in the first quatrain, the speaker states that his

*Central idea.     †Thesis sentence.

friends who are dead are "precious," just as gold and money are precious (line 6). In addition, the speaker has spent much effort on "vanished" sights (line 8), and he moans over the fact that his efforts, like the sights, are gone. He does not make clear just what these sights are, or were, but they obviously refer to people and activities he valued highly, in keeping with the financial imagery.

[4]    Shakespeare pursues the references to money in his third quatrain, and also takes up again the legal imagery of the first quatrain. Thus he grieves "at grievances foregone" in the manner of prosecuting a court case that has already been lost (line 9). As if this were not cause enough for genuine grievance in the sense of sorrow, he counts out his woes like a bank teller counting money, and pays with new woe the woe that he had already paid in the past. In the context of the legal imagery, it is as though his emotions have put him in double jeopardy, for his present emotions overwhelm him for the same reason that he was overwhelmed in the past. There is both ingenuity and truth in this observation, for memory retains just as many regrets as joys.

[5]    It is on the notion of approaching joy that Shakespeare concludes the poem. In the last two lines the speaker asserts that the thought of a present friend has sufficient value to settle all the existing emotional judgments that he has made against himself in his self-analysis. It is as though the friend is a rich benefactor who has rescued him from emotional bankruptcy and the accompanying sentence of emotional misery. The final two lines thus bring together the separate strands of imagery.

[6]    The ingenious pattern of imagery may at first dazzle the reader, but on reflection it continues to unfold many truths. In particular, line 8 ("And moan th'expense of many a vanished sight") carries an idea that living itself requires the spending of a great deal of emotional energy. People cannot have friends and loved ones without emotional commitment; in fact, they can hardly do anything without getting involved. In keeping with the view implied in this image, people could measure life not in months or years but in emotional commitments, for what really is of value is people's total human engagement, not the amount of time they take up on earth. Shakespeare, by freeing the mind to explore the thoughts about human values implicit in his images, has moved toward the very significance of life itself.

★COMMENTARY ON THE THEME

The theme is primarily concerned about the frames of reference of the imagery, and it therefore illustrates the method described in 4, above. Because it also discusses the meaning of the imagery, it also illustrates the method of 1. The last paragraph, by taking the image in one line and developing it extensively, illustrates the sort of development suggested in 6.

SECOND SAMPLE THEME (SYMBOLISM IN A STORY)

### Allegory and Symbolism in Hawthorne's "Young Goodman Brown"

[1]     It is almost impossible to read beyond the third paragraph of "Young Goodman Brown" without seeing allegory and symbolism. The opening is apparently realistic—a man leaves home on an important overnight trip—but his wife's name, "Faith," immediately suggests symbolism or allegory, and before long one is thrust into a semi-real, dreamlike landscape where objective details have extensive moral and psychological meaning. *Hawthorne dramatizes the idea that the overvaluation of an abstract concept of good and evil produces a shortsighted devaluation of human beings; in other words, Hawthorne's idea is that human beings are better than systems.** The story portrays this idea in light of Puritanism in Salem Village early in American history, but the idea also has a timely, broadly humanistic thrust. *Hawthorne expresses these thoughts in the richly suggestive allegory and in the many symbols in the work, particularly the symbolism of the sunset, the walking stick, and the path through the woods.†*

[2]     Hawthorne's allegory is about the process by which a person acquires an overriding and destructive idea. Most of the story up to the last paragraph is dreamlike even though it is generally faithful to chronology. Young Goodman Brown encounters a ritualistic "witch meeting" deep in the forest (p. 406). He is repulsed by the fact that he sees everyone he ever respected at the meeting, and after this vision he spends the remainder of his life in bitterness, measuring his neighbors against an impossibly puritanical standard and condemning them for their shortcomings. This set of events can be applied allegorically to just about all people whose experiences leave them in cynicism or in a form of idealism which is beyond human grasp. By extension, the story applies to all people whose character and experiences lead them to value an abstract system above humanity. No matter what *ism* people follow, to the degree that they are willing to condemn their fellow human beings, to take hostages, sacrifice victims, or destroy houses and land for that *ism*, they are like Goodman Brown with his bitterness and distrust of his fellow villagers.

[3]     This attack on dehumanization may be seen not just in this allegorical reading, but it can be deduced from the many symbols to be found in the work. One might start anywhere, for there are many symbols, but the best place is the beginning. The seventh word in the story, *sunset,* may be seen as symbolic. Sunset indicates the end of the day. Coming at the beginning of the story, however, it suggests that Goodman Brown is

In Laurence Perrine, ed., *Literature: Structure, Sound and Sense,* 2nd. ed. (New York: Harcourt Brace Jovanovich, 1974), pp. 397–407. Parenthetical page numbers refer to this edition.

*Central idea.    †Thesis sentence.

beginning the long night of his misanthropy, a night which for him will never end, because his final days are enshrouded in "gloom" (p. 407). Sunset is a natural symbol for the twilight of life, and here it suggests spiritual death. Hawthorne indicates that Brown, like anyone else who gives up on his fellow human beings, is cut off, enclosed in his own inner world of bitterness, for it is as though the light that guided him will now be gone.

[4]     The process of dehumanization — which is for Hawthorne the real hell for human beings — is assisted by the mysterious guide who resembles Young Goodman Brown's father, and whose walking stick "might almost be seen to twist and wriggle itself like a living serpent" (p. 398). Once Hawthorne has included this description, the reader immediately recalls Satan as the serpent tempting Adam and Eve. Realistically, walking sticks assist people as they go on their way. Symbolically, the very assistance on which people rely is being furnished by the spirit of evil. At one point in the story Hawthorne refers to "the instinct that guides mortal men to evil" (p. 402). In a way, the stick could be representative of this instinct, in psychological terms, or of Satan in mythical terms.

[5]     Whether guided by instinct or by Satan, Brown goes his way to perdition along a symbolic and allusive path through the forest. As Brown follows it, the path grows "wilder and drearier, and more faintly traced," and "at length" the path vanishes (p. 402). This is perhaps like the "way" that is mentioned in the Bible as being "broad" and leading "to destruction" (Matthew, VII.13). In this respect the symbol suggests that of the many options of conduct open to human beings, most are destructive, while a small number (the "narrow" way leading to "life" of Matthew VII.14) are genuinely good. Hawthorne's path for Goodman Brown is at first distinct, as though error is at first unique and unusual, but soon the accumulation of errors becomes so vast that no matter what way he chooses he will end in disaster. Then too, the symbol suggests that as people follow an evil course their perceptions of right and wrong are blurred so that they can no longer see the right way. The implication is that people in the midst of the dark forest of their own misguided preconceptions can no longer distinguish the right way.

[6]     Because "Young Goodman Brown" is so completely allegorical and symbolic, it is difficult to set any precise limits on Hawthorne's meaning. The principal issue raised in the story, however, seems to be a paradox: How can a system that is sincerely believed lead to a bad result which the adherent of the system does not perceive to be bad? How can noble ideals backfire so disastrously? In Brown's case, he leads his life in bitterness against his fellows because he believes so strongly in the accuracy of his own vision. This form of evil is the hardest to remedy no matter what form it takes because the wrongdoer who is convinced of his own virtue is beyond reach. This complication of evil and self-righteousness causes Hawthorne to write that "the fiend in his own shape is less hideous, than when he rages in the breast of man" (p. 403). Young Goodman Brown himself thus emerges as the story's major sym-

bol; he is one of those who walk in darkness but who have forever barred themselves from the light.

★COMMENTARY ON THE THEME

The first paragraph presents justification for treating the allegory and symbolism of the story. In the body of the theme, paragraph 2 treats the allegory, emphasizing the relationship between Young Goodman Brown and people generally who fall into the same pattern of distrust he develops. Paragraphs 3, 4, and 5 treat three major symbols in the story. The emphasis in these paragraphs, and also in paragraph 2, is on the contributions the symbols make to the main idea. The concluding paragraph considers the paradox implicit in the central idea, and shows that Young Goodman Brown himself is a major symbol. Though in a theme of this type there is necessarily a discussion of the ideas of the author, the aim is not so much to expand on the ideas as to show how the allegory and symbolism contribute to the ideas.

**CHAPTER**
# 13

# *The Theme Analyzing Tone*

TONE refers to the means by which a writer conveys attitudes. Although it is a technical subject, in practice the discussion of tone sometimes becomes focused on the attitudes themselves. For this reason, the terms *tone* and *attitude* are often confused. You should remember, however, that tone refers not to attitudes but to that quality of a writer's style that reveals or creates these attitudes. It is important to preserve this distinction.

Studying and describing tone require great alertness, because your understanding will depend largely on your ability to make inferences from the work you are reading (sometimes this process is called "reading between the lines"). Your analysis of tone is, in effect, your analysis of the author's mind at work, and through this analysis you can become aware of the vitality of literature — the creativity of the author's mind as seen in the words. Reading a work of literature without perceiving its tone is like watching a speaker on television with the sound turned off; without tone you can guess at meaning, but cannot understand it fully.

### Tone in Operation

*Tone* in literature has been borrowed from the phrase *tone of voice* in speech. Tone of voice is a reflection of your attitude toward the person or persons whom you are addressing and also toward the subject matter of your discussion. It is made up of many elements: the speed with which you speak, the enthusiasm — or lack of it — that you project into what you say, the pitch and loudness of your speech, your facial expressions, the way you hold your body, and your distance from the person to whom you are speaking.

As a literary example, let us look briefly at this passage from Jonathan Swift's *Gulliver's Travels.*

> Imagine with thy self, courteous reader, how often I then wished for the tongue of Demosthenes or Cicero, that might have enabled me to celebrate the praise of my own dear native country in a style equal to its merits and felicity.[1]

Here is a passage in which Gulliver, Swift's narrator, is perfectly sincere about praising England, whereas Swift the satirist, behind the scenes, is just about to deliver a satiric condemnation of England in 1727. The control of tone makes these contrasting attitudes evident and makes this passage comic. Swift controls the tone by causing Gulliver to refer to the two most famous ancient orators who were known for their ability to speak well but who were also known for their powers to condemn. He also makes Gulliver use the ambiguous phrase "equal to its merits and felicity" and the possibly sarcastic word "celebrate." In conversing with people, you can perceive their tone by all the spoken and "body language" signs; however, in a literary passage like this one you are not aided by anything except what you see on the page. To interpret it properly you have only a dictionary, other reference works, and above all your intelligence.

Tone, of course, may be described in as many ways as there are human moods. Here is a partial list of words that might describe tone in particular passages:

> admiring, worshiping, approving
> strident, subdued, harsh
> disliking, abhorring
> simple, straightforward, direct, unambiguous
> complicated, complex, difficult
> forceful, powerful
> ironic, sardonic, sarcastic
> indirect, understated, evasive
> bitter, grim
> sympathetic, interested
> indifferent, unconcerned, apathetic
> antagonistic, hostile
> violent, outraged, indignant, angry
> elevated, grand, lofty

[1]*Gulliver's Travels and Other Writings*, Louis A. Landa (Boston: Houghton Mifflin, 1960), p. 102.

serious, solemn, sepulchral, ghoulish
comic, jovial, easy, friendly

A thesaurus can supply you with many more words, and it is conceivable that there are, somewhere, literary works to which all the words you discover might be applied.

## Problems in Describing Tone

The study of tone is the study of the ways in which attitudes are manifested in particular literary works. Therefore, when you write a theme about tone, you must attempt to name and describe these attitudes and analyze the means by which they are expressed. Your statements will be based on inferences that you make from the text.

You must also attempt to describe the intensity, the force with which the attitudes are expressed. This task is difficult, but necessary, and it is one of the ways by which you can amplify your statements about the nature of the attitudes. The force of the tone depends on the intrinsic seriousness of the situations, the speakers' degrees of involvement in them, and their control over their expression. You would recognize the differences in intensity between the statements in these two columns:

| 1 | 2 |
|---|---|
| "This report is not what we expected." | "This report is terrible." |
| "Mr. Student, your paper shows promise, but it is not, as yet, up to passing standards." | "Mr. Student, your paper is a slovenly disgrace." |

In describing the difference, you would necessarily concentrate on the differing *intensities* in the quotations. Compare the intensities of these two quotations:

(1) Written on a wall in Panama City: "Yankee, go home."
(2) Written on a wall in Paris: "Yankee, go home—via Air France."

These last quotations bring up another, closely related, element in the consideration of tone—namely, *control*. Writers may feel deeply about a subject, but if they give vent to their feelings completely they are likely to create not a literary work but only an emotional display. They must always control the expression of sentiment, because their appeal must be not only to their readers' sympathies but also to their understanding. A fine example of the control of attitude is *Antony and Cleopatra* (V. ii, 241–281). Cleopatra is about to commit suicide. Just before she does, Shakespeare introduces a country bumpkin on stage to bring her an asp, which will be the cause of her death. The resulting interchange between Cleopatra, serious and about to die, and the stupid but concerned clown is clearly designed to arouse laughter.

*Enter Guardsman and Clown (with Basket).*

GUARD        This is the man.

CLEOPATRA    Avoid, and leave him.

*Exit Guardsman.*

Hast thou the pretty worm of Nilus there
That kills and pains not?

CLOWN        Truly I have him. But I would not be the party that should desire you to touch him, for his biting is immortal. Those that do die of it do seldom or never recover.

CLEOPATRA    Remember'st thou any that have died on't?

CLOWN        Very many, men and women too. I heard of one of them no longer than yesterday; a very honest woman, but something given to lie, as a woman should not do but in the way of honesty—how she died of the biting of it, what pain she felt. Truly, she makes a very good report o' the worm; but he that will believe all that they say shall never be saved by half that they do. But this is most falliable, the worm's an odd worm.

CLEOPATRA    Get thee hence; farewell.

CLOWN        I wish you all joy of the worm.

*(Sets down his basket).*

CLEOPATRA    Farewell. . . .

The problem in interpreting this scene involves Shakespeare's attitude toward Cleopatra and toward his audience. It is likely that Shakespeare introduced the comic scene in order to keep his treatment of Cleopatra from becoming purely sentimental. He knew that one way to produce laughter is to heap misfortune upon misfortune, so that an audience will ultimately respond to additional misfortunes with laughter, not with sympathy. Cleopatra's suicide is the final misfortune, and lest his audience not respond with sorrow, Shakespeare provides the clown to siphon off, as it were, his audience's tension by giving it a legitimate release in laughter. In this way he directs a proper amount of sympathy toward Cleopatra and deepens our concern for her. The situation is complex, but Shakespeare's handling of it indicates the control of the master.

## Laughter, Comedy, and Farce

A major aspect of tone is laughter and the comic and farcical modes. No two critics agree on what exactly makes people laugh but all agree that laughter is essential in a person's psychological well-being. Laughter is an *ad hoc*, unpredictable action; what people find amusing today will not move them tomorrow. The causes of laughter are immeasurably complicated, and difficult to analyze and isolate. However, the major elements in laughter seem to be these:

1. AN OBJECT OF LAUGHTER.   There must be something to laugh at, whether a person, thing, situation, custom, habit of speech or dialect, or arrangement of words.

2. INCONGRUITY.   Human beings have a sense of what to expect under given conditions, and anything that violates these expectations may be a cause of laughter. On a day when the temperature is 100°F., (38°C.), for example, you would reasonably expect people to dress lightly. But if you saw people dressed in heavy overcoats, warm hats, mufflers, and large gloves, who were shivering, waving their arms, and stamping their feet as though to keep them warm, you would likely laugh because those people would have violated your expectation of what sane people would do under the conditions. Their response to the weather is inappropriate or *incongruous*. The standup comedian's story that, "Yesterday afternoon I was walking down the street and turned into a drugstore," is funny because "turned into" can have two incompatible meanings. Here the language itself has furnished its own incongruity. A student once wrote that in high school he had enjoyed singing in the "archipelago choir." This is an inadvertent verbal mistake called a *malapropism*, after Mrs. Malaprop, a character in Richard Brinsley Sheridan's play *The Rivals*. In the student's report about the choir, you expect to see *a capella* — or at least a recognizable misspelling of the word — and when you see *archipelago*, a word that makes sense elsewhere and sounds something like *a capella*, you laugh, or at least smile. Incongruity is the quality common to all these instances of laughter.

3. SAFETY AND/OR GOODWILL.   Seeing people who have just slipped on a banana peel hurtling through the air and about to crack their skull may cause laughter as long as we ourselves are not those people, for our laughter depends on our being insulated from danger and

pain. In farce, where a great deal of physical abuse takes place, such as falling through trapdoors or being hit in the face by cream pies, the abuse never harms the participants. The incongruity of such situations causes laughter, and one's safety from personal consequences — together with the insulation from pain of the participants — prevents the interference of more grave or even horrified responses. The element of goodwill enters into laughter in romantic comedy or in works where you are drawn into general sympathy with the major figures. Here the infectiousness of laughter and happiness influences your responses. As the characters make their way toward success, your involvement with them will produce a general sense of happiness which may cause you to smile and also may cause you to laugh sympathetically.

4. Unfamiliarity, newness, uniqueness, spontaneity. Laughter depends on seeing something new or unique, or in experiencing a known thing freshly. Laughter usually occurs in a flash of insight or revelation, and the situation producing laughter must always possess spontaneity. Perhaps you have had a joke or funny situation explained to you, and found that the explanation dampened the spontaneity that would have enabled you to laugh. Although spontaneity is most often a quality of the unfamiliar, it is not lost just because a thing becomes familiar. A good joke, comic incident, or story may retain the power to provoke laughter because of its uniqueness or because of the merit of its views of life. Jokes of this type assume the status of "standing jokes." Novels like *Huckleberry Finn* and Henry Fielding's *Joseph Andrews* retain their wit and spontaneity and thus are always comic. The quality of writing and structuring in works of this type is an element of tone and would provide a suitable topic for study in a theme.

## Irony

One of the most human traits is the capacity to have two or more attitudes toward something. You might love someone but on occasion express your affection by insults rather than praise. A large number of contemporary greeting cards feature witty insults, because many people cannot stand the sentimentality of the "straight" cards, and send the insulting card in the expectation that the person receiving it will be amused and will recognize genuine fondness on the sender's part. Expressions in which one attitude is conveyed by its opposite are *ironic*. *Irony* may be defined as a mode of ambiguous or indirect expression; it is natural to human beings who are aware of the possibilities and complexities in life. Irony is a function of the realization that life does not always measure up to promise, that friends and loved ones may sometimes be angry and bitter toward each other, that the universe offers mysteries that human beings cannot comprehend, that doubt exists even in the face of certainty, and that character is built through chagrin, regret, and pain as much as through emulation and praise. In expressing ideas ironically, writers pay the greatest compliment to their readers, for they assume that they have sufficient skill and understanding to see through the surface statement into the seriousness or levity beneath.

The major types of irony are *verbal, situational,* and *dramatic.* One of the American astronauts was once asked how he would feel if all his reentry safety equipment failed as his space vehicle was falling toward earth. He responded, "A thing like that could ruin your whole day." This is *understatement* or *litotes. Overstatement,* or *hyperbole,* is exaggeration for effect, as in statements like, "If I've told you once, I've told you a million times."

The term *situational irony,* or *irony of situation,* refers to human conditions that are measured against forces that transcend and overpower human capacities. These forces may be social, political, or environmental. If situational irony is connected with a pessimistic or fatalistic view of life it is sometimes called *irony of fate* or *cosmic irony.* Thomas Hardy was adept at creating this sort of irony, for he set up little accidents, chances, or misunderstandings that played a role, usually calamitous, far beyond their ordinary significance. Thus, in *The Return of the Native,* Eustacia appears at the window of her home briefly and glances at the visiting Mrs. Yeobright outside. Because a former suitor is visiting Eustacia, and also because she believes that her husband Clym will answer the door, she does not admit Mrs. Yeobright. Mrs. Yeobright has seen Eustacia at the window and misinterprets Eustacia's motives; she is disheartened and leaves for home, only to meet death on the heath. All subsequent disasters in the novel stem from this incident, and their effect on the tone of the novel is that the ill consequences are much more pathetic because they could have been easily avoided. The implication is that human beings are caught in a web of circumstances and that their lives are largely determined by these conditions, regardless of what they themselves do.

Situational irony could of course work in a more optimistic way. For example, a good person could go through a set of difficult circumstances and be on the verge of losing everything in life, but through someone's perversity or through luck, might emerge successfully. Such a situation could reflect an author's conception of a benevolent universe. Most often, however, cosmic irony is more like that in Hardy.

*Dramatic irony* applies when a character perceives a situation in a limited way while the audience sees it in greater perspective. The audience sees double meaning whereas the character sees only one. The classic example of dramatic irony is found in *Oedipus Rex,* where Oedipus thinks he is about to discover that someone else murdered his father, while the audience knows all along that he himself is the murderer and that as he condemns the murderer he condemns himself. In Hemingway's story "My Old Man," dramatic irony is utilized skillfully. This story is told by a son about his father who is a jockey but who also becomes involved in deals to fix horse races. During the first part of the story the narrator does not know the significance of the events he is describing, while the reader can see that the father is guilty of fixing races. During the latter half of the story, Hemingway subtly employs dramatic irony to focus on the son's attempts to mask from himself the significance of the father's actions and also to avoid the realization that his father has undergone physical and moral deterioration. The father's death at the end of the story, and the comments by the two "guys" about the father, finally and brutally force the boy to face the truth. Hemingway thus creates a poignant account of a loss of innocence, and he does so by using dramatic irony to show that the boy possessed innocence that could be lost.

**Irony, Laughter, and Tragedy**

If you conclude that the incongruity of laughter and the ambiguity of irony are closely linked together, you are right. Laughter is one product of irony, though more often of ironic expressions than ironic situations. In fact, however, many ironic situations verge on tragedy. In tragedy, all bright hopes for the future are blasted; the good people are brought to destruction by the forces unleashed around them. Tragic irony is thus based on a discrepancy between great potential and disastrous consequences. If there is laughter in tragedy, it is not the participants or the spectators who laugh, but some set of detached, remote, inhuman beings. Shakespeare's Gloucester in *King Lear* (IV.i, 42–43) describes this situation well:

> As flies to wanton boys are we to th' gods,
> They kill us for their sport.

**Studying Tone**

The study of tone requires studying everything in a work that contributes to more than denotative statement. To perceive tone you should be constantly aware of the general impression that a passage leaves with you, and analytical enough to study the particular ways by which this effect is achieved. You must understand all the words and all the situations. Read the work carefully, and then study the passages you select for discussion to determine the connotations of the words and the rhythms of the cadence groups. Because many things in the work may affect tone, you should be alert to everything.

To see how everything can work at once, let us look at another passage from Swift's *Gulliver's Travels*. In the fourth voyage, Swift causes Gulliver to describe with pride the most recent weaponry, methods, and achievements in warfare:

> . . . being no stranger to the art of war, I gave . . . a description of cannons, culverins, muskets, carabines, pistols, bullets, powder, swords, bayonets, battles, sieges, retreats, attacks, undermines, countermines, bombardments, sea-fights; ships sunk with a thousand men, twenty thousand killed on each side; dying groans, limbs flying in the air, smoke, noise, confusion, trampling to death under horses' feet; flight, pursuit, victory; fields strewed with carcasses left for food to dogs, and wolves, and birds of prey; plundering, stripping, ravishing, burning and destroying. And to set forth the valour of my own dear countrymen, I assured him, that I had seen them blow up a hundred enemies at once in a siege, and as many in a ship, and beheld the dead bodies drop down in pieces from the clouds, to the great diversion of all the spectators.[2]

The tone is that of condemnation, angry but cold. Swift is in control. He achieves his tone in a number of ways. First, Gulliver thinks he is praising war while the sensitive reader receives entirely different signals. The reader and Swift provide a humane political and moral context against which Gulliver's words are to be measured. Thus we have an example of situational irony. Second, the texture of the passage is one of accumulation. Swift has Gulliver list all the death-dealing weapons and all the horrible consequences of warfare. The condemnation of war is achieved by the multiplication of examples alone, virtually overcoming all possible opposing views. Third, there is verbal irony in phrases like "the valour of my own dear countrymen" and "to the great diversion of all the spectators." This is hyperbole that cuttingly exposes the callousness to suffering that usually accompanies war. Fourth, the passage is capable of producing laughter—not happy laughter, but laughter of amazement and repulsion at the incongruity caused by the common moral pretensions of many people and their dereliction of these pretensions during warfare. When you read the passage you respond to everything at once, yet analysis reveals a passage of high complexity. Swift's control of tone is the cause of your responses.

## Your Approach to Tone

Your main problem in reading the work assigned is to determine to your satisfaction what the dominant tone is. You must therefore carefully examine not only what is said but the context in which it is

[2]*Gulliver's Travels and Other Writings*, ed. Landa, pp. 200–201.

said. In order to support your claim about tone, you will need to study those factors (style, structure, idea) that cause the particular tone that you have noted.

The amount of analysis you do will depend on the length of the work. In a long work you might analyze representative passages that support your central idea. If the work is short, you might very well attempt to analyze the entire work.

Once you have decided on your interpretation of the tone, you should state that as your central idea. Then, without making distortions, you should gather material that will support your central idea. Let the material produce the idea, and do not neglect material that opposes your idea. So long as what you analyze has bearing on your central idea, you might bring in considerations of style, ambiguity, accumulation of evidence — all at one time. Just remember to point your discussion toward your basic argument.

## Organizing Your Theme

### INTRODUCTION

State your central idea. You should not only define the tone briefly but also describe the force and conviction of the tone. Your thesis sentence should be a statement about the areas in which you plan to develop your discussion. If there are any particular obstacles to the proper determination of the tone, either in the work or in your personal attitudes, you should state these in your introduction also.

### BODY

The body should be a pointed discussion of the major elements in the work that caused you to arrive at your central idea. You are free to organize this section in any way you wish. Following are two suggested methods:

1. If there is a unity of tone throughout the work, you should organize the body to show the scope of the tone; that is, you would show that various sections of the work are similar in tone. Or you might wish to analyze and discuss the tone in one or more representative passages, to show the characteristic methods by which the author controls tone. If you are considering comic elements or laughter, try to show the principal means by which the writer has created humor. Are incongrous situations mainly worked with, or is comic language relied on? Consider the structuring of the humor, first by carefully recording those places where you laughed, and second by determining the way in which the author prepared you for those moments of laughter. The idea is that

you do not laugh in a vacuum, but respond to an arrangement of materials which is climaxed in laughter. Determine this arrangement.

2. If there is a complexity or plurality of attitudes in the work, attempt to describe and interpret the author's method. Irony, of course, depends on a complexity of attitudes. In considering irony you should determine the type. If your topic is dramatic irony, how is this achieved by the writer? Why is the presentation effective? In verbal irony, can you classify the types (overstatement, understatement, sarcasm) and the moods (admiration, sympathy, cynicism, etc.)? In cosmic irony, what kind of attitude does the author express about people and about the universe?

## CONCLUSION

The principal object of your conclusion is to relate the question of tone to your understanding and evaluation of the work. Elements to consider in evaluation are (1) the intensity and (2) the control over attitudes.

SAMPLE THEME

### Tone in Stephen Crane's "The Open Boat"

[1]     *In "The Open Boat" Stephen Crane shows admiration and sympathy for four men cast adrift in a small boat (and, symbolically, for the plight of humankind generally), and he also exhibits bafflement and mild scorn at the apparent indifference, hostility, and arbitrariness of the universe.** The story is divided into seven sections that mark the developing action but have little to do with the tone except that Crane's admiration for the characters and arguments against the universe are stronger at the end of the story than at the beginning. The two attitudes exist simultaneously throughout the story, just as the essential conflict in the story is between the men in the boat and the apparently arbitrary and capricious forces preventing them from reaching land easily. *Crane renders his admiration and scorn through his descriptions of the men, his commentary on the situation in the boat, and his irony.*†

[2]     Crane's descriptions of the men emphasize their admirable, cooperative spirit. Every reference made to Billie the oiler, for example, is in language of approval. When Billie is asked by the correspondent to take over the rowing, Billie's response is a quick "Sure," even though he has been doing more than his share already (p. 234). On other occasions Billie

In Walter K. Gordon, *Literature in Critical Perspectives* (Englewood Cliffs, N.J.: Prentice-Hall, Inc., 1968), pp. 225–237. Parenthetical page numbers refer to this edition.

*Central idea.     †Thesis sentence.

is shown as a man who is "busy" with the affairs of the boat (p. 226) and also as a "wily surfman" (p. 229) and a person capable of making sound conclusions and judgments (p. 228). When the men leave the boat for shore, it is clear that Crane invites us to see that Billie has left the piece of life preserver for the correspondent, in a spirit of selfless cooperation. Although Crane focuses admiration on Billie, he also surrounds his descriptions of the other men with the same fondness. He shows that the Captain is always awake and in command, and that even the cook does his share during the long night by warming the tired rowers after they have been spelled from their back-breaking duty. Similarly, the correspondent works along with the others despite the fact that a person of his profession would probably not be accustomed to hard labor. The tone is admiration for all the men.

[3]     Superimposed upon these descriptions of the men is Crane's running commentary on the action, which indicates sympathy for the men and a shared set of values with them. Crane verbalizes what could have been expressed by the men had they been more articulate. He emphasizes their spiritual kinship, for example, at the beginning of section III:

> It would be difficult to describe the subtle brotherhood of men that was here established on the seas. No one said that it was so. No one mentioned it. But it dwelt in the boat, and each man felt it warm him (p. 227).

Throughout the story such commentaries suggest the closeness of the narrator and the men. It is as though the speaker has become so much a part of the situation that he moves from his own stance as narrator into the language and speech patterns of the men. The teeth of the shivering correspondent, for example, play "all the popular airs" (p. 234). Such an ironic overstatement would be more typical of the men than of an uninvolved narrator. Similar also are the commentaries (a) comparing moving in the boat to the difficulties of stealing eggs from under a hen (p. 227), (b) claiming that the coldness of the water was "tragic" (p. 236), (c) complaining that the backaches of a man rowing are more numerous than the aches that might befall a regiment of men (p. 230), and others. These commentaries, wry and almost comic as they are, fit the pattern of Crane's admiration for the men.

[4]     To be contrasted with this admiration is the irony pervading the story. Crane makes plain that his four shipwrecked men are actors in a great cosmic play which is for the most part incomprehensible. He makes the sea seem hostile, with its waves constantly threatening to swamp the small boat and with the "ugly brute" of a seagull (p. 227) and the threatening fins of the shark (p. 233). These are physical manifestations of the sea's hostility, and Crane goes beyond them into a larger, cosmic fabric illustrating the helpless lot of humankind in a bleak, indifferent universe. His commentary about throwing "bricks at the temple" (p. 233) in anger and frustration, his frequent interjections about the unfairness of drowning within view of sand and trees (pp. 229, 231, 233), the reference to the "ninny-woman, Fate" (p. 229), together with the claim that "the whole affair is absurd" (p. 229) indicate his derision of the seemingly arbitrary

universe in which the strongest man, Billie the oiler, can drown. There
may be an additional irony here, for it is clear that Billie has performed so
selflessly and heroically that he may have weakened himself beyond his
capacity to save himself. Here the irony is that heroism and kindness,
rather than being rewarded, are the precise cause of a person's destruction. As the old saying goes, "No good deed shall go unpunished."

[5]     There are many other ironies in the story—such as the fact that
Billie reaches his goal only after he has drowned, when his forehead
touches the sand "that was periodically, between each wave, clear of the
sea" (p. 237), or the understatement that when the men first come in sight
of land the correspondent "for some reason" wishes to see it—but the
main thrust of the irony is that Crane is using "The Open Boat" as a
symbol of human life. Bafflement, helplessness, anger, disillusion,
bitterness, despair, scorn—all these attitudes seem to be suggested by
the arbitrary death of Billie. Crane expresses nothing positive when he
considers the sea and the universe. But when he looks inwardly toward
humankind, he finds hope. It is, at the end, the man who performs the act
of rescue who has the halo "about his head" (p. 237). Crane seems to be
in the position of asking questions but receiving no answers that lead to
any orderly purpose. In the absence of answers from without, he seeks
them from within, and therefore "The Open Boat" shows that admiration
is deserved only by those who promote our survival through assistance
and cooperation. The author's attitudes show that he is not removed from
the plight of the men and of the human race generally, but is an integral
part of it.

★COMMENTARY ON THE THEME

Paragraphs 2 and 3 illustrate the means by which one might discuss a straightforward, unambiguous tone. Paragraph 2 emphasizes
the author's admiration for one character—Billie the oiler—and for
brevity's sake refers to the other three characters rapidly. Paragraph 3
shows, in effect, that Crane is so closely identified with the characters
that his point of view virtually merges with their outlook on their own
circumstances. The author becomes the speaker for those he admires.

The fourth paragraph shows how one might consider situational
irony. It is necessary to view the general situation in relationship to
some larger set of circumstances. In this case the circumstance is Crane's
portrait of a bleak, indifferent universe. The concluding paragraph
shows how verbal irony might be handled, and it also shows how an
unambiguous tone may be combined with irony for discussion.

CHAPTER
# 14

# The Theme Analyzing Prosody

PROSODY is the word commonly used to refer to the study of sound and rhythm in poetry. Other equally descriptive words are *metrics, versification, mechanics of verse,* and *numbers.* (*Numbers* is not common at present, but it was current in Pope's time. Longfellow also used it.) Some persons call sound and rhythm the *music* of poetry.

Although sound and rhythm are the primary concern of prosodic study, these elements are never to be discussed in a vacuum. They are always an integral part of every good poem and are important only as they are related to the other parts. Alexander Pope indicated that "the sound must seem an echo to the sense." This idea is important. In poetry each word must count. Everything should work to convey ideas and attitudes—not just the meanings of the words but their sounds and their positions in lines and in the entire poem. Words must be placed in the most effective location, and major ideas must be arranged for the maximum effect. The poet utilizes every linguistic skill to strike your mind and spirit, to fix the poem in your memory. Thus, prosodic study is an attempt to determine how the poet has arranged sound in the interests of sense.

The two major categories to be considered in prosodic analysis are rhythm and sound.

### Rhythm

Rhythm refers to the relationship of words in groups. Large units are sentences and paragraphs; smaller units are *cadence groups* and *metrical feet.* Principally we will be concerned here with cadence groups and feet, for these form the basic blocks of rhythmical analysis.

**CADENCE GROUPS**

Words do not function alone but take on meaning only as they form a part of phrases or clauses. This is an inescapable fact of any language, and one should never ignore it in a consideration of a poet's prosodic technique. The term used to describe a functioning group of words is *cadence group* (also discussed briefly in Chapter 15). The word *in*, for example, is a preposition, but is not very meaningful alone. In phrases like *in the dooryard* and *in the night*, however, it becomes part of an indissoluble unit of meaning—prepositional phrases that are also cadence groups. The word *star* conveys a certain amount of meaning, but *the great star* forms a syntactic and rhythmical unit, a cadence group. When you speak you do not utter words separately, but rather put them together into cadence groups which coincide syntactically, rhythmically, and semantically. If we use spaces to indicate the vocal pauses, noticeable and slight, that separate cadence groups, we can see approximately how individual sentences are comprised of these units of both rhythm and meaning:

> Fourscore and seven years ago     our fathers brought forth
> on this continent     a new nation     conceived in liberty
> and dedicated to the proposition     that all men     are created equal.

This is of course famous prose, and you can see that it would be impossible to read it without bunching the words together approximately as it is laid out. The following lines by Walt Whitman are spaced according to such cadence groups:

> When lilacs last     in the dooryard bloom'd,
> And the great star     early droop'd     in the western sky     in the night.

Such groups may or may not correspond to regular rhythmical demands in poetry. Here is an example of poetry in which the cadence groups are contained within a rhythmical norm:

> What passing-bells     for these who die as cattle?
> Only the monstrous anger     of the guns.
> Only the stuttering rifles     rapid rattle
> Can patter out     their hasty orisons.
> —Wilfred Owen, "Anthem for Doomed Youth"[1]

You may perceive a rhythmical similarity between the groups *What passing bells* and *can patter out;* the second and fourth syllables are more heavily pronounced (stressed) than the first and third. You may also perceive the rhythmical similarity (augmented by verbal repetition) of

*Only the monstrous anger* and *Only the stuttering rifles.* This kind of poetry, in which cadence groups form part of a recurring pattern, is loosely called *traditional.* Poetry like Whitman's however, in which cadence groups behave more or less arbitrarily according to meaning and the poet's apparent wishes rather than to rhythmical regularity, is called *free verse.* Poets of both free and traditional verse share the desire to create effective, moving ideas through the manipulation of cadence groups. The difference between them is that the free-verse poet relies almost exclusively on the arrangement of cadence groups while the traditional poet merges cadence groups and rhythmical regularity. Thus, free verse takes no definite shape; lines may be long or short, as the poet wishes to expand or concentrate the ideas. Traditional verse takes on a more formal appearance, and its rhythms can be systematically measured.

### METRICAL FEET

When you speak, you naturally give more force or loudness to some syllables than you give to others. The syllables to which you give more force are *heavily stressed,* and those to which you give less are *lightly stressed.* In most English poetry poets have distributed the heavily and lightly stressed syllables into patterns called *feet.* They usually fill the lines with a specific number of the same feet, and that number determines the *meter* of the line. Thus five feet in a line make *pentameter,* four are *tetrameter,* three are *trimeter,* and two are *dimeter.* Frequently, rhetorical needs lead poets to substitute other feet for the regular feet. Whether there is *substitution* or not, the number and kind of feet in each line constitute the metrical description of that line. In order to discover the prevailing metrical system in any poem, you *scan* that poem. The act of scanning is called *scansion.*

Your first problem in scansion is to recognize where syllables are and to distinguish one syllable from another. Experience has shown that students who in the early grades have been taught to read by the "word-recognition" method, as contrasted with the "syllable" method, often find it hard to distinguish syllables. This difficulty is unfortunate, because an understanding of syllables is the first requirement in developing feeling for rhythms in poetry. You must therefore be especially cautious and realize that words like *merrier* and *terrier,* for example, are three-syllable words, as is *solitude.* If you find difficulty in perceiving the syllables in lines of poetry, a good idea is to read each word aloud separately, pronouncing every syllable, before reading the words in poetic context. The practice of reading poetry aloud is good in any event. If you have been encouraged to read for speed, you must abandon this approach when you read poetry.

The next step in preparation for your theme is to interpret *stress* or *accent*. You are concerned with showing the syllables that receive major and light stress, and you need a system for showing these syllables. In scansion a heavy or primary accent is commonly indicated by a prime mark ('), whereas a light accent may be indicated by a circle or degree sign (°).

Once you have determined the relationship of light and heavy accents, you are ready to mark out your poem into the recurring metrical pattern. The names of the various metrical feet are derived from Greek poetry. In English, the most important are the two-syllable foot, the three-syllable foot, and the imperfect (or one-syllable) foot.

The Two-Syllable Foot

1. Iamb.    A light stress followed by a heavy stress, as in

be - have

The iamb is the most common foot in English poetry because it is capable of great variation. Within the same line of five iambic feet, each foot can be slightly different in intensity from the others. In this line from Wordsworth, each foot is unique:

The winds / that will / be howl - / ing at / all hours.

Even though *will* and *at* are stressed syllables, they are not as heavily stressed as *winds, howl-,* and *hours.* Such variability, approximating the rhythms of actual speech, makes the iambic foot suitable for just about any purpose, serious or light. The iamb therefore assists poets in focusing attention on their ideas and emotions. If they use it with skill, it never becomes monotonous, for it does not distract the reader by drawing attention to its own rhythm.

2. Trochee.    A heavy accent followed by a light, as in

u - nit

The iamb and the trochee deserve special attention. Most English words of two syllables are trochaic, for example:

region, doctrine, author, willow, morning, early

Words of two syllables having an iambic pattern usually have prefixes or else they are borrowed from a foreign language and their pronunciation is unchanged in English:

control, because, despair, sublime
machine, garage, technique

Because trochaic rhythm is often called *falling, dying, anticlimactic,* and *feminine* (this term was used before the advent of modern feminism), and because iambic rhythm is usually called *rising, elevating, climactic,* and *masculine,* a major problem in English poetry has been to fit many trochaic words into iambic patterns. A common way to solve the problem — and a way consistent with the natural word order of the language — is to place a definite or indefinite article or a possessive pronoun, or some other single-syllable word, before a trochaic word, for example:

$$\text{the búilding; a frámework; their númber}$$

Such additions produce an iamb followed by the light stress needed for the next iamb. For example, Thomas Gray, in the third line of his "Elegy Written in a Country Churchyard," introduced an article before the word *ploughman.* Next he introduced a two-syllable adverb, *homeward,* which is also trochaic. After this he placed *plods,* a one-syllable verb, and completed the line with a three-word phrase, *his weary way.* Notice his use of a single-syllable pronoun before the trochaic word *weary* in order to fit this word into the iambic pattern. The complete line is a perfectly regular iambic line of five feet (iambic pentameter):

$$\text{The plóugh - / man hóme - / ward plóds / his wéar - / y wáy.}$$

Shakespeare did virtually the same thing in this line from his sonnet "Let Me Not to the Marriage of True Minds":

$$\text{With - ín / his bénd - / ing síck - / le's cóm - / pass cóme./}$$

Notice that Shakespeare began the second foot with the possessive pronoun *his,* a one-syllable word that enabled him to include three successive trochaic words within the iambic pattern. The inclusion of the single syllable *come* at the end of the line completes the pattern and makes the line perfectly regular iambic pentameter.

Another obvious means of using trochaic words is to substitute them for iambs, a device often used at the beginning of a line, as Yeats did here:

$$\text{Túrn - ing / and túrn - / ing ín / a wíd - / en - ing gýre.}$$

Often poets avoid the problem entirely by reducing the number of polysyllabic words in their lines and by relying heavily on one-syllable words, as Oliver Goldsmith did in this line:

$$\text{A bréath / can máke / them ás / a bréath / has máde.}$$

In studying prosody, you might consider the number of polysyllabic words, as has been done here, and observe the methods by which the poet has arranged them to fit or conflict with a basic metrical pattern.

3. PYRRHIC.   Two unstressed syllables, as in *on their* in Pope's line:

Now sleep - / ing flocks / on their / soft fleec - / es lie.

The pyrrhic is usually substituted for an iamb or trochee and usually consists of weakly accented words like prepositions and articles. For this reason it is impossible in English for an entire poem to consist of pyrrhics.

4. SPONDEE.   Two heavy accents, as in *rough winds* in Shakespeare's line:

Rough winds / do shake / the dar - / ling buds / of May.

Like the pyrrhic, the spondee is primarily a substitute foot in English. An acceptable way to draw attention to a spondee is to link the two syllables with a chevronlike mark, as shown. Spondees seem to create special difficulty in prosodic analysis. A principal reason is that quite often *pitch* is confused with *stress,* as in the following example:

Such seems / your beau - / ty still.

Although *beauty still* may easily be spoken at one pitch, there is a definite weakening of stress over the *y,* so that *beauty* is definitely not a spondee.

Another problem with spondees occurs if they are mistaken for pyrrhic feet. A spondee is the juxtaposition of two syllables of equally *heavy* stress, not of equally *light* stress.

THE THREE-SYLLABLE FOOT

1. ANAPAEST.   Two light stresses followed by a heavy:

By the dawn's / ear - ly light

2. DACTYL.   A heavy stress followed by two lights:

might - i - est

THE IMPERFECT FOOT

The imperfect foot consists of a single syllable: (°) by itself, or (′) by itself. This foot is a variant or substitute occurring in a poem in which one of the major feet forms the metrical pattern. The second line of "The Star-Spangled Banner," for example, is anapaestic, but it contains an imperfect foot at the end:

What so proud - / ly we hailed / at the twi - / light's last gleam - / ing.

Most scansion of English verse can be carried out with reference to the metrical feet described above. The following nonce lines illustrate all the feet listed.

TROCHEE      IAMB           IAMB          ANAPAEST        SPONDEE

How in / my thoughts / those hap - / pi - est days / shine forth —

TROCHEE      DACTYL          IAMB          PYRRHIC      SPONDEE

Days of / mel - o - dy / and love / and a / great dream.

## UNCOMMON METERS

In many poems you might encounter variants other than those described above. Poets like Browning, Tennyson, Poe, and Swinburne experimented with uncommon meters. Other poets manipulated pauses or *caesurae* (discussed below) to create the effects of uncommon meters. For these reasons, you might need to refer to other metrical feet, such as the following:

1. AMPHIBRACH. A light, heavy, and light, as in the following line from Swinburne's "Dolores":

Ah, feed me / and fill me / with plea - sure.

The amphibrach is the major foot in Browning's "How They Brought the Good News from Ghent to Aix"; for instance:

And in - to / the mid - night / we gal - loped / a - breast.

2. AMPHIMACER OR CRETIC. A heavy, light, and heavy, as in Browning's lines: *Love is best*   and   *praise and pray.*

The amphimacer occurs mainly in short lines or refrains, and also may be seen as a substitute foot, as in the last foot of this line from Tennyson's "Locksley Hall":

In the / spring a / young man's / fan - cy / light - ly / turns to / thoughts of love.

3. BACCHIUS OR BACCHIC. A light followed by two heavy stresses, as in *Some late lark* in W. E. Henley's line:

Some late lark / sing - ing.

The bacchius often occurs as a substitute for an anapaest, as in the last foot of this line from Browning's "Saul":

Where the long / grass - es sti - /fle the wa - /ter with - in / the stream's bed.

Note: In scanning a poem to determine its formal meter, always try to explain the lines simply, by reference to the more common feet, before turning to the less common ones. If a line can be analyzed as iambic, for example, do not attempt to fit the bacchius or the amphibrach to it unless these feet are unmistakably indicated. The following line is iambic:

The file / of men / róde forth / a - móng / the hills. /

It would be a mistake to scan it thus:

The / file of men / róde / forth a - móng / the hills. /

This incorrect analysis correctly accents *file of men* and *forth among*, but by describing these phrases as two amphimacers, respectively, it must resort to the explanation that *The* and *rode* are imperfect feet. Such an analysis creates unnecessary complications.

### THE CAESURA, OR PAUSE

If you refer to the passages from Lincoln, Whitman, and Owen in the discussion of cadence groups (p. 175), you will recall that the various cadence groups were separated by vocal pauses or breaks in the speech. In linguistic study these pauses are called *junctures;* in prosodic study the pause is called a *caesura* (the plural is *caesurae*). For scansion, the caesura is indicated by two diagonal lines or virgules (//) to distinguish it from the single virgule separating feet. The following line by Ben Jonson contains two caesurae:

Thou are not, // *Penshurst,* // built to envious show.

If a caesura follows an accented syllable, it may be called a *masculine,* or *stressed* caesura; if it follows an unaccented syllable, *feminine* or *falling*. In the following line from William Blake, a stressed caesura follows the word *divine:*

With hands / divine // he mov'd / the gen - / tle Sod.

The following line from the same poem ("To Mrs. Anna Flaxman") contains a falling caesura after the word *lovely:*

Its form / was love - / ly // but / its col - / ours pale.

The word *caesura* is usually reserved for references to junctures within lines, but when a juncture ends a line—usually marked by a comma, semicolon, or period—such a line is *end-stopped*. If you are writing about a poet's use of pauses, you should treat not only the caesurae but also the end-stopping; you might use the double virgules to show the concluding pause, as in the following line:

A thing of beauty // is a joy forever: //

If a line has no punctuation at the end and runs over to the next line, it is called *run-on*. A term also used to indicate run-on lines is *enjambement:*

> Its loveliness increases; // it will never
> Pass into nothingness; // but still will keep
> A bower quiet for us, // and a sleep
> Full of sweet dreams, // . . .
>
> —Keats, *Endymion*, lines 1–5

### EMPHASIS BY FORMAL SUBSTITUTION

Most poems are written in a pattern that can readily be perceived. Thus Shakespeare's plays usually follow the pattern of *blank verse* (unrhymed iambic pentameter) and Milton's *Paradise Lost* follows this same pattern. Such a pattern is no more than a rhythmical norm, however. For interest and emphasis (and perhaps because of the very nature of the English language) the norm is varied by *substituting* other feet for the normal feet.

The following line is from the "January" eclogue of Spenser's *Shepherd's Calendar*. Although the abstract pattern of the line is iambic pentameter, it is varied by the substitution of two other feet:

All in / a sun - / shine day, // as did / be - fall.

*All in* is a trochee, and *shine day* is a spondee. This line shows formal substitution; that is, a separate, formally structured foot is substituted for one of the original feet. The effect of these substitutions is to enable one's voice to emphasize *all* as a strong syllable, almost a separate imperfect foot. Then the phrase *in a sun* rolls off the tongue as an anapaest, and the spondee on *shine day* enables the voice to emphasize the words. In the context, Spenser has just been stressing the miseries of winter, and this line with its substitutions encourages the reader to think of spring as the voice lingers on the words:

> A shepherd's boy (no better do him call)
> When winter's wasteful spite was almost spent,
> All in a sunshine day, as did befall,
> Led forth his flock, that had been long ypent [enclosed].

When you study rhythm, try in this way to relate the substitutions to the ideas and attitudes the poet is apparently expressing.

### EMPHASIS BY RHETORICAL VARIATION

The effect of formal substitution is to create opposing or contrasting internal rhythms. The same effect is also achieved by the manipulation of the caesura. Placing the caesura in a perfectly regular line has the same effect, in speaking the line, as if formal substitution had occurred. This variation may be called *rhetorical substitution.* A noteworthy example in an iambic pentameter line is this one by Pope:

His ac - / tions', // pas - / sions', // be - / ing's, // use / and end;

Ordinarily there is one caesura in a line of this type, but in this one there are three, each producing a strong pause. The line is regularly iambic and should be scanned as regular. But in reading, the effect is different. Because of the pauses in the middle of the second, third, and fourth feet, the line is actually read as an amphibrach, a trochee, a trochee, and an amphimacer, thus:

His ac - tions', // pas - sions', // be - ing's, // use and end;

Although the line is regular, the practical effect — the rhetorical effect — is of variation and tension. In the following well-known line from Shakespeare's *Twelfth Night,* rhetorical substitution may also be seen:

If music // be the food of love, // play on!

This line is regularly iambic except, perhaps, for a spondee in *play on,* but the reading of the line conflicts with the formal pattern. Thus, *If music* may be read as an amphibrach and *be the food* is in practice an anapaest because of the short pause after *music* and the light stress on the word *be* following the caesura. The words stressed in the line are *music, food, love,* and the command *play on.* The line reads like normal speech even though it is in a formal rhythmical structure, and Shakespeare has provided us with the best of both worlds.

In whatever poetry you study, your main concern in noting substitutions is to determine the formal metrical pattern and then to analyze the formal and rhetorical variations on the pattern and the principal causes and effects of these variations. Always show how these variations have assisted the poet in achieving emphasis.

### EMPHASIS BY RHYTHMICAL TENSION

The basic working units of meaning are phrases, clauses, and sentences, and the basic rhythmical unit, as we have seen, is the cadence group. In poetry there is a complexity because regular metrical patterns frequently conflict with these units. Some poets (e.g., Milton, Chaucer, Wordsworth) create emphasis and tension in their poetry by making strong demands for sentence structure over and against an established metrical pattern. Here, for example, is a short passage from Wordsworth, laid out as prose:

And I have felt a presence that disturbs me with the joy of elevated thoughts; a sense sublime of something far more deeply interfused, whose

dwelling is the light of setting suns, and the round ocean and the living air, and the blue sky, and in the mind of man.
—"Tintern Abbey," lines 93–99

It is difficult, yet not impossible, to perceive the actual line divisions in this example. Wordsworth is superimposing an extended sentence structure on the metrical structure, a characteristic habit that is perfectly in keeping with meditative or philosophic poetry. Similarly, Milton is famous for his extended verse paragraphs in blank verse.

Other poets, by contrast, blend their sentence structure almost completely into their rhythmical pattern. Take, for example, this passage from Pope, which is also laid out as prose:

Nor public flame, nor private, dares to shine; nor human spark is left, nor glimpse divine! Lo! thy dread empire, Chaos, is restored; light dies before thy uncreating word: thy hand, great Anarch! lets the curtain fall; and universal darkness buries all.
— *The Dunciad*, IV, 651–656

The sentences are perfectly fitted to the lines, making the counting of feet comparatively easy, and we could determine the length of each line easily, without the aid of the rhyme. As a result, Pope and poets like him have frequently been accused of too much "boring regularity," whereas poets like Wordsworth and Milton have been praised for their greater "freedom." In actuality, the principles of variation are used by all these poets, with Wordsworth and Milton adding extensive syntactic variation to metrical variations.

## Sound

Just as poetry involves particular attention to rhythm, it requires special emphasis on the sounds of individual words. These sounds have been classified by modern students of language as "segments." For example, in the word *soft* there are four segments, or individual meaningful sounds, formed by the letters *s, o, f,* and *t*. In this word, each letter that spells (*graphs*) the word also indicates a *segment* of sound. But this is not always the case. In the word *enough,* for example, there are only four segments, formed by *e, n, ou,* and *gh;* the last two segments require two letters each.

The segments are usually divided into *vowel sounds* (including *semivowels*) and *consonant sounds.* It is important to emphasize the word *sound* as distinguished from the letters of the alphabet, for, as you will see, the same letters often represent different sounds. You should have some acceptable notational system for indicating sounds. The most readily available systems of pronunciation are those in the dictionary;

many take into account regional differences in pronunciation. If you have questions about syllabication and the position of stresses, you can use the dictionary as an authority. Two other systems of indicating sounds are based upon more recent scientific analyses. The first is the *International Phonetic Alphabet* as adapted for use in English, and the second is a system called *phonemic.*[2] The great virtue of these notational systems is that they are more descriptive than those in the dictionaries. The phonemic system is especially useful because it presents a satisfactory method of analyzing not only sounds but also *stress, pitch,* and *juncture.* These are the so-called "suprasegmental phonemes"; that is, they are those elements of speech production other than segments that contribute to meaning. Because both the phonetic and phonemic systems would require chapter-length explanation and because the dictionary systems are readily available, the dictionaries will be the guide in the following discussion and sample theme.

### VOWEL SOUNDS

Vowel sounds are produced by vocal vibrations resonating in the space between the tongue and the top of the mouth. The tongue is held in one position during the entire production of the sound. It is possible to hold a vowel sound for a considerable length of time (e.g., *whee-e-e-e-e*) and for a short time (e.g., *whit*). There are two systems operating in the pronunciation of vowel sounds: first is *front-central-back;* second is *high-mid-low.* These terms are derived from the position of the tongue during the pronunciation of a vowel sound. For most purposes in your analysis of prosody, you need to consider only the extremes of *high-front* and *low-back.* Observe that the vowel sounds *ē, i, ā,* are all produced in a narrow space between the tongue and the hard palate. These sounds are both *front* and *high.* By contrast, pronounce the *ä* in *arm.* Notice that your tongue is still in a front position, but that it has dropped far down in your mouth. This *ä,* in other words, is a *low-front* vowel sound. Now pronounce the vowel sound *ō* as in *coal.* Notice that your tongue has stayed high, but has dropped *back* in your throat. The *ō* sound is a *high, back,* and *rounded* sound. Now pronounce the *ô* in *orphan,* and the *ōo* in *troop.* Notice that these are both *low, back,* and *rounded* sounds.

[2]For a lucid discussion of English phonetics, see W. Nelson Francis, *The Structure of American English* (New York: Ronald Press Co., 1958), pp. 51–118. For the phonemic system, see Francis, pp. 119–161, and Donald J. Lloyd and Harry R. Warfel, *American English in Its Cultural Setting* (New York: Alfred A. Knopf, 1956), pp. 294–318. For a discussion of the contributions that linguistic study can make to the study of prosody, see Ronald Sutherland, "Structural Linguistics and English Prosody," *College English,* XX (1958), 12–17, reprinted in Harold B. Allen, ed., *Readings in Applied English Linguistics,* 2nd ed. (Englewood Cliffs, N. J.: Prentice-Hall, Inc., 1964), pp. 492–499.

### SEMIVOWEL SOUNDS

The semivowels are *w*, *y*, and *h*. These are segments that (1) begin in a vowel position but glide into a following vowel, thus performing the function of a consonant, as in *w*ind, *u*nion, *y*es; or (2) begin the central vowel of a syllable but glide into a new position, thus in effect forming the second part of a diphthong, as in *go* (go*w*) and *weigh* (wa*y*); or (3) begin in the position for a following or preceding vowel sound but add aspiration (breathy air) to the sound, as in *hearty* and *ahem* (but notice that the *h* is frequently silent, as in *honor*).

### CONSONANT SOUNDS

There are various classifications but basically the consonant sounds are of two types: (1) Stop sounds are made either by the momentary stoppage and release of breath when the lips touch each other or when the tongue touches the teeth or palate. The stop sounds are *p, b, t, d, k, g*. (2) Spirant or continuant sounds are produced by the breath in conjunction with certain positioning of the tongue in relation to the teeth and palate, as in *n, l, th (thorn), th̶ (the), s, z, ch (chew), j (jaw), sh (sharp), zh (pleasure)*, and *ng;* or in conjunction with a touching of the lower lip and upper teeth for the sounds *f* and *v*, or of both lips for the sound *m*. Another way of classifying consonant sounds is according to whether they are *voiced*, that is, produced with vibration of the vocal chords *(b, d, v, z)* or *voiceless*, produced by the breath alone *(p, t, f, s)*. The nature of consonant sounds is meaningless with reference to their context. The *s*, for example, in a context of rage, can augment the rage, but in a quiet context it can produce a drowsy, sleepy effect, as in the lines quoted from Spenser on p. 182.

### SPELLING VERSUS SOUND

When discussing segments you must be careful to distinguish between spelling or *graphics*, and pronunciation or *phonetics*. Thus the letter *s* in the words *sweet, sugar,* and *flows* has three very different sounds: *s, sh,* and *z*. Similarly, the words *shape, ocean, nation, sure,* and *machine* use different letters or combinations of letters to spell the same *sh* sound.

Also, vowel sounds may be spelled in different ways. The *e* sound, for example, can be spelled with *i* in *machine, ee* in *feet, ea* in *eat, e* in *even, y* in *funny*, yet the vowel sounds in *eat* and *break* are not the same, even though they are spelled the same. Always be on the alert.

### SEGMENTAL POETIC DEVICES

You are now ready to apply some of your knowledge of segments to actual poems. A poet may use words containing the same segments and thereby impress your memory by merging sound and idea. In descriptive poetry, the segments may actually combine, with rhythm, to imitate some of the things being described. The segmental devices are *assonance, alliteration, onomatopoeia,* and *rhyme.*

ASSONANCE. The repetition of identical vowel sounds in different words—for example, short *i* in "swift Cami*l*la ski*m*s," is called assonance. It is a strong means of emphasis, as in the following line, where the *u* sound connects the two words *lull* and *slumber,* and the short *i* connects *him, in,* and *his:*

> And more, to lull him in his slumber soft

In some cases you may discover that the poet has used assonance quite elaborately, as in this line from Pope:

> 'Tis hard to say, if greater want of skill

Here the line is framed and balanced with the short *i* in *'Tis, if,* and *skill.* The *ä* in *hard* and *want* forms another, internal frame, and the *a* in *say* and *greater* creates still another. Such a balanced use of vowels is unusual, however, for in most lines the assonance will be a means by which the poet emphasizes certain words by making them stand out phonetically.

In looking for assonance, be cautious about equating sounds like the *e* in *depart* with the *ē* in *tree;* the *e* in *depart* is not a true long *ē,* but rather a half-long *e,* and some would maintain that it is a *schwa* (a sound like the *a* in *sofa*). Also, you should not select isolated instances of a sound in your description of assonance. If, for example, you find three words in the same line that include a long *ā* sound, these form a pattern and are worthy of mention as an instance of assonance; but, if you find a word six lines later that includes a long *ā,* this word is too far away from the pattern to be significant.

ALLITERATION. Like assonance, alliteration is a means of highlighting ideas by the selection of words containing the same consonant sound—for example, the repeated *m* in "*m*ixed with a *m*urmuring wind," or the *s* sound in "your never-failing *s*word made war to *c*ease," which emphasizes the connection between the words *sword* and *cease.*

There are three kinds of alliteration. (1) Most commonly, alliteration is regarded as the repetition of identical consonant sounds that begin syllables in relatively close patterns—for example, "*L*aborious, heavy, *b*usy, *b*old, and *b*lind," and "While *p*ensive *p*oets *p*ainful vigils keep." Used sparingly, alliteration gives strength to a poem by emphasizing key words, but too much can cause comic consequences. (2) A special kind of alliteration known as *consonance* uses the repetition of words that contain the exact patterns of two or more identical consonant sounds—for example, *gr/nd* in *groaned, ground; t/r/r* in *terror, terrier;*

*gr/b* in *grab, grub*, and so on. This device does not occur very often in most of the poems you will encounter, for it calls attention to itself and might detract from an important idea. (3) Another form of alliteration occurs when a poet repeats identical or similar consonant sounds that do not begin syllables but that create a pattern and thereby have prosodic importance — for example, the *z* sound in the line "In these places freezing breezes easily cause sneezes." Such a pattern is hard to overlook. In "The *p*ebbles in the *b*ubbling *p*ool," both *p* and *b* are *labial* consonant sounds, that is, they are made by a momentary stoppage of breath at the lips; *p* is a *voiceless* stopped sound, whereas *b* is a *voiced* stopped sound. Because of the similarity, the two sounds should be mentioned as part of a pattern of alliteration.

ONOMATOPOEIA.    Onomatopeia is the blending of consonant and vowel sounds with rhythm to create the effect either of imitating the sound of a thing being described or of suggesting a certain activity or condition. It is thus a remarkably colorful augmentation of a poet's ideas. Often onomatopoeia depends on the fact that many words in English are *echoic*, that is, they are verbal echoes of the thing they mean, such as *buzz, bump, slap*, and so on. Here is a passage from John Donne's sonnet, "Batter My Heart," which uses this sort of onomatopoeia:

> Batter my heart, three-personed God; for you
> As yet but knock, breathe, shine, and seek to mend,
> That I may rise, and stand, o'erthrow me, and bend
> Your force, to break, blow, burn, and make me new.

Notice here the words *batter, knock, bend, break, blow*, and *burn*, the sounds of which actually are like the spiritual violence the speaker is imploring God to effect on him. Shakespeare created a noteworthy effect with the following line, spoken by Cleopatra in *Antony and Cleopatra* (V.ii. 284–285) just before she commits suicide to avoid the disgrace of being captured:

> Now no *m*ore
> The juice of Egy*p*t's gra*p*e shall *m*oist this li*p*.

Here Shakespeare uses words with *m* and *p*, both of which are bilabial sounds (made with both lips), to suggest the action of putting a glass of wine to the lips. Here is a virtuosic passage from Spenser's *Faerie Queene* (I.41) onomatopoeically suggesting a sleepy, lulling scene:

> And more, to lull him in his slumber soft,
>   A trickling stream from high rock tumbling down
> And ever-drizzling rain upon the loft,
>   Mixed with a murmuring wind, much like the sowne [sound]
> Of swarming bees, did cast him in a swowne [swoon, faint].

Here the *s, l, m,* and *w* consonants and the *i, ô,* and *u* vowels all combine in the context to create an effect of drowsiness.

RHYME. Rhyme, the most easily recognized characteristic of poetry, refers to the recurrence of phonetically identical syllables in *different* words, usually words ending lines. It is therefore a combination of assonance and identical consonant sounds. When you describe a rhyme scheme, use letters (*a, b, c,* etc.). Each new letter indicates a new sound; a repeated letter indicates a rhyme. In a Shakespearean sonnet, for example, the rhyme scheme is *abab cdcd efef gg.* The rhyme scheme of an Italian or Petrarchan sonnet is *abba abba cd cd cd.*

Whenever rhyme occurs you should analyze its effects and the way these are achieved. Observe the grammatical forms of the rhyming words. If poets rhyme only nouns, for example, their rhymes are likely to be monotonous, for they should show some variety in the grammatical forms. Another area of study is whether the rhymes are unusual or surprising. If poets relied on "sure returns of still expected rhymes" (like the *breeze* blowing through the *trees*), their rhymes would be obvious and dull. Observe in the following couplet by Byron that the rhyming words are verbs, and that wit and surprise result from the riddle in the first line and the meaning of the final word:

'Tis strange—the Hebrew noun which means "I am" [i.e., *God*],
The English always use to govern d–n [i.e., *damn*].
—*Don Juan*, I, xiv, 111–112

Although few rhymes will furnish the irony of this one, you should observe the method of rhyming in the poems you study. As you make further analyses you will be impressed with the way in which your understanding of the craft of poetry will grow.

In connection with rhyme, the following terms are important. In *eye rhyme* or *sight rhyme* the rhyming words look the same but are pronounced differently—for example, "Broken is the clock I *wind*" and "I am frozen by the *wind.*" In *slant rhyme* the rhyming vowel sounds are different in quality whereas the consonant sounds are identical—for example, *could* and *solitude.* Rhymes falling on a strong accent are commonly called *masculine,* though you might prefer to use terms like *heavy-stress rhyme* or *single-syllable rhyme* instead. Heavy-stress rhyme may be seen in these lines from Robert Frost's "Stopping by Woods on a Snowy Evening":

Whose woods / these are / I think / I know.

His house / is in / the vil - / lage though.

Rhymes falling on a light stress, either on a trochee, a dactyl, or an amphibrach, are called *feminine,* though you could as conveniently refer to *falling rhyme, dying rhyme, trochaic rhyme, dactyllic rhyme* (or *triple rhyme*). The second and fourth lines of the first stanza of "Miniver Cheevy" by Edwin Arlington Robinson conclude with a falling rhyme:

> Miniver Cheevy, child of scorn,
>> Grew lean while he assailed the *séasŏns;*
> He wept that he was ever born
>> And he had *réasŏns.*

Dactyllic or triple rhyme is scarce, though it may be seen in these lines from Browning's "The Pied Piper of Hamelin":

> Small feet were *páttĕrĭng,* wooden shoes *cláttĕrĭng,*
> Little hands clapping and little tongues *cháttĕrĭng.*
> And, like fowls in a farm-yard when barley is *scáttĕrĭng,* . . .

Usually, but not necessarily, heavy-stress rhyme is appropriate to serious purposes, while falling and triple rhymes lend themselves easily to comic effects.


## Organizing Your Theme

Depending on your assignment, you might wish to show the operation of all these component elements of prosody, or you may wish to focus on just one aspect. It would be possible, for example, to devote an entire theme to the discussion of (1) regular meter, (2) one particular variation, such as the anapaest or spondee, (3) the use of the caesura, (4) alliteration, (5) assonance, (6) onomatopoeia, or (7) rhyme. The following plan assumes a comprehensive theme, which you might vary according to your needs.

### INTRODUCTION

The introduction should establish the scope of your discussion. Begin by making a statement about the relationship of the content of the poem or passage to the poet's prosodic technique. What is particularly noteworthy about the poem? Is it descriptive, lyric, narrative? What attitudes are present in the poem? Are any actions or objects described? Does the poem have rhyme? Is the use of rhyme particularly interesting or arresting? Conclude with a thesis sentence indicating the areas of prosody you plan to treat.

### BODY

Here you carry out your detailed discussion of the rhythmical and segmental techniques of the passage or poem. Describe the formal metrical pattern first. Does the poet seem to move naturally and effectively within the confines of poetic meter, or does the thought seem at war with the meter? How successfully are important words or syllables placed in positions of stress? Are meter and subject matter successfully shaped into suitable climaxes? How effectively are caesurae controlled? Do the pauses seem to occur haphazardly, or as part of a controlled pattern of variation? What formal substitutions occur in the pattern of verse? What rhetorical substitutions occur? How are they achieved, and what end do they serve?

In discussing segmental aspects you will be referring to assonance, alliteration, consonance, onomatopoeia, and rhyme (if rhyme is present in the poem you are studying). What is the relationship between assonance or alliteration and the poet's thoughts and descriptions? How does the poet use these devices to throw emphasis on certain words and ideas? Can you determine if the poet has used onomatopoeia? How effective is it? If the poet has used rhyme, what sorts of words are rhymed? What is the relationship of the rhythm to the rhyme? Are there any unusual rhymes, comic rhymes? Does the poet create any climaxes with the use of rhyme?

### CONCLUSION

Here you evaluate the success of the passage. Did the prosody seem appropriate to the rhetorical situation? Did it conflict, and if so, does that conflict provide grounds for an adverse judgment? Did the prosody augment the idea of the passage? Did it give the passage more power than the idea alone would give it? In short, answer the question of how well the sounds and the rhythms succeeded in being an instrument of communication and a device by which the poet may evoke the proper emotions in the reader.

### HINTS ON PROCEDURE

1. At the beginning of your theme you should provide a triple-spaced version of the passage under analysis. Make at least two carbon or Xerox copies for various analytical purposes.

2. Number each line of the passage, regardless of its length.

3. Analyze the passage as follows:

   a. Establish the formal pattern of the verse and note where all the formal substitutions occur.

      (1) Indicate the separate feet by a diagonal line or virgule (/). Indicate caesurae by double diagonals (//).

      (2) Indicate lightly stressed syllables by the circle or degree sign (°). Show heavily stressed syllables by the prime (').

   b. Read the passage for rhetorical substitutions; make notes about where they occur and about how the poet creates them.

   c. Discover the various segmental poetic devices. Circle letters indicating a pattern of alliteration and assonance, and draw lines indicating the connection. Different colored pencils or magic markers are effective in distinguishing the various patterns. If you use only one pencil or pen, you might set up a system of dotted, dashed, and unbroken lines (see the sample theme). Any easily recognized system that is convenient for you is acceptable. It is also a good idea to circle the metrical variations such as the anapaests and trochees, so that you can identify them easily when you begin to write your theme.

4. At the bottom of your pages or below your analysis, provide an explanatory key to your circles and lines.

5. For your discussion of sounds, it is best to use a standard pronunciation guide. If you have had formal linguistic study, use the phonemic or phonetic systems; otherwise you will probably find one of the standard collegiate dictionaries more convenient.

6. Underline all sounds to which you are calling attention. If you refer to a sound within a word (for instance, the *l* in *calling*), underline only that sound. Be sure to provide illustrations to make your discussion clear.

If you prepare these prosodic worksheets with care, half your job is over. All you need do after this preparation is to describe what you have analyzed and noted. Here your dotted or colored lines can help you immeasurably to spot the variations and devices of sound you have observed.

SAMPLE THEME

## A Prosodic Analysis of Lines 232–243 of Tennyson's "Morte D'Arthur"

### METRICAL VARIATION

But the o- / ther swift- / ly strode // from ridge / to ridge, //          1

Clothed with / his breath, // and look- / ing, // as / he walk'd, //          2

Lar-ger / than hu- / man // on / the fro- / zen hills. //          3

He heard / the deep / be-hind / him, // and / a cry          4

Be-fore. // His own / thought drove / him // like / a goad. //          5

Dry clash'd / his har- / ness // in / the i- / cy caves          6

And bar-    ren / chasms, // and all / to left / and right          7

The bare / black cliff / clang'd round / him, // as / he based          8

His feet / on juts / of slip- / pe-ry crag // that rang          9

Sharp- smit- / ten // with / the dint / of ar- / med heels— //          10

And on / a sud- / den, // lo! // the lev- / el lake, //          11

And the / long glor- / ies // of / the win- / ter moon. //          12

[1] = Anapaest, or effect of anapaest.  [4] = Effect of imperfect feet.
[2] = Amphibrach, or the effect of amphibrach.  [5] = Pyrrhic.
[3] = Spondee.  [6] = Trochee, or the effect of trochee.

*The Complete Poetical Works of Tennyson,* ed. W. J. Rolfe (Cambridge, Mass.: Houghton Mifflin Co., 1898), p. 66.

ALLITERATION

But the other ⓢwiftly ⓢtrode from ridge to ridge,                                      1

Clothed with his breath, and looking, as ⓗe walk'd,                                     2

Larger than ⓗuman on the frozen ⓗills.                                                 3

Ⓗe ⓗeard the deep beⓗind ⓗim, and a cry                                              4

Before. Ⓗis own thought drove him like a goad.                                         5

Dry Ⓒlash'd ⓗis ⓗarness in the icy Ⓒaves                                             6

And ⓑarren ⓒhasms, and all to left and right                                         7

The ⓑare ⓑlack Ⓒliff Ⓒlang'd round him, as he ⓑased                                8

His feet on juts of slippery Ⓒrag that rang                                           9

Sharp-smitten with the dint of armed heels—                                          10

And on a sudden, Ⓛo! the Ⓛevel Ⓛake,                                               11

And the Ⓛong gⓁories of the winter moon.                                            12

⁓⁓⁓⁓ = s                                    ——————— = b

— — — — — = h aspirate                      —·—·—·— = l

•••••••••• = k

ASSONANCE

But the other swiftly str(o)de from ridge to ridge,     1

Cl(o)thed with his breath, and looking, as he walk'd,     2

Larger than human on the fr(o)zen hills.     3

He heard the deep beh(i)nd him, and a cr(y)     4

Before. His (ow)n thought dr(o)ve him l(i)ke a g(oa)d.     5

Dr(y) clash'd his harness in the (i)cy caves     6

And barren ch(a)sms, and all to left and r(i)ght     7

The bare bl(a)ck cliff cl(a)ng'd round him, as he based     8

His feet on juts of slippery cr(a)g that r(a)ng     9

Sh(ar)p-sm(i)tten w(i)th the d(i)nt of (ar)med heels—     10

And on a sudden, lo! the level lake,     11

And the long glories of the winter moon.     12

———————— = ō*          —·—·—·—·—· = ä

— — — — — = ī          ∿∿∿∿ = i

•••••••••• = a

*Pronunciation symbols as in *Webster's New World Dictionary,* 2nd ed.

[1]       This passage from Tennyson's "Morte D'Arthur" describes the ordeal of Sir Bedivere as he carries the dying Arthur from the mountainous heights, where he was wounded, down to the lake, where the king will be sent to his final rest. Tennyson devotes great attention to the almost ghostly, deserted landscape, emphasizing the bleakness and hostility of the scenes through which Bedivere carries his royal burden. The passage is in unrhymed iambic pentameter—blank verse—as one might expect for descriptive or meditative poetry. *But Tennyson's verse is alive; it constantly augments his descriptions and conveys an impression of Bedivere's mood, whether of anguish or relaxation.\* The control over prosody enables a true blending of sound and sense, as may be seen in Tennyson's use of rhythm and in his manipulation of segmental devices, including onomatopoeia.†*

[2]       Tennyson controls his meter to emphasize Bedivere's exertions and moods. In line 1 the meter is fairly regular, except for an anapaest in the first foot. This regularity may be interpreted as emphasizing the swiftness and surefootedness of Bedivere when walking. But he is about to undergo a severe test, and the rhythm quickly becomes irregular, as though Tennyson wants to strain the pentameter verse in illustration of the superhuman exertions Bedivere is going through. Tennyson therefore uses variations to highlight certain key words that carry much rhetorical weight. For example, he uses the effect of anapaests in a number of lines. In line 2 he emphasizes the chill air and Bedivere's vitality in the following way:

Clothed with / his breath, //

The image is one of being surrounded by one's own breath that vaporizes on hitting the cold air, and the rhythmical variation—a trochaic substitution in the first foot—enables the voice to build up to the word *breath*, a most effective internal climax.

[3]       Tennyson uses something like the same rhythmical effect in line 3, where he emphasizes the *frozen hills* by creating a caesura in the middle of the third foot, and then by making the heavy stress of the third foot fall on the preposition *on*, which with *the* creates in effect the two unstressed syllables of an anapaest including the first, stressed, syllable of *frozen*. The effect is that the voice builds up to the word and thus emphasizes the extreme conditions in which Bedivere is walking:

// on / the fro - / zen hills.//

Tennyson uses this effect twelve times in the passage. It thus is one of his major means of rhetorical emphasis.

[4]       Perhaps the most effective metrical variation is the spondee, which appears in lines 5, 6, 8 (twice), 10, and 12. These substitutions, occurring mainly in the section in which Sir Bedivere is forcing his way down the frozen hills, permit the lines to ring out, as in:

The bare / black cliff / clang'd round /

---

*Central idea.     †Thesis sentence.

and

$$\text{Dry clash'd / his hår- / ness.}$$

The best use of the spondee is in line 5, where the stresses accumulate and reach a climax on the word *drove*, which suggests the torment Bedivere is feeling:

$$\text{His own / thought drove / him //}$$

To put a case, let us suppose that Tennyson had been an inferior poet, and had written instead, "He was goaded by his thought," or "His thought was like a goad to him." When one realizes how inferior such choices are, Tennyson's achievement stands out even more.

[5]     There is much other substitution, too, both formal and rhetorical, and the tension these variations create keeps the responsive reader aware of Bedivere's tasks. One type of variation is the appearance of amphibrachic rhythm, which is produced in lines 2, 3, 4, 6, 7, and 11. The effect is achieved by a pattern which complements the rhetorical anapaests. A caesura in the middle of a foot leaves the three preceding syllables as a light, heavy, and light, the rhythmical form of the amphibrach. In line 2, for example, it appears thus:

$$\text{// and look- / ing //}$$

In line 6 it takes this form:

$$\text{/ his har- / ness //}$$

[6]     Still another related variation is that of the apparently imperfect feet in lines 5, 8, 11, and 12. These imperfect feet are usually produced by a caesura, which isolates the syllable from any other effective rhythm. The syllable is thus left unstressed, as *him* is in line 8:

$$\text{The bare / black cliff / clang'd round / him, //}$$

In line 11 the syllable (on the word *lo!*) is surrounded by two caesurae, and is therefore thrust into a position of great stress:

$$\text{And on / a sud-/den // lo! // the lev- / el lake}$$

Other, less significant substitutions are the trochees in lines 3 and 7, and the pyrrhic in line 12. All the described variations support the grand, free conception of the heroic action described in the passage.

[7]     Many of the variations described are produced by Tennyson's free handling of his sentence structure, which results in a free placement of the caesurae and in a free use of end-stopping and enjambement. It is interesting that four of the first five lines are end-stopped (two by commas, two by periods). Bedivere is walking but exerting himself during these lines and apparently he is making short tests to gather strength for his ordeal. The ordeal comes during the next four lines, when he makes his precarious descent; none of the lines containing this description is end-

stopped. Bedivere is disturbed (being goaded by "his own thought"), but he must keep going, and we may presume that the free sentence structure and the free metrical variation enforce the difficulty and mental disturbance he is experiencing. But in the last two lines, when he has reached the lake and therefore his goal, the lines "relax" with falling caesurae exactly following the fifth syllables. In other words, the sentence structure of the last two lines is fairly regular, an effect designed to indicate the return to order and beauty after the previous, rugged chaos.

[8]       This rhythmical virtuosity is accompanied by a similarly brilliant control over segmental devices. Alliteration is the most obvious, permitting Tennyson to tie key words and their signifying actions together, as in the *s*'s in "*s*wiftly *s*trode in line 1, or the *b*'s in *b*arren, *b*are, *b*lack, and *b*ased in lines 7 and 8. Other notable examples are the aspirated *h*'s in lines 2–6 (*h*e, *h*uman, *h*ills, *h*eard, *b*e*h*ind, *h*im, *h*is, *h*arness); the *k*'s in lines 6–9 (*c*lash'd, *c*aves, *c*hasms, *c*liff, *c*lang'd, *c*rag); and the *l*'s in lines 11 and 12 (*l*o, *l*evel, *l*ake, *l*ong, g*l*ories). One might compare these *l*'s with the *l*'s in the more anguished context of lines 8 and 9, where the sounds appear as the second segment in the heavy, ringing words there (b*l*ack, c*l*iff, c*l*ang'd, s*l*ippery). The sounds are the same, and the emphasis is similar, but the contrasting effects are noteworthy.

[9]       Assonance is also present throughout the passage, and where it appears it adds strength. In the first five lines, for example, the $\bar{o}$ appears in six words. The first three $\bar{o}$'s are in descriptive or metaphoric words (str*o*de, cl*o*thed, fr*o*zen), while the last three are in words describing the pain and anguish that Bedivere experiences as a result of his efforts in the barren landscape (*o*wn, dr*o*ve, g*o*ad). The *o* therefore linguistically ties the physical to the psychological. Other patterns of assonance are the *a* in lines 7, 8, and 9 (ch*a*sms, cl*a*ng'd, bl*a*ck, cr*a*g, r*a*ng), the *ä* of line 10 (sh*a*rp, *a*rmed), the *ī* of lines 4–7 (beh*i*nd, cr*y*, l*i*ke, dr*y*, *i*cy, r*i*ght), and the short *i* of line 10 (sm*i*tten, w*i*th, d*i*nt). One might remark also that there are many high-front vowel sounds ($\bar{e}$, $\bar{a}$, *i*, *a*) in the first ten lines. But in the last two lines, which describe the level lake and the moon, Tennyson introduces a number of low-back vowels ($\hat{o}$, $u$, $\bar{o}$, $\hat{o}$, $\hat{o}$, $u$, $\overline{oo}$). The striking effect of the vowels in these last two lines can be pointed out only when they are heard immediately after the two preceding lines:

> . . . as he based
> His feet on juts of slippery crag that rang
> Sharp-smitten with the dint of armed heels—
> And on a sudden, lo! the level lake,
> And the long glories of the winter moon.

As these last two lines are read, their low-back vowels make possible a lowering of vocal pitch and a relaxation of vocal tension, and thereby they are eminently appropriate at this point in the poem, when Sir Bedivere has attained his goal.

[10]       The last two lines are, in fact, almost totally onomatopoeic, since the liquid *l* sounds suggest the gentle lapping of waves on a lake shore. There are other examples of onomatopoeia in this short passage, too. In line 2

Tennyson brings out the detail of Sir Bedivere's walking in the presumably cold air "Clothed with his breath," and in the following five lines Tennyson employs many words with the aspirate *h* (e.g., *his harness*); in this context, these sounds suggest Sir Bedivere's labored breath as he carries his royal burden. Similarly, the explosive stops *b* and *k, d,* and *t* in lines 6–10 seem to be imitative of the sounds of Sir Bedivere's feet as he places them on the "juts of slippery crag."

[11]      This short passage is a mine of prosodic skill. The sounds and the rhythms of the words and lines themselves, put into this context by Tennyson, actually speak along with the meaning; they emphasize the grandeur of Arthur and his faithful follower, and for one brief moment bring out the magic that Tennyson associated with the fading past. In the poem, the outright glory of this passage makes understandable Sir Bedivere's previous reluctance to cast away King Arthur's sword. Such glory is not to be thrown away easily; but now it is gone, and we can regain it only in our imagination, or in Tennyson's poem.


★COMMENTARY ON THE THEME


This theme presents a full discussion of the prosody of the passage from Tennyson. Paragraphs 2 through 7 discuss the relationship of the rhythm to the content. Note that prosody is not discussed in isolation, but as it serves Tennyson's purpose in describing the action and scenes of the passage. Thus, paragraph 4 refers to the use of the spondee as a means of reinforcing the ideas. In this paragraph there is also a short comparison of alternative ways of saying what Tennyson says so well. While such speculative comparison should not be attempted often, it is effective here in highlighting Tennyson's prosodic excellence.

Paragraphs 8 and 9 present a discussion of the alliteration and assonance of the passage, and paragraph 10 considers onomatopoeia.

# CHAPTER 15

# *The Theme Analyzing Prose Style*

STYLE is usually understood to mean the way in which writers employ their words, phrases, and sentences to achieve the desired effects. It should be distinguished from *structure*, which is concerned with the organization and arrangement of the work as a whole. Although *style* may be used loosely to comprise the writer's entire craft, for this theme you will be concerned with the word in its narrow sense.

The object of your theme is to make you aware of style: what it is, how to discuss it, how to evaluate it, how to relate it to the achievement of the literary work as a whole, how to define the characteristics of each writer's style. Because style is concerned with diction, phrases, sentences, and sound and rhythm, you will have to wrestle with sentences and words, and from time to time you may be thrown on your ear. But if you persist you will develop the ability to make some accurate and useful observations about a writer's style, and you will be well on the way toward a dependable means of evaluating literature.

## Limitations

In your analysis you will not be able to make observations about an entire work because of limited space. To write this assignment, you need to consider only a short passage—a single paragraph is best, although a passage of dialogue is also satisfactory. As with the prosodic analysis, it is usually best to select a well-written passage or else one that conveys a good deal of the writer's argument, for authors will have devoted their best skill and energy to such passages. You must be aware that the discussion of one paragraph does not necessarily apply to the whole work. But if you make these points — that your method of analysis would be the same for any passage in the whole book and that the paragraph is important in the book — the generalizations you make will have implications for the entire work.

## Control

You may encounter a problem when you first undertake to study a writer's style. Suppose you choose to analyze a piece of dramatic prose or a passage of dialogue from a novel; or suppose you select a passage from a novel that is told from the first-person point of view. When you speak about the style of these passages, are you describing the *writer's* style or the *speaker's* style? Suppose that you analyze, in the same work, two passages that are dissimilar in style. Did the writer's style change, or was it adapted to fit the different places or speakers? And if it was so adapted, what are you trying to discover by an analysis of style?

The answer seems obvious. In your analysis you are trying to determine the degree of the writer's *control* over the subject matter. Control is what matters. If you discover that writers adhere to the same style throughout their work, that fact might lead you to conclude that they have inadequate control over their subject. But you should ask some further questions. Do they have some definite end in view in using this one style? If so, what is it? Are they successful? The aim of your analysis is always to describe specific characteristics and to make at least partial judgments of why these characteristics appear and what they contribute to the work.

To see how this aim might be fulfilled, look at the following example, from *The Merchant of Venice*, Act I, Scene ii:

> If to do were as easy as to know what were good to do, chapels had been churches and poor men's cottages princes' palaces. It is a good divine that follows his own instructions: I can easier teach twenty what were good to be done, than to be one of the twenty to follow mine own teaching. . . .

From the style of this passage, it seems clear that Portia (the speaker) is a woman with a rapid mind, well befitting her masquerade as an intelligent lawyer-judge later in the play. Her first sentence uses simple diction in a complex structure. Of her first fourteen words, six compose infinitives and two are verbs; a total of eight words out of fourteen, or over 55 per cent, serve as verbs or verbals. Her mind, in other words, is active. The first fourteen words are also part of an if-clause, dependent on the verb in the following main clause. The ability to use subordination in sentences is regarded as the mark of a good mind and a good style. Portia, too, shows an ability to use rhetoric — in this sentence the rhetorical device called *zeugma* (the use of a single word with double grammatical weight). The main clause of the first sentence is equivalent to two clauses, but the verb is used only once: "chapels had been churches and poor men's cottages [had been] princes' palaces." Portia's language is exceedingly simple, but she shows a fine sense of rhetorical and logical balance.

To be contrasted with Portia's speech is this one by Ophelia in *Hamlet,* Act IV, Scene v, 40–42:

> Well, God 'ild you. They say, the owl was a baker's daughter. Lord, we know what we are, but know not what we may be. God be at your table.

Ophelia makes this speech after she has become insane. Her words are simple, and her sentences are disconnected. Just when she seems to become coherent (in sentence three) her thought is swiftly broken, and her last sentence seems as random as her first. Had Shakespeare introduced the intellectual toughness of Portia's speech here, he would not have shown a broken mind but an alert one in all its powers. Thus he gave Ophelia these disconnected sentences, so unlike her coherent speeches in poetry earlier in the play.

The point about these two passages is that although they differ in style, Shakespeare's control and artistry do not. In fact, the passages show his mastery of dramatic prose. The study of style should aim toward a description of writers' abilities to control their words to serve their needs.

## Approaches to Style

The four ways to describe style are (1) the analysis of diction, (2) the analysis of grammar, (3) the analysis of rhythm and sound, and (4) the analysis of rhetoric.

### DICTION

A study of diction does not simply rely on dictionary definitions, but goes beyond the meanings of the words to a study of their relationships in context. Words rarely exist by themselves but are in a context in which one word affects another, and your interest here should be to observe and record these relationships.

Look at the words in passages and see where they take you. You are on an exploration and may or may not discover something valuable. Some guidelines for your itinerary might be the following questions: What are the speakers? Are they the authors, some aspect of the authors' personalities, or some separate speakers with their own characteristics? What kinds of backgrounds do the speakers have? How old are they? Do they use standard English? Substandard? Slang? Dialect? Profanity? Do they seem to be articulate or relatively inarticulate? As an exercise you might try to characterize the diction of speakers such as Huckleberry Finn, Holden Caulfield (from Salinger's *Catcher in the Rye*), Jane Eyre, or of authors such as Erica Jong, Piri Thomas, Woody Allen, Thomas Hardy, or Jean Stafford.

In describing events or situations, do the writers or speakers use specific words or general words? In the discussion of ideas, are the words concrete or abstract? Do the writers provide specific examples to illustrate ideas? Let us take, as an example, the following passages, the first from Hemingway's *A Farewell to Arms*, and the second from Theodore Dreiser's *The Titan*:

> [1] In the late summer of that year we lived in a house in a village that looked across the river and the plain to the mountains.   [2] In the bed of the river there were pebbles and boulders, dry and white in the sun, and the water was clear and swiftly moving and blue in the channels. [3] Troops went by the house and down the road and the dust they raised powdered the leaves of the trees.   [4] The trunks of the trees too were dusty and the leaves fell early that year and we saw the troops marching along the road and the dust rising and leaves, stirred by the breeze, falling and the soldiers marching and afterward the road bare and white except for the leaves.[1]

> From New York, Vermont, New Hampshire, Maine had come a strange company, earnest, patient, determined, unschooled in even the primer of refinement, hungry for something the significance of which, when they had it, they could not even guess, anxious to be called great, determined so to be without ever knowing how.[2]

Hemingway's diction is here very specific: words such as *house, river, mountains, pebbles, trees, leaves,* and *dust* refer to something real. When Hemingway wishes to describe something about this scene his words are concrete, as in *dry, clear, swiftly moving, dusty, stirred, falling, marching,* and *bare.* With this diction you may contrast Dreiser's words, such as *strange, earnest, patient, determined, hungry, significance,* and *anxious.* Obviously the passages are on different topics, and both in their way are quite successful, but the diction indicates a specific visualization of things on Hemingway's part and an attempt at psychological penetration on Dreiser's. In whatever passage you study, look for such characteristics.

Another fruitful area of discussion is that of the *denotations* and

---

[1]Reprinted with the permission of Charles Scribner's Sons and Jonathan Cape Ltd. from *A Farewell to Arms* by Ernest Hemingway, p. 3. Copyright 1929 Charles Scribner's Sons. Renewal copyright © 1957 Ernest Hemingway.

[2]New York: Dell Publishing Co., Inc. (Copyright World Publishing Co.), 1959, p. 25.

*connotations* of words. The denotation is what a word signifies, and the connotation is what a word suggests. Compare these passages:

1. I'll think about it.
2. I'll try to find a solution.
3. I will plan to devote my utmost diligence to the consideration of this problem.

Without a context it is difficult to know the real meaning of any of these statements, but on their surfaces the first and the third promise not much at all — they are more appropriate for dismissing consideration than for promising it — while the second indicates that the speaker probably will study the problem and try to come up with a solution. Study this passage, the conclusion of Joseph Conrad's novel *Nostromo:*

> In that true cry of love and grief that seemed to ring aloud from Punta Mala to Azuera and away to the bright line of the horizon, overhung by a big white cloud shining like a mass of solid silver, the genius of the magnificent *capataz de cargadores* dominated the dark gulf containing his conquests of treasure and love.[3]

What has happened here is that a woman has cried aloud because the man she loved has died. But Conrad has attempted in this description to elevate the man, Nostromo, to the category almost of a demi-god. A careful study of the words, such as *bright line, shining, solid silver,* and *conquests,* would make this connotation plain.

There are other aspects of diction that you might also wish to consider. Sometimes writers may use many *allusions* as they write, thereby suggesting other contexts in which their work may be placed or with which their ideas may be compared. If you do not have a wide command of the sources yourself, or if your book is not well annotated, you will not be able to do much with this topic, but if your writer refers to something you know well, say the Bible, you might be able to work out a theme on the use of allusion alone. In a discussion devoted to style it is also permissible to consider images and symbols, but such a discussion can lead away from style and become an end in itself. As long as your treatment of imagery does not dominate your discussion it would be in order to bring it in as a part of style.

## GRAMMAR

The nomenclature of grammar is a useful tool in describing a writer's sentences. If you find many short sentences in one writer's work and long ones in another writer's, for example, it is not very informative to make these observations in a vacuum. But if you can

[3]New York: Modern Library, 1951, p. 631.

connect them to a description of the writers' grammatical control, you are on the way to something meaningful. As an example, refer again to the passage from Hemingway. You will observe that Hemingway's sentences are medium length to lengthy, but more can be done than this. In the paragraph Hemingway uses the word *and* many times. Of the four sentences, the last three are all compound sentences (independent clauses joined by *and*), whereas the first one is complex. Usually compound sentences do not demonstrate cause-and-effect or other relations and so are best used in narrative description. A number of compound sentences tend to declare, rather than to analyze (similarities between Hemingway's passage and parts of the King James Bible have been noticed in this connection). Also, compound sentences strung together may, under some circumstances, suggest resignation on the speaker's part. These remarks apply here.

In this passage there are also many prepositional phrases. There are sixteen phrases, to be exact (one with a compound object). Of these sixteen, twelve are adverbial, and of these twelve, eight modify verbs. This number is to be contrasted with the number of single-word adverbs — three. The proportion of phrases is so high that you might justifiably conclude that the characteristic method of modification in the passage is the use of phrases. Prepositional phrases usually require many *in*'s, *of*'s, and *the*'s; so a passage with many phrases would likely contain many monosyllabic words. In this passage, there are 126 words; 103 have one syllable; 22 have two syllables; and one has three syllables. The method of modification thus has a close relationship to the simple, rather stark diction of the passage, for if Hemingway had relied on single-word adverbs he would necessarily have used more polysyllabic words. (Notice that the three single-word adverbs are all polysyllabic: *swiftly, early, afterward.* The longest word in the passage is an adverb.)

You can see that a knowledge of grammatical terms (in this example, a knowledge of conjunctions, compound sentences, complex sentences, adverbs, phrases, nouns) aids in the analysis, description, and evaluation of style.

Because the application of grammar to style may seem unusual to you, let us refer again to the passage from Dreiser, also quoted above. The sentence begins with a prepositional phrase used adverbially, with four objects of the preposition. Then Dreiser introduces the verb *(had come),* and then the subject of the verb *(strange company).* Immediately after the subject there are three adjectives that modify it. There is then a fourth adjective *(unschooled)* modified by an adverb phrase *(in even the primer),* and the object of the preposition is modified by an adjective phrase *(of refinement).* Then there is a fifth adjective *(hungry)* modifying the subject of the sentence. This fifth adjective has complex modification; first there is an adverb phrase *(for something),* and then the noun *something* is modified by an adjective clause, which in turn has with it an adverb clause *(the significance of which, when they had it, they could not even guess).* The original series of adjectives is resumed with *anxious,* which is modified by the adverbial infinitive *to be called great.* The adjective series ends with the seventh, *determined,* which is modified by the adverbial infinitive phrase *so to be,* which is modified by the adverbial *without ever knowing how.*

If you have been confused by this grammatical description, you will readily agree that the sentence begins simply but unusually and becomes difficult and involved. It is inverted and rhetorically dramatic; it depends for its full effect on close study in its context on the printed page, whereas the example from Hemingway could be readily followed if someone read it aloud. In Dreiser's defense, you might say that the sentence explores a difficult avenue of thought: Dreiser is describing the makeup of a giant, a *titan,* and theoretically his language should therefore be grand and sweeping. In fact, this sentence fits into his design, for its seven adjectives build up to a cumulative impression of bigness.

## RHYTHM AND SOUND

RHYTHM.    Prose rhythm is difficult to analyze and describe, but if you alert your ear and if you can combine the results of your hearing with the analysis of grammar in a passage, you can arrive at accurate and useful generalizations. The nomenclature of metrical feet (*iambs, trochees,* and so on) is generally not applicable for prose, because words that are part of a metrical pattern in poetry may become part of a larger rhythmic pattern in prose. The rhythm of prose, in short, is generally vaster than that of poetry, in keeping with prose writers' general intention to develop their thoughts extensively. To feel prose rhythm, read this passage, which opens Nathaniel Hawthorne's story "The Hollow of the Three Hills."

> [1] In those strange old times when fantastic dreams and madmen's reveries were realized among the actual circumstances of life, two persons met together at an appointed hour and place.   [2] One was a lady, graceful in form and fair of feature, though pale and troubled, and smitten with an untimely blight in what should have been the fullest bloom of her years; the other was an ancient and meanly dressed woman, of ill-favored aspect, and so withered, shrunken and decrepit that even the space since she began to decay must have exceeded the ordinary term of human existence.   [3] In the spot where they encountered no mortal could observe them.   [4] Three little hills stood by each other, and down in the midst of them sunk a hollow basin, almost mathematically circular, two or three hundred feet in breadth, and of such depth that a stately cedar might but just be visible above the sides. . . .[4]

[4]In Myron Matlaw and Leonard Lief, eds., *Story and Critic* (New York: Harper & Row, 1963), p. 64.

Although these sentences could easily be scanned as iambs, anapaests, and the other poetical feet, you will notice that it is more accurate to submerge many of the accents in larger prose rhythms; that is:

> Thrée líttle híalls stood bý each other,
> and dówn in the mídst of them sunk a hóllow básin.

In hearing the rhythm of these fragments, notice that stresses are placed on fewer syllables than in a verse passage of comparable length. There is less stress because in prose the individual *cadence groups,* or *phraseological groups,* are the basic developmental and rhythmical units. A typical sentence is usually made up of two or more cadence groups.[5]

What you should do in analyzing prose style for rhythm is to mark the cadence groups in order to observe whether they range from short and rapid to long and leisurely or to something in between. Rely on your own vocal pauses as you read, being careful to mark the ends and beginnings of groups as suggested by punctuation marks, and the natural, if slight, pauses *(junctures)* between subjects and predicates, compound subjects, and so on. As you analyze the various groups you might arrange them spatially to show how they are spoken. Thus one unit, say an opening phrase, might go on a separate line to indicate its uniqueness, and a clause might take an entire line but have extra long spaces between words to show where junctures occur. Let us see how the first sentence of "The Hollow of the Three Hills" might be laid out:

> In those strange old times
> when fantastic dreams     and madmen's reveries
> were realized
> among the actual circumstances     of life,
> two persons met together     at an appointed hour and place.

With this layout may be compared a spatial arrangement of two sentences from Katherine Anne Porter's story "He":

> He did grow     and he never got hurt.
> A plank blew off the chicken house     and struck him on the head
> and he never seemed to know it.[6]

While it is unwise to make extensive generalizations from only these two sentences, it is possible to observe in Hawthorne a tendency toward longer sentences, resulting in rhythmical units that are not self-contained clauses. Hawthorne's rhythmical units are embodied in phrases like the beginning prepositional-adverb phrase ("In those strange old times"), and the sentence is so extensive that it is made up of eight units. The rhythmical units in Katherine Anne Porter's sentences, by contrast, are coincidental with complete sentence structures.

---

[5]Cadence groups are also discussed in Chapter 14.
[6]In Sean O'Faolain, ed., *Short Stories: A Study in Pleasure* (Boston: Little, Brown and Co., 1961), p. 255.

It is also possible to see in Hawthorne a tendency to arrange his diction and his stresses in patterns of two (e.g., *strange old; dreams . . . reveries;* and *hour and place*). Only an analysis of a greater number of sentences, however, would confirm whether these tentative conclusions have any validity. Your job in analyzing a prose passage is to make a similar attempt to discover and to characterize its rhythms. As a means of self-assistance, you should read the passage aloud and listen for its rises and falls, its lengths of utterance. It is also helpful to have another student read the passages aloud to you, so that you will be better able to observe its rhythms.

SOUND.   Despite the differences between poetry and prose, the various "poetic" devices such as alliteration, assonance, and onomatopoeia may also be at work in prose (see pp. 187–189). You should be alert for them. Look at the example from Hemingway again. If you listen, you will hear that Hemingway employs assonance in sentence 2 (m*o*ving, bl*ue*); in sentence 3 (h*ou*se, d*ow*n, p*ow*dered); and sentences 3 and 4 (l*ea*ves, br*ee*ze, w*e*, tr*ee*s). The passage from Hawthorne's "The Hollow of the Three Hills" utilizes assonance and also a good deal of alliteration. In sentence 1, for example, you may notice "*m*et to*g*ether" and "*r*everies we*r*e *r*ealized." In sentence 2 there is "*f*raceful in *f*orm and *f*air of *f*eature," and "*bl*ight" and "*bl*oom." A closer study would reveal a number of other segmental devices. The effect of this attention to sound should be to make the reader stop and listen, and to concentrate on the suggestions and the connotations of the prose. In commenting on passages like these you should certainly establish their similarity to poetry and should also include this fact in your evaluation of the style.

### RHETORIC

The point at which diction, grammar, and rhythm and sound merge is described by the very broad word *rhetoric*, which may be defined as the art of persuasive writing. The three areas of analysis become important only as they reveal characteristic features and skills of the writer you are studying. You might use your grammatical analysis, for example, to show the simplicity or complexity of the writer's style. You should observe whether the sentences fall into patterns. Are most of the sentences simple, compound, or complex, or is there a mixture? Can you determine any relationship between the patterns and the ideas or descriptions? Are there any rhetorical devices used that can be described grammatically? Are the sentences mainly *loose* (simply declarative) or *periodic* (arranged to achieve a climax), and why?

The idea of talking about rhetoric is to tie your analysis to a consideration of the effectiveness of the writer's sentences. Let us take an example of a famous sentence, from Samuel Johnson's letter to Lord

Chesterfield, in which Johnson rejected the Lord's belated offer of financial assistance:

> The notice which you have been pleased to take of my labours, had it been early, had been kind; but it has been delayed till I am indifferent, and cannot enjoy it; till I am solitary, and cannot impart it; till I am known, and do not want it.

Notice here that Johnson uses a number of parallel constructions. (A parallel construction is the repetition of the same grammatical form both to conserve the number of words in a sentence and also to promote interest.) He uses "had it been . . . had been," and then uses the "till I am . . . and cannot" pattern three times. The last time, he varies the "cannot" with a "do not." The sentence is both simple, direct, and effective because of this combination of parallelism, variation, and climax.

In any discussion of style you should try to concern yourself with the ways in which the writer puts all the elements together. Words such as *climax* and *parallelism* should figure heavily in your analysis. It might be helpful to take the original sentence and try to paraphrase it. The comparison can help you in your perception of the author's skill. Let us take the following sentence from Franklin D. Roosevelt's first inaugural address:

> So, first of all, let me assert my firm belief that the only thing we have to fear is fear itself—nameless, unreasoning, unjustified terror which paralyzes needed efforts to convert retreat into advance.

Let us try a paraphrase:

> I firmly believe that our only fear is to be afraid of terror which prevents us from advancing.

In comparison, Roosevelt's original assumes an even better light than at first reading. His sentence uses some effective repetitions: he changes the infinitive *to fear* to the noun *fear;* then he sets up the noun *terror* in apposition to *fear* and precedes it with three adjectives which point out his belief that the terror is irrational. The concluding clause builds up to the word *advance,* which aptly defines the goals he wanted the country to follow in 1933. You might wonder if Roosevelt would ever have persuaded many people to accept his programs if he had written his sentence in the manner of our paraphrase. What counts is the arrangement of his words and their power to interest and arouse his listeners.

You should recognize that *rhetoric* is a very comprehensive word. Segmental repetitions such as alliteration are rhetorical devices, because they assist the writer in making the words and ideas effective. The selection of one word in preference to another is also rhetorical because the aim is to render an idea or description accurately and sometimes colorfully. Many elements of rhetoric have been classified and named, and a good glossary of literary terms will provide you with a knowledge of these. (Also, you might observe that in the sample theme an instance of *chiasmus* or *antimetabole* is described in the passage by William Congreve.)

## Organizing Your Theme

### INTRODUCTION

You should begin by relating your passage to the work as a whole. Where does the passage appear, and what are the circumstances? What does the passage show about characters, ideas, or things that may also be shown in the entire work? Your aim should be not to answer these questions in great detail, but only to provide as much information as is necessary to make your discussion of style meaningful. Develop a central idea about the style of the passage, and conclude with your thesis sentence.

### BODY

Governing the entire body of your theme should be your attempt to show the effectiveness or ineffectiveness of the author's writing. The sample theme opens with a description of a rhetorical figure, and throughout the theme there is an emphasis on matters such as climax, emphasis, and the appropriateness of the prose to the speaker.

You might wish to single out one aspect of style in your discussion, or to discuss everything, as you wish. In a discussion of diction you should consider things like the degree of specificity, generality, concreteness, abstractness, levels of simplicity or difficulty, and appropriateness. In grammar, consider things like length and subordination, and also any rhetorical devices that can be described grammatically. In rhythm and sound, try to determine characteristic rhythms and the assistance that rhythm and sound give to the content of the passage.

To assist your analysis, you should make good notes about word counts, grammatical characteristics, qualities of diction, cadence groups, and so on. Use the dictionary for help with various words. Sometimes you can transfer material from your notes directly to your theme, with only minor modifications.

### CONCLUSION

Make a concluding evaluation of the style. If you have any additional observations, make them here. Try to conclude on a note of how successfully the style of the passage contributed to the content.

## HINTS ON PROCEDURE

1. This theme is designed to increase your perceptions, sensitivity, and appreciation. Listen carefully; read carefully; try to feel the full force of the passage you select.
2. Make a copy of your passage and place it at the start of your theme.
3. Number each sentence in your passage.
4. When you write, use quotations to illustrate your points. Do not just quote in a vacuum, however, but explain your point and make your analysis before or immediately after your quotation.
5. Underline all elements to which you wish to draw attention.
6. Always indicate the sentence numbers of your quotations.

SAMPLE THEME

### A Study of the Style in Mirabell's Speech in Act I, Scene I, of William Congreve's Comedy *The Way of the World* (1700)

FAINALL.    For a passionate lover, methinks you are somewhat too discerning in the failings of your mistress.

MIRABELL.    [1] And for a discerning man, somewhat too passionate a lover; for I like her with all her faults; nay, like her for her faults.    [2] Her follies are so natural, or so artful, that they become her; and those affectations which in another woman would be odious, serve but to make her more agreeable.    [3] I'll tell thee, Fainall, she once used me with that insolence, that in revenge I took her to pieces; sifted her and separated her failings; I studied 'em and got 'em by rote.    [4] The catalogue was so large that I was not without hopes one day or other to hate her heartily: to which end I so used myself to think of 'em that at length, contrary to my design and expectation, they gave me every hour less and less disturbance; till in a few days it became habitual to me to remember 'em without being displeased.    [5] They are now grown as familiar to me as my own frailties; and in all probability, in a little time longer I shall like 'em as well.

[1]     This stylistically successful passage is spoken by Mirabell early in *The Way of the World,* before he becomes enmeshed in the strategies in which he must engage to win Millamant, the woman he loves. *He is here talking about Millamant, and Congreve designs the speech, on the one hand, to show his love for her and his own mental powers, and, on the other, to*

Kathleen M. Lynch, ed. (Lincoln: University of Nebraska Press, 1965), pp. 17–18.

*cause the audience to laugh.*\* The comic strain is implicit in the incongruity that Mirabell describes: He knows all Millamant's shortcomings but loves her not only in spite of them but *because* of them. The speech then comically describes how he got into the predicament. *Obviously the passage is doing many things at once, and its success depends on Congreve's stylistic control, a control which may be seen in the opening rhetorical figure, in the grammar of the passage, and in the diction, rhythms, and segmental repetitions.*†

[2]     The very first sentence, in which Mirabell creates a rhetorical figure begun unintentionally by Fainall, shows Mirabell's mental quickness. Fainall speaks of *passion* and *discernment.* in a 1-2 order, and Mirabell then creates a 2-1 repetition of *discernment* and *passion.* Rhetorically, Mirabell has composed a *chiasmus* or *antimetabole.* Such a figure is effective when it is used in a prepared speech (i.e., "Ask not what *your country* can do for *you,* but what *you* can do for *your country*"), but when one considers that this speech is supposedly impromptu, the only conclusion is that Congreve is using style to show Mirabell's superior mind. Here Mirabell takes Fainall's words and builds upon them, displaying a superiority which may be seen to foreshadow his overcoming Fainall at the end of the play. Also, his taking an observation and completing it rhetorically will be duplicated in Act IV, just before the "proviso scene," when he finishes the couplet that Millamant had begun quoting. Such readiness of expression illustrates a mind operating at the highest level.

[3]     Even though Mirabell is demonstrably able intellectually, he is caught by his emotions, and this complex state dictates the rhetorical and grammatical structure of the speech. Essentially the form is one of comparison, developing from the contrast between passion and discernment in sentence 1. Both sentences 1 and 5, for example, are similar because both refer to the dual state. Sentence 1 has compound verbs *(like, like),* and sentence 5 is a conventional compound sentence, balanced easily on both sides of a semicolon. These sentences serve as the topic sentence and concluding sentence of the speech. The interior sentences develop the contradictions inherent in Mirabell's condition, each of them using a "so . . . that" type of construction to indicate (a) an extreme of emotion and (b) some kind of decision or outcome. Thus, in sentence 2 it is Millamant's "follies" which are "so natural, or so artful, that they become her." In sentence 3 it is Millamant's "insolence" that causes Mirabell in "revenge" to study her faults. The same grammatical pattern appears twice in sentence 4, once in reference to the large catalogue of faults and again in reference to Mirabell's inadvertent realization that the faults have become a part of her charm. Just as Mirabell is aware of the conflict between his discernment and his passion, the structure of each of the sentences is shaped as reflecting the conflict.

[4]     The grammar not only complements Mirabell's paradoxical state, but it also is arranged toward climaxes designed to produce laughter. The end of the first sentence shows such an arrangement:

nay, like her for her faults.

\*Central idea.        †Thesis sentence.

The contrast between *like* and *faults* is made so quickly and plainly that laughter is an almost certain result. Congreve makes all the sentences clear and uncomplicated, so that the comic interest is foremost. Even the most difficult of his sentences, sentence 4, contains three internal climaxes ending with *heartily, disturbance,* and *displeased.* Each one of these constructions builds up to the concluding word which, when delivered properly, would effectively trigger laughter. Indeed, though the entire sentence is 64 words long, it is divided by these climaxes into three separate sentences, the first two being complex and the last simple. Thus, Congreve creates humor by highlighting the lover's contradictory state within simplified and climactic sentence structures.

[5]    Congreve is successful in maintaining the same simplicity in Mirabell's diction, which is surprisingly easy even though the speech deals with complicated emotional and intellectual states. Only a few of the words and idioms are now outdated, such as *nay, that insolence* (for "so much insolence") and *used myself to think* (for thought). The only words that may offer difficulty for a modern reader are perhaps *affectation, artful,* and *insolence. Discerning* in the sense of *penetrating* or *discriminating* might be regarded as difficult, but Mirabell picks up this word from Fainall's previous sentence, and develops the idea throughout his own speech, repeating the meaning of discernment in the words *sifted* and *separated.* Also, throughout the speech he contrasts his discernment with his love for Millamant, so that any initial difficulty with the word should be overcome well before the last word is spoken. Thus the context itself clarifies any difficulty.

[6]    For the most part, however, Mirabell's words themselves are clear to any audience. His most straightforward language is his direct declaration of love for Millamant, which he makes in the second half of the first sentence.

for I like her with all her faults; nay, like her for her faults.

This sentence contains fourteen words, and each one is from the language of everyday speech. With no words of more than one syllable, the sentence is a model of simplicity and directness. The sentence, too, is important to the remainder of the play, for there is no qualification in these words. One presumably should remember them later on because in all the cynicism and subterfuge it is possible that Mirabell's love for Millamant might seem to be buried. But here he has stated his love as clearly and unequivocally as any lover ever could.

[7]    Even in his handling of abstract ideas, Mirabell's diction is under control. Since he is describing his emotional state, he must necessarily use the appropriate words, such as *faults, passionate, affectations, agreeable, design, expectation, disturbance, displeased,* and *familiar.* Despite the abstract quality of these words, they become clear in the context. One of the reasons they do not fly out of comprehension is that Mirabell uses very simple and specific verbs. In sentence 3, for example, there are seven verbs, all of them active and vivid *(tell, used, took, sifted, separated, studied,* and *got).* This sentence is the most lively one, but the verbs in

each of the other sentences also keep the subject on a plain, real level, well within the ready grasp necessary at a first hearing, which is the experience of most people in an audience.

[8]     Consistent with the aim of easy audience comprehension, Congreve keeps the rhythmical units relatively short; obviously he designed them to be heard rather than to be read. One might look at sentence 3 in this regard. The sentence has 33 words in it, but in speech it would break into ten separate cadence groups, as follows:

|                  |                           |
|-----------------:|---------------------------|
| I'll tell thee,  | Fainall                   |
| she once used me | with that insolence,      |
| that in revenge  | I took her to pieces;     |
| sifted her       | and separated her failings; |
| I studied 'em    | and got 'em by rote.      |

In such an arrangement the units are quite intelligible. In the same way, in sentence 2 Congreve solves a problem where complexity could possibly interfere with an audience's comprehension. The second half of the sentence contains a subject that is separated from the verb by a seven-word adjective clause ("which in another woman would be odious"). Such an interruption might possible diffuse the thought and thereby lose Congreve's comic point, but he keeps control by finishing the sentence in seven words, six of which are of one syllable. Here is the entire section:

|                        |                        |
|------------------------|------------------------|
| and those affectations |                        |
| which in another woman | would be odious        |
| serve                  | but to make her more agreeable. |

Here the last word, *agreeable,* having four syllables, is the most complicated word in the group, but because the previous six words comprise six syllables, the entire phrase is simple and immediately intelligible. One could hardly imagine better dramatic prose.

[9]     Undergirding all the qualities of style so far mentioned is the barely noticeable presence of various segmental repetitions. It is hard to know the true effect of alliteration and assonance in prose, for these devices are not readily apparent and the casual reader may simply neglect them. But if one is truly aware of sound as sound, the devices may produce a psychological awareness of the words and the ideas which they express. Sentences 1 and 5, which have already been noted as forming a structural frame for the paragraph, contain similar patterns of alliteration. In sentence 1 there are *l*'s in *lover* and *like,* while in 5 the *l*'s appear in *little, longer,* and *like.* Also, in 1 there is an *f* in *for* and *faults,* while in 5 the *f* may be heard in *familiar* and *frailties.* In addition, both sentences contain internal rhymes: *all* and *faults* in sentence 1, and *grown* and *own* in 5. Inobtrusive as these similarities are in the total context of the passage, they add a complementary unity of sound to the paralleling of the structures and thought of the two sentences.

[10]     Congreve uses alliteration in each of the other sentences as well. In 2 there are *m*'s (*make, more*) and *w*'s (*woman, would,* and [with aspiration] *which*). Sentence 3 has *s*'s (*sifted, separated,* and *studied*). The most

complicated sentence is 4, which also contains the greatest number of segmental repetitions. There is an *h* pattern (*h*opes, *h*ate, *h*eartily) and an *ng* pattern (thi*ng*, le*ng*th), and also a pattern of assonance in *ä* (*la*rge and h*ea*rtily, with the *r* also being repeated), *i* (t*i*ll, *i*t, hab*i*tual), *ē* (m*e*, b*e*ing, displ*ea*sed), and particularly *e* (*e*nd, mys*e*lf, l*e*ngth, *e*xp*e*ctation, *e*v*e*ry, l*e*ss, l*e*ss, and rem*e*mber).

[11]     This passage is evidence of Congreve's great skill as a master of dramatic prose. If style is truly the mark of a person's character, then the highest tribute one could give to the passage is that Mirabell comes alive in it. Congreve shows his hero as a person capable of winning the world — and on the world's terms. He also shows Mirabell as a lively and introspective person, enmeshed in love and aware of his powerlessness against his emotions, but also fascinated and slightly amused at himself. His keenness of insight is accompanied by directness of expression. When his emotions are allowed to surface they are stated in the simplest, most direct language. Congreve thus reveals Mirabell as a mind in full power and a soul in love. His control over Mirabell's speech is such that he brings his audience to laugh not at Mirabell, but with him.

## ★COMMENTARY ON THE THEME

Like the sample theme on prosody (Chapter 14), this theme is comprehensive for illustrative purposes. The first paragraph locates the passage in the entire play, and also indicates the main ideas in the passage. Paragraph 2 discusses how the passage is launched by a rhetorical figure, and it relates this figure to the character Mirabell's brilliance, a point made in the central idea. Paragraphs 3 and 4 discuss the grammar of the passage, noting features such as the parallel structures of the opening and closing sentences, the common patterns of the three internal sentences, and the pointing of the sentences to create laughter. Paragraphs 5, 6, and 7 discuss the diction, emphasizing the simplicity and appropriateness of the words, and noting that some of the abstract words are kept from obscurity by the active, plain verbs. Paragraph 8 contains a brief analysis of the rhythms of the passage, pointing out the relationship between the shortness of the cadence groups and the dramatic function of the speech. Paragraphs 9 and 10 present a discussion of segments, particularly relating the repetitions to the parallelism of the opening and closing sentences in the passage. The last paragraph contains a final tribute to the style, emphasizing that the speaker's character is realized as he talks himself alive.

Note that any one of the four approaches illustrated in this theme could serve as the basis for an entire theme on style.

# CHAPTER
# 16

# *The Theme of Evaluation*

EVALUATION is the ultimate goal of all literary study. Evaluation is closely allied with *judgment,* which is the faculty by which we can distinguish between good and bad, right and wrong, plausibility and implausibility, and so on. As used here, *evaluation* means the act of deciding what is good, bad, or mediocre. It requires a steady pursuit of the best — to be satisfied with less is to deny the best efforts of our greatest writers. Evaluation implies that there are ideal standards of excellence by which decisions about quality can be made, but it must be remembered that these standards are flexible in their application and may be applicable to works of literature written in all places and ages.

You may sometimes find that works commonly adjudged to be good do not seem good to you. If such is the case, try to live with the work for a time. If you have ever played in a band or orchestra, or sung in a chorus, you may have found some musical composition distasteful when you first read it through, but discovered, as you worked on it and learned it, that you finally became fond of the work. This process confirms the statement that you will learn to understand and like a good work of art when you have the opportunity to do so. If, however, you find that despite prolonged exposure to the work, you still do not concur in the general favorable judgment, be as certain as you can that your reaction is based on rational and logically defensible grounds.

Of course your ability to judge will be increased as you learn about more and more fine works. You must read and learn as much as you can, in order to establish the qualities of good literature firmly in your mind, and as these qualities become clearer to you, you will be able to evaluate with greater ease. Now, you have the task of evaluating a single work for your theme. This single assignment should have a definite bearing on your judgment in future years, because careful effort now will permanently improve your critical faculties.


## Rationale of Evaluation

There is no precise answer to the problem of how to justify an evaluation. Evaluation is the most abstract, philosophical, and difficult writing you will do about literature, just as it is the most necessary. Standards of taste, social mores, and even morals differ from society to society and age to age; nonetheless, some works of art have been adjudged good or even great by generation after generation, whereas others have not. The student therefore asks, "By what standards may a work be judged a good or great work?" and, "How do I make this judgment by myself?"


## Standards for Evaluation

There are many standards to help you evaluate a literary work. Some of the major ones are described below, and many have been suggested in earlier chapters. The terms involved are used and defined here in the sense in which they are usually used in regard to literature.

### TRUTH

Although *truth* or *truthful* is used in speaking of literature to mean *realism* or *realistic* (e.g., does Flaubert give a truthful picture of Emma Bovary's society?), its meaning here is restricted carefully. To speak of the truth is to imply generality and universality. Let us take a concrete illustration.

Sophocles's *Antigone* is a play that has survived the passage of 2,400 years. It concerns a society (the Greek city-state with a ruling monarch) that no longer exists; it deals with a religious belief (that the souls of the unburied dead never find rest) that passed from currency centuries ago; it involves an idea (of a curse following an entire family) accepted now only by the least educated members of our society. Wherein, then, lies the appeal, the truth, of *Antigone*, which makes it as much alive for our age as it was for the Greeks of more than 2,000 years ago?

The answer is at least partly in the permanence of the human problem that Antigone faces: "How do I reconcile my duty to obey the state with my duty to obey my conscience? And if the two conflict, which do I follow?" This dilemma, and the suffering inevitable for any persons caught in it, regardless of which choice they make, is one that human beings have faced since the beginning of time; while humanity and states exist, this conflict between laws and conscience will endure. In short, the play embodies, lives in terms of, and comments on, one of the great *truths* of human life. It measures up to one standard we use in deciding whether a work of art is good or bad, great or mediocre.

## AFFIRMATIVENESS

*Affirmativeness* means here that human beings are worth caring about and writing about, no matter how debased the condition in which they live or how totally they abuse their state. All art should be affirmative. Although many works apparently say "no" to life, most say "yes," and a good argument can be made that the "no" works indirectly present a "yes." Thus, if a character like Macbeth or Hurstwood falls to the depths of misfortune, despair, and death, the author must demonstrate that there is a loss of some sort worth lamenting. Human worth is here affirmed even as a major character loses it. If a character like Mirabell in Congreve's play *The Way of the World* is happy and in good estate at the end of the work, the author must show that the character's qualities have justified the good fortune. Life is again affirmed. If an unworthy character is fortunate at the end, like Joe Gowland in A. J. Cronin's *The Stars Look Down*, the author still affirms human worth by suggesting a world in which such worth may become triumphant. In short, authors may portray the use and abuse of life, the love and the hate, the heights and depths, but their vision is always that life is valuable and worthy of respect and dignity. The best works are those that make this affirmation forcefully, without being platitudinous or didactic.

### "THE JOINT FORCE AND FULL RESULT OF ALL"

This quotation is from Pope's *Essay on Criticism,* in which most of what can be said about evaluation is said. Pope insisted that a critic should not judge a work simply by its parts but should judge the *whole,* the entirety of the work. You can profit from Pope's wisdom. You should carefully consider the total effect of the work, both as an artistic form and as a cause of impressions and emotions in yourself. James Joyce used the concepts "whatness" and "radiance" in describing the totality of a work; that is, when a work seems to be entirely itself, the force of its totality impresses the reader in a moment of revelation, or radiance. Bear in mind that a great work may be imperfect, but if the sum total of the work is impressive, the flaws assume minor importance. In other words, even if the author can be attacked on technical matters, the total effect of the work may overshadow the adverse criticism. Thomas Hardy and Theordore Dreiser are two authors in point; their language frequently‚be shown to be at fault, but a reading of their best works reveals them to be superior novelists.

So one cannot judge a work as good or bad by referring to only one element within it. An interesting plot, a carefully handled structure, a touching love story, a valid moral—none of these attributes alone can justify a total judgment of "good." One can say, for example, that Dickens's *Oliver Twist* has an extremely ingenious plot and that it arouses our emotions effectively. But to evaluate the novel fully one must take into consideration several questions. Foremost among them are these: How does the character of Oliver withstand modern knowledge of child development? Could a child subjected from birth to the brutal experiences that Oliver endures develop into the person that Dickens presents? You cannot make a final judgment on the work as a whole without taking all its important aspects into account.

Another important phase of the "joint force and full result of all" is the way in which you become involved as you read. Most of what you read, if it has merit, will cause you to become emotionally involved with the characters and actions. You have perhaps observed that characters in some works seem real to you or that incidents are described so vividly that you feel as though you had witnessed them. In these cases you were experiencing the pleasure of involvement. The problem here is whether your pleasure was fleeting and momentary ("just kicks"), or whether it has assumed more permanence (whether it resulted from a passage that is permanently, or spiritually, satisfying).

Closely integrated with the idea of involvement is the Aristotelian theory of *purgation* or *catharsis* in tragedy. How do you regard the character of Macbeth when he kills Duncan, or of Othello when he strangles Desdemona? Shakespeare causes you to become involved with both heroes, and when they perform evil deeds your own conscience cries out for them to stop. The result, when the play is over, is a "purgation" of your emotions; that is, if you experience these plays well, you will also have experienced an emotional "drain." You can see that the use to which a writer puts your involvement is important in your judgment of the work.

## VITALITY

A good work of literature has a life of its own and can be compared to a human being. You know that your friends are always changing and growing, and that you learn more and more about them as your friendship progresses. A work of literature can grow in the sense that your repeated experience with it will produce insights that you did not have in your previous readings. A classic example of such a work is *Huckleberry Finn*, known to children as an exciting and funny story of adventure but known to adults as a profound story about the growth of a human soul. Another example is *Gulliver's Travels,* in which critics for two centuries have been finding new insights and beauties. It is naturally difficult for you to predict the future, but if you have based your present opinion on reasonable grounds and have determined that the work is good, you may conclude that within the work there will be what Wordsworth called "food for future years."

### BEAUTY

Whole books have been devoted to an attempt to define *beauty.* Briefly, beauty is closely allied with unity, symmetry, harmony, and proportion. To discover the relationship of parts to whole — their logical and chronological and associational functions within the work — is to perceive beauty in a work.

In the eighteenth century there was an idea that "variety within order" constituted beauty; the extent to which Pope's couplets vary within the pattern of the neoclassic couplet is an illustration of the eighteenth-century ideal. The Romantic and post-Romantic periods held that beauty could be found only through greater freedom. This belief in freedom has produced such characteristics of modern literature as originality for its own sake, experimentation in verse and prose forms, freedom of syntax, stream-of-consciousness narration, and personal diction. Despite the apparent change of emphasis, however, the concepts of unity and proportion are still valid and applicable. Studies of style, structure, point of view, tone, and imagery are therefore all means to the goal of determining whether works are beautiful. Any one of these studies is an avenue toward evaluation. Remember, however, that an excellence in any one of them does not make a work excellent. Frequently critics use such terms as "facile" and "surface excellence" to describe what they judge to be technically correct but artistically imperfect works.

### YOUR PREFERENCES

Although personal likes and dislikes are the least valid criteria for judgment, they are not to be excluded. They are the principal guides to what you read, but they are valueless when purely whimsical — without any basis in thought or knowledge. They become more valuable as they reflect mature thoughts based on knowledge. The more knowledge behind a preference, the more reliable it is, because the preference then stems not from a vacuum but from a deeply ingrained basis of comparison.

In writing, you should carefully distinguish between evaluating a work and merely liking or disliking it. You will readily admit that you might dislike works that everyone maintains are good; similarly, you may like some works that you would admit were worthless. You have heard people say "Everyone to his or her taste," or "I know what I like," and thus justify their preferences on unreasonable grounds. Of course, preference plays a part in evaluation and appreciation, but if you are to become a literate, disciplined reader, you will realize that pure subjectivism is inadequate. Evaluation must be based on solid grounds, grounds on which most human beings, despite personality differences, can agree.

In your theme you do not need to emphasize your likes and dislikes as a separate point, but your discussion should permit you to make your feelings clear by implication. The only exception occurs if you are asserting a preference despite faults, or a dislike despite excellences, and even then you must develop valid criteria to justify your responses.

## Organizing Your Theme

In your theme you will attempt to answer the question of whether the work you have studied is good or not. If so, why? If not, why not? The grounds for your evaluation must be artistic. Although some works may be good pieces of political argument, or successfully controversial, your business is to judge them as works of art.

### INTRODUCTION

In the introduction you briefly encapsulate your evaluation, which will be your central idea, and list the points by which you expect to demonstrate your central idea. To assist your reader's comprehension of your ideas, you should provide any unique facts or background about the work you are evaluating.

### BODY

In the body you attempt to demonstrate the grounds for your evaluation. Your principal points will be the excellences or deficiencies of the work you are evaluating. Such excellences might be qualities of style, idea, structure, character portrayal, logic, point of view, and so on. Your discussion will analyze the probability, truth, force, or power with which the work embodies these excellences.

Avoid analysis for its own sake, and do not merely retell stories. If you are showing the excellence or deficiency of a character portrayal, you must necessarily bring in a description of the character, but remember that your discussion of the character is to be pointed toward *evaluation*, not *description*, of the work as a whole. Therefore you must select details for discussion that will illustrate whether the work is good or bad. Similarly, suppose you are evaluating a sonnet of Shakespeare and mention that the imagery is superb. At this point you might introduce some of the imagery, but your purpose is not to analyze imagery as such; it should be used only for illustration. If you remember, as a cardinal rule, to keep your thematic purpose foremost, you should have little difficulty in making your discussion relate to your central idea.

### CONCLUSION

The conclusion should be a statement on the total result of the work you are evaluating. Your concern here is with total impressions. This part of evaluation should underline your central idea.

SAMPLE THEME

### *A People's Dream: An Evaluation of Black Elk Speaks*

[1]         Those who read *Black Elk Speaks* might recall the excitement of discovery that Keats felt when he first read Chapman's translation of Homer. *The book is authenticity itself, a unique and powerful record of responses and recollections of an Oglala Sioux warrior and visionary, Black Elk.** The period described is that between about 1867 and 1890, when the westward expansion produced the defeat and finally the humiliation of the Indian nations that had owned the western prairies before that time. In 1931, Black Elk, then a man of 68, related his story to his son, who translated it into English to be transcribed by John G. Neihardt. The account — is it autobiography, history, meditation, revelation, or all four? — is therefore both a translation and a transcription. *Though the entire work is unique, Black Elk's reality and authenticity may be seen in his view of the Indian wars, his faith in his mystic powers, his value for life and the land, and his simple eloquence.*†

[2]         As an historic account, *Black Elk Speaks* presents a view of history that is a truthful antidote to the view of the Indian wars that the western movie has promoted. As Black Elk saw it, the *Wasichu's* (White person's) thirst for gold and land produced violence, conquest, and broken promises. The military defeats by the U.S. Army turned Indian against Indian, and resulted in impoverishment, flight, and death by starvation or massacre. With their buffalo and their ponies gone, the Indians had little choice but move onto reservations. Though the victor has always made "right," it has rarely been little more than half right, and the direct, personal account of Black Elk provides a truthful restorative.

All quotations and parenthetical page numbers refer to *Black Elk Speaks: Being the Life Story of a Holy Man of the Oglala Sioux, as told through John Neihardt (Flaming Rainbow), Illustrated by Standing Bear* (New York: Pocket Books, 1972).

*Central idea.       †Thesis sentence.

[3]     The work is also an account of Black Elk's inner vision of truth. Feeling that he had a unique role to play in the betterment of his Sioux nation, he apparently thought that the descriptions of his visions—the most important being his great revelation at the age of nine—were of principal value. He was a man with mystic powers, and apparently used them to effect cures and to predict the future. Many sophisticated readers might dismiss this aspect of the work as superstition, but in an age of "Transcendental Meditation" and the "Relaxed Response," more and more people are coming to recognize the mysterious, hidden sources of human power. It would therefore be arbitrary to deny the authenticity of Black Elk's descriptions of his mysterious powers.

[4]     While Black Elk's visions may be admittedly controversial, there can be no controversy about the power and wisdom of his values. Principally he expresses belief in valor and endurance and respect for life and for the land. Almost a thesis in his account is his claim that the Indians were living on their own land and desired only to be left alone, in a cooperative harmony between "two legs" (human beings) and "four legs" (the other animals). With such a value, it is natural that he would look with horror at the slaughter of the buffalo herds—a deliberate policy, incidentally, that the American government carried out in order to render the Indians helpless:

> . . . I can remember when the bison were so many that they could not be counted, but more and more Wasichus came to kill them until there were only heaps of bones scattered where they used to be. The Wasichus did not kill them to eat; they killed them for the metal that makes them crazy [gold], and they took only the hides to sell. Sometimes they did not even take the hides, only the tongues; and I have heard that fire-boats came down the Missouri River loaded with dried bison tongues. You can see that the men who did this were crazy. Sometimes they did not even take the tongues; they just killed and killed because they liked to do that. When we hunted bison, we killed only what we needed. And when there was nothing left but heaps of bones, the Wasichus came and gathered up even the bones and sold them (p. 181).

It is difficult to see how anyone with a grain of respect for life could see the slaughter in any other way, and yet, through such actions, the west was "won." But perhaps the gentler values of Black Elk, who provided shelter for a family of porcupines on a freezing night (p. 130) and who described his attitudes with such directness, may eventually become prominent.

[5]     It is, finally, Black Elk's straightforward, direct eloquence that is the best, most convincing aspect of the book. Everything that one might require from a great writer is here: conciseness, accuracy, strong feeling, irony, humor, pathos, use of images, vividness. Nothing is done to excess; Black Elk is a lover of detail, but just the right amount, and he did not engage in his emotions to the point of sentimentality. For example, his description of the dead after the senseless slaughter at Wounded Knee (December 29, 1890) displays controlled bitterness and pathos:

It was a good winter day when all this happened. The sun was shining. But after the soldiers marched away from their dirty work, a heavy snow began to fall. The wind came up in the night. There was a big blizzard, and it grew very cold. The snow drifted deep in the crooked gulch, and it was one long grave of butchered women and children and babies, who had never done any harm and were only trying to run away (p. 223).

One might quote many other examples from the book to show Black Elk's mastery. Especially unforgettable are his description of the power of a circle (pp. 164 f.) and his lament over the loss of his people's dream (p. 230).

[6]    An evaluation of *Black Elk Speaks* would not be complete without an emphasis on its power to evoke an almost overwhelming sorrow and regret over the loss that it describes. Today people are finding much value in a pluralistic culture, and as a result the values represented by Black Elk seem more worthy than ever of being followed and cherished. It is painful, almost too painful for words, to read in Black Elk's narrative just how the civilization that held these values was snuffed out. Truly, a book that so successfully provokes these thoughts is worthy of being enshrined in one's heart. *Black Elk Speaks* demonstrates that there is a whole tradition that has been ignored in our histories of literature.

★COMMENTARY ON THE THEME

The elements in any evaluation can be listed for convenience only. In an evaluation itself, they are all brought together, as they are in this theme. The principal standard of evaluation here, however, is truth or authenticity, which may also be regarded, almost mystically, as the sort of "radiance" spoken of by Joyce (see p. 218).

Paragraph 1 includes the central idea and a brief description of what the book, *Black Elk Speaks,* is like. Paragraphs 2 and 3 emphasize Black Elk's adherence to historical and subjective truth. The fourth paragraph asserts the value of Black Elk's love of life and the land, and paragraph 5 discusses the directness of his style. The last paragraph praises the book for its power to stimulate sympathy and love of life.

# CHAPTER
# 17

# *The Review*

THE REVIEW is a general essay on a literary work. It may also be thought of as a "critique," a "critical review," or simply an "essay." It is a free form, for in a review virtually everything is relevant—subject matter, technique, social and intellectual background, biographical facts, relationship to other works by the same author or by different authors, historical importance, and everything else. Because your aim in writing a review should be to judge generally the author's performance, the theme closest in purpose to the review is the theme of evaluation (Chapter 16). The review is different, however, because of its general nature, and in this respect is like the report (Chapter 3). In the review, evaluation is only one of the aims, for there may be other elements of the work under surveillance that should be mentioned, special difficulties that you want to explain and special features that you want to note.

Since the review is so free, it is also a challenge to the skills you have developed thus far as a disciplined reader. Much of your school experience to date has been assimilation—acquiring information and applying certain skills; your tasks have been mainly doing and deciding what to do. But with a review, you are left to your own devices; you must decide what to write about as well as what to say. Freedom of choice should be a constant goal, and it is important for you to realize that your experience is equipping you more and more to know what to do with this freedom. You should be able to synthesize the knowledge you are acquiring; you should not only know how to answer questions but should also decide on the questions to be asked.

Because the review is the most personal as well as general theme about literature, and also because of a close tie with the commercial side of literature and other forms of entertainment, it is one of the most common forms of critical writing. Most of the professional writing about literature in America today is reviewing. Performances of plays, musical compositions, art works, scholarly performances, scientific works, and of course works of imaginative literature are all subject to review. Of all the themes described in this book, the review is the one that you are most likely to be called on to write in your post-college careers, either by general publications or by publications of various organizations.

The review may be thought of as the "first wave" of criticism, with other, more deeply considered criticism to follow later. One immediate problem of the review is therefore to keep it from becoming too hasty, too superficial. Alexander Pope was probably considering this problem when he wrote the following couplet about the frequency of reviews and the stupidity of some of the reviewers (in the passage, substitute "works of art" for "verse," and "reviews" for "prose"):

> A *Fool* might once *himself* alone expose,
> Now *One* in *Verse* makes many more in *Prose.*
> — *Essay on Criticism,* 1.7,8

## Types of Reviews

1. GENERAL.    Most reviews that you will be called on to write are general. For these you may assume that your readers are concerned not with specific occupational or professional matters, but with ideals, aspirations, daily living, success or failure, emotional well-being, and human relationships generally. If you touch on social, economic, or religious problems in your review, your focus should be broadly moral or ethical, not specifically political or sectarian. That is, you may be discussing a problem that has been treated by the political party you favor, but for your review you should keep in mind that many readers will have political views different from yours, and may dismiss everything you write if you argue partially. Hence you should discuss the political problem in such a way that you appeal to a wide spectrum of political thought, not just to a narrow one.

2. SPECIALIZED.    There is often a need for a specialized type of review. Suppose, for example, that you are planning to write reviews of the same non-fictional work for two magazines, one for psychologists and the other for a religious group. You will immediately see that your reviews would be different. The one for the psychologists would emphasize the psychological implications of the work, while the other would stress the religious ones. You might also be called on in another course to write a review, say in sociology or history. Each discipline

would require a different approach and selection of detail. Or it might be that you are writing a review of a recent novel—normally a subject for a general review—but your audience is to be a group of criminologists. While for the general reader you would focus on common human concerns, for the criminologists you would probably stress those conditions described in the novel that seemingly lead characters into delinquency and crime. You can see that the materials you select for discussion will necessarily be dictated by the group you are trying to reach.

3. PERSONAL.  In a personal review, reviewers are less interested in pointing out features of the work itself than in presenting their own train of thought prompted by the occasion of the reading of the work. A review of this type is not so much a review as an artistic, moral, religious, or political essay, or a combination of these. Such an essay may take the following forms: (a) A consideration of the implications of the work being reviewed. In such an essay, writers first refer to an idea or ideas in the work, and then develop their own ideas as augmentations of these. (b) A discussion stemming out of disagreement with something in the original work. Writers may take one major idea and contradict that, or they may wish to rebut a series of statements in the work. Needless to say, both forms are difficult to manage, but if they are done well they can achieve their own independent interest and value.

## Your Readers and Your Selection of Material

No matter what type of review you write, you should perceive your role for the review as a guide and commentator. Do not try to make your review a substitute for the work itself. Thus it is necessary to refer to events or principal ideas in the work, but you should not make an exhaustive description. If the book you are reviewing has a surprise ending, it would be unforgivable to spoil the book for your readers by disclosing this ending, but you might justifiably intrigue your readers by indicating that they will be surprised when they come to the end of the work. If the author draws a number of important conclusions, do not describe every one. Concentrate only on one or two, leaving the rest for your readers themselves. If your subject is a book of poems, concentrate only on those poems that seem important or typical.

Perhaps the best frame of mind you can muster before you begin to write is this: imagine that you are preparing your readers to read the work themselves; imagine that you are providing them with parachute and rip cord, protective clothing, and the airplane ride, but that they must make the jump.

## Organizing Your Theme

Your review should include the following elements, formed into a thematic structure.

### INTRODUCTION

In this section you should place the work in perspective. In what period was it written? What is the nationality of the author (if of another nationality)? What kind of background knowledge is needed for an understanding of the work, or what kind, and how much, is supplied by the author (for example—a knowledge of oil drilling, of conditions in the old West, etc.)? To what genre does the work belong? What general issues need explaining before you begin your discussion of the work? Although most frequently you will be asked to review a play or novel, it is good to bear in mind that you may also be reviewing techniques of acting and staging a play. If you are reviewing a new edition of an old work, you may be judging the relevance of the past to the present and also the scholarly helps provided by the editor (if you have a scholarly edition to review). Try always to show that your work has relevance to the present group of readers. Be sure to include your central idea and thesis sentence.

### BODY

In the body of your theme you should try to arouse interest in the work you are reviewing or else to discourage readers from reading the work, if the work itself dictates this conclusion. Beyond providing the introductory information, your principal objective is to describe the strengths and weaknesses of the work. To write such a description you must call into play just about everything you have learned about analyzing literature for ideas, form, and style. In a sense, the review can be as specific as you wish to make it, for the greatest part of the body should be given to analysis. In this analysis, you may bring out your own strengths and interests as a critical reader. It may be, for example, that you have become proficient in discussing structure. If we suppose that you have observed a tightly knit structure in the work you are reviewing, you might choose to discuss that element in the body of your review, thereby appealing to your reader's response to artistic excellence. You should always recognize, however, that your discussion should be of limited extent. There is no need for a detailed, word-by-word analysis. It is not a theme on structure that you want, but a review emphasizing this element.

For specialized reviews you might call into play those disciplines that have interested you thus far in your high school career. Your study of economics, for example, may have led you to feel competent in handling ideas connected with that subject. Hence, in your review of a novel you might bring your awareness of economics to bear on the work. Or you may have developed an interest in social studies, and may wish to treat the characters in a work according to your understanding of social problems.

Whatever your personal interests and specialties, however, the best guide for the subject matter of the body is the work itself, which may very well force you to make certain considerations. Obvious characteristics may necessitate the form of your discussion. In the sample theme, for example, the unusual features of the characters and the dialogue in Pinter's play *The Homecoming* literally shape the form of the review. The sample theme therefore touches on aspects of *character analysis* (Chapter 4) and *style* (Chapter 15), even though it is by no means a complete essay on either of these topics. Many readers of literature would probably also choose in a review to emphasize the characters and dialogue, but many might choose to discuss the bizarre humor, or the connection with existential philosophy, and so on.

**CONCLUSION**

Your conclusion should be an attempt at evaluation of the work, certainly not as extensive as that in a theme of evaluation, but at least an outline of your responses and a suggestion to your readers of how they might respond, granted that you have shown that your interests coincide approximately with theirs. If the body of your review has emphasized evaluation, you should close your essay with a simple résumé of your points. If you are ever asked to review a work in, say, no more than 150 words, the greatest part of the review, about 130 words, should be devoted to evaluation.

SAMPLE THEME

### The Homecoming and the Articulation of Silence: The Sound of One Hand Clapping

[1]        *The Homecoming* is in the tradition of the theater of the absurd. To some readers, this fact may suggest grotesque characters, maimed in body and soul, who reside in garbage cans and do very little or who live in never-never lands and do very little as they wait for other characters who never appear. It may also suggest that the inarticulateness of the characters and the static action may at play's end create muteness and puzzlement in the audience. To a great extent, *The Homecoming* (1965) by

Harold Pinter, *The Homecoming* (New York: Grove Press, 1965 and 1966).

the British dramatist Harold Pinter, shares these forbidding characteristics, but the play is also good theater; in fact, it is fascinating theater.
*It compels by virtue of its very inaction, and it reveals provocative insights
into modern life.*\* *To gain these insights, however, students of literature
must devote themselves to understanding Pinter's characters and his unusual
techniques and conventions, for once these are studied, the play becomes
richly suggestive and powerful.*†

[2]     The most dominating and pervasive character in the play is Max,
a seventy-year-old ex-butcher, whose drab London home serves as the
setting. Max is given no surname, an absence, like so many other ab-
sences in the play, that is part of Pinter's method to suggest the root-
lessness — the aimlessness and facelessness — of modern persons. The
namelessness both intrigues and alienates readers, for at the same time
that they come to know the characters intimately, they are aware of
how little they know about them and how much more they would like
to know. But Pinter nevertheless presents many intimate and fascinating details: Living with Max are two of his sons, Lenny and Joey, and
his sixty-three-year-old brother, Sam. Lenny is a sadist. Joey does de-
molition work during the day and is attempting a career as a professional boxer at night. Sam is a chauffeur and also, apparently, a
deviant personality (at least, Max thinks he has a deviant personality).
The play receives its name because Teddy, Max's lethargic eldest son,
who has become a professor of philosophy in America and has been
away for six years, returns home with his wife Ruth, a pensive woman
who formerly worked as a photographer's model.

[3]     One may expect no lessons in polite social behavior from such a set
of characters. Gracious they are not. All the veneer of civilization is
stripped away from them. It is almost as though Pinter has created the
bare human consciousness, the stream of thoughts and reflections that
are suppressed in ordinary human relationships, although they are nevertheless present. Here there are no artificial enthusiasms, no etiquette,
where no kindness is; or, where there is a conventionally polite or meaningless comment, it is inappropriate, and it merely underlies the uncon-
ventionality of the situation. Thus, when Teddy unexpectedly returns
home and is seen by Lenny, there is no warm greeting, no laughter, no
inquiry into the past six years of separation, no merriment, no cordiality;
there are only two minimally courteous but hollow "hullo's." Similarly,
Teddy walks calmly away from his wife without a word of goodbye or
reproach. Does the author suggest that human beings would behave thus
if they did not feel compelled to follow the conventions of polite society?
Is there a discrepancy between wishes and action, and if the two were
fused, would human beings be like the characters in *The Homecoming?* If
so, Pinter is presenting a revealing although not a happy truth about life.

[4]     The key to understanding the characters, in fact, and the cause for
their appeal despite their shortcomings as fully rounded human beings,
is that Pinter has made their behavior almost solely a function of their
thoughts. He has taken a simple human incident, and has apparently

\*Central idea.          †Thesis sentence.

asked this question about it: "What would happen under these circumstances if all the characters behaved exactly as they felt?" *The Homecoming* is his answer. The reader could easily envisage another set of matching incidents going on simultaneously, in which all the social graces would be causing the characters to behave conventionally. Much of the theatrical effectiveness of *The Homecoming* results from this unspoken but nevertheless real contrast between the stage action and the conventional action that might be expected under the same conditions.

[5]    One might pursue this avenue of speculation, for in the realm of suggestion and fantasy the play is a rich fabric of "could be's" and "might be's." The characters contribute to the richness of the play in many ways, one of these being their names. At the outset, we learn that Max is now old though once powerful, and this his brother "Uncle Sam," is tired after chauffering people around all day. Could this be taken as Pinter's observation that the roles of England and America as world powers are nearing their end? Similarly, there is temptation to inquire into the meaning of the Biblical names. The dead Jessie was Max's wife and mother of his sons. Biblically, Jesse was the grandson of Ruth and the father of King David, from whose line the Messiah was to derive. Samuel (Sam) was influential in selecting David as king. According to some views, Joseph (Joey) was the father of Jesus, but according to others, he was no more than the husband of Mary (in this play, Joey gets no "gravy"; if this fact is intended as a Biblical allusion, what bizarre humor!). All these relations are of course mixed up in *The Homecoming*, and the names, except for Jessie, are common enough (and Teddy and Lenny are nonBiblical names). Because of the discussion between Lenny and Teddy, however, and also because of the general spiritual drift of Pinter's characters, the names may very well be a means of enforcing the assertion that people in the twentieth century have lost their certainty. The heroes of Biblical times are a far cry from the antiheroes of today; the world is minimal, everywhere minimal.

[6]    The play's action is similarly minimal. It would be difficult to maintain that there is any action at all, as that word is usually understood, except for the brief violence at the end of the first act. The action in the second, concluding act involves not so much action as the development of an incredible scheme, hatched by the younger sons and the father, that involves Ruth. The most surprising action, which is the play's climax—if it has one—consists simply in Teddy's consenting to the scheme and his consequent departure. In short, the action is absurd.

[7]    This apparent senselessness or absurdity is also characteristic of other aspects of the play, the most obvious of which is Pinter's dialogue. The speech is sparse and laconic, interspersed with occasional rhapsodic outbursts as various characters become emotionally stimulated. Frequently the dialogue contains apparently illogical and irrelevant changes of subject, and in this regard it is perhaps more naturalistic than what appears in most other plays. Also realistic, in the sense of lifelike even though not "literary," are the many pauses that break up the speeches. These pauses are carefully written into the directions and on the stage would

[8]

certainly produce a slow-moving, monolithic pace. The pauses also underline the essential solitude of most of the characters. As a particular character speaks, and hears no response, he waits a moment, then goes on, but the effect is to show that the other characters, instead of forming a responsive audience, really are part of an indifferent and self-occupied universe. Once again, the dialogue suggests, what would people say if they spoke as they really felt?

Out of such characteristics of *The Homecoming* one may find the same suggestiveness, ambiguity, and beauty of traditional literature. Symbolically, here are people living without illusions, with their ties to tradition cut; they have no reverence, as Lenny says, for the unknown, no faith. Knowledge and philosophy have filtered into irrelevant and snobbish channels, as with Teddy, and present no chance for nourishing the desiccated plants of life. The significant pauses in the speeches dramatize the conflict between man, on the one hand, and nothingness, on the other. In the world of Max and his sullen sons, there is little if anything to fill up the void — a family group with no real internal loyalty but much hostility. Through these characters and their strange dialogue and behavior, Pinter suggests that many families are such in name only, and that many homes are no more than places where people live together. To come home to such a place is not to receive warmth or love or strength with which to face the world.

[9]

In fact, *The Homecoming* is very much like a sporting event in which the team one supports is losing, except that in the play there is no winner. We see no victors dashing down the field in glory, only characters in a perpetual pose, like the retreating Teddy, walking away from an increasing series of defeats. Certainly one cannot leave such a play in a mood of great cheer, but one must recognize that Pinter has created a world that is consistent with an important interpretation of modern life. There are many other diversionary pursuits that may provide the happy endings we enjoy witnessing, but Pinter's play is not one of these. As drama, *The Homecoming* successfully creates conflict, tension, and emotional release. As philosophy, it creates the perplexity that a great segment of humanity is feeling today. One cannot expect more from the theater.

★COMMENTARY ON THE THEME

The central idea of the review is that *The Homecoming* is a compelling play with provocative insights. The introduction relates the play to the movement of the theater of the absurd, and this relationship is stressed again in paragraph 6. Paragraphs 2, 3, 4, and 5 are devoted to the characters (one aspect of study indicated in the thesis sentence). Paragraph 2 describes the characters briefly, and paragraphs 3 and 4 consider their unusual behavior. Paragraph 5 treats the names of the characters as symbols. The second half of the body of the review, dealing with "unusual techniques and conventions," comprises paragraphs

6, 7, and 8. These respectively treat the unusual action, the unusual dialogue, and the relationship of the unusual characters and actions to more normal aspects of literature. The conclusion emphasizes again the compelling ability of the play to arouse speculation about the nature of modern life.

The audience proposed for reading this sample review is a general, not a specialized one. Therefore the review considers the play as it interests people generally concerned about life. Had the review been designed for, say, an audience of Catholics or Presbyterians, it might have related both the bleak view of the characters and their generally Biblical names to the Christian philosophies of these two groups. Similarly, if the review had been written for an audience of psychiatrists, it might have emphasized the detached, paranoid, and somewhat autistic personalities of some of the characters. Remember again, however, that unless you have a specialized audience in mind, you should direct your review to the general reader.

# 18

# *The Theme on Film*

FILM has today become the respected word for movies and motion pictures. It is a highly specialized kind of drama, utilizing, like drama, the techniques of dialogue, monologue, and action. Like drama also, it employs spectacle and pantomime. Unlike drama it embodies many additional techniques that are peculiarly a result of the technology of photography, editing, film development, and sound. If you are planning to write about film, many of your considerations may be purely literary, such as structure, tone, ideas, imagery, style. In addition, the techniques of film are so specialized—so much of an extension of what you normally see on a printed page—that a discussion of film requires more technical awareness than is normally needed by the disciplined reader.

## Film and Other Literary Forms

Film may be likened to a dramatic production. A typical production is a realization on stage of a dramatic text. The producer and director, together with actors, artists, scene designers, costume-makers, carpenters, choreographers, and lighting technicians, attempt to bring a dramatic text to life. Though occasionally a stage production may employ brief sections of film, slides, and tape recordings for special effects (e.g., the witches in *Macbeth,* the ghost in *Hamlet*), the stage itself limits the freedom of the production. Aside from budget, the makers of film have few such limitations. In this respect film is like the novel or the story, in which the absence of any restrictions beside the writer's imagination permits the inclusion of any detail whatever, from the description of a chase to the re-enactment of a scene in the Napoleonic wars. In reading, when you attempt to visualize a scene, you are using your imagination. When you look at a film, the film-maker has in effect provided you with a ready-made imagination. Is there to be a scene on a desert island? The film-maker has gone on location to such an island, and in the film presents the island itself, complete with beach, sand dunes, palm trees, native huts, and authentic natives-turned-actors. Little is left to your imagination. Is there to be a scene on a distant planet? Obviously the film-maker cannot go on location there, but a working location will be created in the studio, with lighting, props, and costumes. Film, in short, enables a dramatic production to achieve something approaching the complete freedom that one finds in novels and stories.

### Film and Art

To the degree that film is confined to a screen, it may visually be compared with the art of the painter or the still photographer. There is a whole language of visual art. Paintings and photographs have compositional balance. One object may appear in relationship to another as a background forces the eye upon a visual center of attention. A color used in one part of a painting may be balanced with the same color, or its complement, in another part of the painting. The use of certain details may have particularly symbolic significance. Paintings may become allegorical by including certain mythical figures or other objects in the background. Particular effects may be achieved with the use of the textures of the paint. The techniques and effects are virtually endless.

Still photographers have many of the same resources as painters, except that they cannot create quite the same textures with their cameras and their developers that painters can with their paints. Basically photographers transfer an image of reality to a finished print or slide. But they do have freedom of focus with their lenses, and can throw one object into focus while putting others out. They also have the freedom to select camera speeds, and can either stop an action at 1/1,000 a second, or let it remain blurred at 1/25 of a second. With the exacting control of developers, they can create many monochromatic, polychromatic, blurred, textured surfaces, and with techniques such as these they truly have a great deal of interpretive freedom in handling the initial photographic reality that is the basis of their art.

The film-maker is able to utilize almost all the resources of the still photographer, and most of those of the painter. Artistically, the most confining aspect of film is the rectangular screen, but aside from that, film is quite free. With a basis in a dramatic text called a "script" or "film-script," it employs words and their effects, but it also employs the language of art and especially the particular verisimilitude and effectiveness of moving pictures. In discussing a film, then, you should see that film communicates not just by words, but also by use of its unique and various techniques. You can treat the ideas, the problems, the symbolism in a film, but while treating them you should recognize that the visual presentation is inseparable from the medium of film itself.

## Techniques

There are many techniques of film, and a full description and documentation of them could, and has, become extensive.[1] In preparing to write a theme about film, however, you should try to familiarize yourself only with those aspects of technique that have an immediate bearing on your responses to the film and your interpretations of it. Film is both visual and audial.

### VISUAL

Camera technique permits great freedom in presenting scenes. If you are seeing a stage production of a play, your distance from the actors is fixed by your seat in the theater. In a film, on the other hand, the visual viewpoint is constantly shifting. The film may begin with a distant shot of the actors — a "longshot" — much like the sight you might have on a stage. But then the camera may zoom in or out to present you with a sudden closeup or panorama. Usually an actor speaking will be the subject of a closeup, but the camera may also show closeups of other actors who are reacting to the first actor's statements. You must decide on the effects of closeups and longshots yourself, but it should be plain that the frequent use of either — or of middle-distance photographs — is a means by which film directors specifically convey meaning.

The camera may also be moved rapidly, or slowly, from character to character, or from character to some natural or manufactured object. In this way a film may show a series of reactions to an event. It may also show visually the attitude of particular characters or it may represent a visual commentary on their actions. If a young couple is in love, as an example, the camera may shift from the couple to flowers, trees, and water, thus associating their love visually with objects of beauty and growth. Should the flowers be wilted, and the trees be without leaves, and the water brackish, the visual commentary might well be that the love is doomed and hopeless. Because characters are constantly seen in settings, real or symbolic, you should always be aware that the cinematic manipulation of setting is even more a part of the statement of

---

[1]See, for example, Rudolph Arnheim, *Film as Art* (Berkeley: University of California Press, 1969); Daniel Talbot, ed., *Film: An Anthology* (Berkeley: University of California Press, 1969); and Louis D. Giannetti, *Understanding Movies* (Englewood Cliffs, N.J.: Prentice-Hall, Inc., 1972).

the film than it might be in a story, in which even an alert reader may often lose awareness of such relationships.

The camera may also be used to create effects that no other medium can convey. Slow motion, for example, can focus on a certain aspect of a person's character. A girl running in slow motion happily through a meadow enables the viewer to concentrate on the possible joy conveyed by the slow rhythms of her body and the patterns of her dress and her hair. In Sydney Pollack's *They Shoot Horses, Don't They?* a sequence early in the film shows a horse with a broken leg being shot. This sequence is done in slow motion, a fact that has great significance at the end of the film when a young man with a slow-moving mind cooperates with a depressed young girl as she tries to commit suicide. It is clear that the shooting of the horse occurred when the young man was a child, and that the scene somehow has influenced him to pull the trigger when the girl asks him to. The slow-motion technique of both shootings is designed to show how they are linked in the young man's befuddled mind.

There are many other techniques of camera use and of editing that also have a bearing on action and character. The focus may be made sharp at one point, fuzzy at another. Moving speaking characters out of focus may suggest that their listeners are beginning to disregard them. The use of sharp or fuzzy focus may also visually show that characters have seen things exactly or inexactly. In an action sequence, the camera may follow moving characters, a technique that is called "tracking." It is possible to track from a car or truck, which may follow the movement of running human beings or horses, or the movement of cars. A camera operator on foot may be the tracker, or the camera may shoot movement from a helicopter or an airplane. Movement may also be captured by a fixed camera that follows a character from one point to another in panoramic view. Then, too, the camera may be held fixed and moving characters may simply walk, run, or ride across the screen. If they are moving in a car, the car may become blurred. For special comic effects, the film may be reversed in order to emphasize the illogicality of the actions being filmed. Reversing, of course, is a result of the developing, editing, and cutting process, which is a means by which film-makers can create many other visual effects, such as *fading* or *dissolving* from one scene to another, or superimposing one scene upon another.

The process of editing deserves special consideration, for it is the soul of the film-maker's art. A typical film is made up of many separate sequences, all put together during editing sessions. In one scene a character may be seen boarding a plane. Then there may be a scene showing the plane taking off, then flying. Then may follow a scene landing, followed by the character getting off the plane. The entire action may conclude with several different views of the character riding in a taxi to a specific destination. In the film, the whole sequence may take no more than half a minute, yet the episode may consist of perhaps a dozen separate views from the camera. It is editing that puts everything together. The camera records many views; the director selects from among these in creating a film.

## LIGHT, SHADOW, COLOR

As in the theater, the film-maker utilizes light, shadow, and color as a means of communication. Characters filmed in a bright light are presumably being examined fully, whereas characters in shadow or darkness may be hiding some of their motives. The use of flashing light might show a changeable, mercurial, and perhaps sinister character or situation. In color, the use of greenish-tinted light may suggest ghoulish motivations. Colors of course have much the same meaning that they have in any other artistic medium. Always, colors are carefully arranged. Like the stage director, the film-maker will arrange the blocking of the characters and scenery to create a pleasing arrangement and complementing of colors. However, clashing colors may be used to suggest a disharmony in the mind of one or several of the characters. Light may also be employed for similar effects. A scene in sunshine, which brings out all the colors, and the same scene in rain and clouds or in twilight, all of which mute the colors, create different moods.

## PANTOMIME AND ACTION

In film there are often many periods in which action takes place with no dialogue. The camera may show a man reacting to a situation, or a boy running through a woods, or a couple walking in a park. The scene may run on for several minutes, with all the footage being devoted to movement. Such wordless action is essentially *pantomime* rather than drama. To some degree, all actors employ pantomime by gesture and facial expression. In a dramatic production, pantomime is featured mainly as "business," and many dramas call for pageantry and swordplay. The unspoken devices of the stage are soon exhausted, however (unless the production happens to be ballet or actual pantomime), and any production must soon return to spoken dialogue. But in film there is great potentiality for rhapsodical focus on movement. In addition, musical accompaniments can be so interwoven with the action that dramatic statement can be rendered effectively without the use of the spoken word.

The strength of film has always been the portrayal of direct action. Love affairs, chases, trick effects, fights, ambushes, movement of all sorts—all these make an immediate appeal to the viewer's sense of reality. Actions of love and violence are immediately stimulating. Obviously one of the things you should look for in film is the effectiveness of the portrayal of the action: What is the relationship of the action to the theme of the film? Does the action have any bearing on the characters, or does it seem to have departed from character into an indulgence in action for its own sake? Is the action particularly realistic? Does the camera stay at a distance, showing the persons as relatively small in a vast natural or artificial world? Do closeups show smiles, frowns, eagerness, or anxiety? Is any attempt made to render temperature by action, say cold by characters' stamping their feet, or warmth by characters' removing their coats or shirts? Does the action show any changing of mood, from sadness to happiness, or from indecision to decision? What particular aspects of the action point toward these changes?

Closely related to the portrayal of action is the way in which the film shows the human body. The closeup is a technique for rendering certain aspects of the drama. Other methods, too, can be employed. A photograph showing an actor in complete proportion may be emphasizing the normality of that person, or it may show the views toward humanity of the film-maker. The film may also create certain distortions. The "fisheye" lens creates such a distortion, usually of the center of a face, which often shows a character's view of another character, or shows the film-maker's thoughts about a character. Sometimes the view creates bodily distortions, emphasizing certain limbs or other parts of the body, or focusing on a scolding mouth or a suspicious eye. If distortion is used, it invites interpretation: perhaps the film-maker is attempting to show that certain human beings, even when supposedly normal, bear weaknesses and even psychological disturbances.

### MONTAGE

Montage is to film as imagery is to literature; it may demonstrate a character's thoughts or dreams, or it may embody the director's commentary on situation or character. Physically, montage refers to an abrupt changing of scene, but it should be distinguished from a narrative change of scene and also from camera movement for narrative purposes. Exclusively a result of editing and therefore a unique property of film, montage provides commentary or illustration by association. For example, an early sequence in Sir Charles Chaplin's *Modern Times* shows a large group of workingmen rushing to their factory jobs. Immediately following this scene is a view of a large, milling herd of sheep. By this montage, Chaplin is suggesting that the men are being herded and dehumanized by modern industry. A similar effect is created at the opening of Nicolas Roeg's 1971 film *Walkabout*. A man is shown going to his job at the office; montage is then used to show a scene of a simple brick wall. The association suggests that the man has reached a psychological impasse; he is figuratively up against a wall and does not know where to turn. This montage prepares the viewer for a sequence early in the film, in which the man goes berserk and tries to kill his two children and himself. At the end of the film, the man's daughter is shown in her home, and again the brick wall is flashed on the screen to suggest that now she too has reached an impasse in her life.

While montage is different from a narrative change of scene, it may be used as a "flashback" to explain present, ongoing actions or characteristics. In this respect it retains its nature as a mode of commentary or explanation. Thus, characters suffering from amnesia may suddenly undergo brief recollections from their unremembered past, and these may be shown in brief, almost subliminal montages. A famous montage occurs in *Citizen Kane*, by Orson Welles. One of the final scenes shows the protagonist Kane's boyhood sled, which bore the brand name "Rosebud." This montage clarifies Kane's dying word by indicating that he still maintained a fond connection with the long-departed innocence of his youth.

### SOUND

The first business of the sound track in a film is naturally to include the spoken dialogue. But there are many other effects that become a part of the sound track. Music is selected to suit the mood of the film. Special sound effects are used to augment the action; the sound of a blow, for example, will be enhanced electronically in order to cause an impact on the viewer's ears that is similar to the force of the blow itself. If characters are engaged in introspection, muted strings may create a mellow sound to complement their mood. But if they are verging on a psychosis, the sound may become percussive and cacophonous. At times the sound may be placed through a mechanical appartus of some sort in order to create weird or ghostly effects. Often characters' words will be echoed rapidly and sickeningly in order to show their dismay or anguish. In a word, sound is a vital part of film. Once you leave the theater, or the television set if you have been watching the late show, it is difficult to remember all aspects of sound, say a certain melody that serves as mood or background to the action, but you should make the effort to observe some of the various uses to which the sound is put.

### Preparing Your Theme

Obviously the first requirement is to see a film. It is wise to see it twice or more if you can, because it is reasonable to assume that your discussion will take on value the more thoroughly you know the material. It is difficult to take notes in a darkened theater, but you should make an immediate effort, after leaving, to take notes on the various aspects of the film that impressed you. Take the program or write down the names of the director and the principal actresses and actors. Try to make your notes as complete as you can, for when you write your theme you will not be able to verify details and make illustrative quotations as you can with a written work that you can recheck. If any particular speeches were worth quoting from the movie, you should try to remember the general circumstances of the quotation, and also, if possible, any key words. Try to recall uses of costume and color, or (if the film was in black and white) particularly impressive uses of light and shade. An effort of memory will be required in writing a theme on film.

**Organizing Your Theme**

### INTRODUCTION

Here state your central idea and thesis sentence as usual. You should also include background information necessary for understanding what you will bring out in the body of your theme. It is appropriate to include here the names of the director, or director-producer, and the actresses and actors worthy in your judgment of particular mention.

### BODY

The most difficult choice that you will face in writing about film is deciding on a topic. If you have no other instructions, you might conveniently decide on subjects like those described in other chapters of this book—e.g., characterization, ideas, structure, problems. Remember, however, to widen your discussion of such topics to a consideration of the techniques of film as well as to the dialogue.

Then, too, you may choose to confine your attention to special cinematographic techniques, stressing their relationship to the theme of the film, their appropriateness, and their quality. If you have never paid particular attention to techniques of film or to photography, you might find some difficulties here. But if you concentrate on certain scenes, you may be able to recall enough to describe some of the techniques, particularly if you have helped yourself with good notes.

In judging a film you might also choose to emphasize the quality of the acting. How well did the actors adapt to the medium of film? How convincing were their performances? Did they possess good control over their facial expressions? Did their appearance lend anything to your understanding of the characters they portrayed? How well did they control bodily motion? Were they graceful? Awkward? Did it seem that the actors were genuinely creating their roles, or just reading through the parts?

Or you may wish to write a general review, bringing in all these various aspects that go into the total package that is the film. If you write a review, consult Chapter 17 for ideas on how to proceed.

## CONCLUSION

You might best conclude by evaluating the effectiveness of the cinematographic form to the story and to the idea. Were all the devices of film used in the best possible way? Was anything particularly overdone? Was anything underplayed? Was the film good, bad, or indifferent up to a point, and then did it change? Why? How? The development of answers to questions like these will be appropriate in the conclusion of your theme.

---

SAMPLE THEME

---

### Ingmar Bergman's *Virgin Spring*: An Affirmation of Complexity

[1]    *Virgin Spring,* a black-and-white film in Swedish with English subtitles, is directed by Ingmar Bergman and written by Ulla Isaksson. *It is a complex but affirmative rendering of an old Scandinavian folk tale.** It first appeared in 1960, and has been shown many times since by various film societies and clubs. It is well acted, with particularly strong performances by Max von Sydow as the father, Töre, and by Birgitta Pettersson as the daughter, Karin. The fabric of the film is woven of violence, horror, revenge, and mystery; against this background, however, there emerges a pattern of purpose and affirmation. On the surface the story of the film is simple enough. In medieval times a young girl is permitted to ride alone to the church to deliver candles, but on her way she is murdered by three herdsmen. The three men take her garments and ask shelter for the night at her home, where they try to sell the clothes to her parents. The father concludes that the three men have murdered his daughter, and he murders them in revenge. Going to recover his daughter's body, the father vows to build a church on the spot where she fell. When the body is removed, a spring of water gushes forth from the point where her head lay. *While the film could thus be regarded as an inspiring miracle play, designed to confirm religious faith, the impact of the characterization and cinematic techniques is that any faith, or any commitment whatsoever, is a difficult and sometimes self-contradictory struggle.†*

[2]    The characterization brings out the complexity. The servant girl, for example, is ostensibly a malcontent, a dark-haired figure of evil committed to Odin, the god of battles and death. She is to be contrasted with

---

*Central idea.    †Thesis sentence.

the fair-haired Karin, the daughter, who is a figure of goodness and purity. But the servant girl is not seen so simplistically, for she is shown as a menial whose freedom is restricted and whose potential beauty is useless. Desiring fine clothes and servants herself, she has nothing. Her approaching motherhood will not be accompanied by marriage. Her resentment, and her worship of the mysterious Odin, which presumably brings down disaster on the family she serves, are therefore not unmitigated evil but understandable responses to an undesirable condition. Her placing the frog in the bread loaf is not an act of evil, despite its consequences, but rather an extreme act of spitefulness, frustration, and disgust. Such complexity marks Bergman's uniquely modern handling of an old story.

[3]        The same complexity may be seen in Karin, the daughter. She is the sacrificial victim, and her ultimate death arouses the horror and indignation that one feels at seeing purposeless violence. But at her home, before she goes on her journey, she is shown with some of the haughtiness and spitefulness that characterize a spoiled person. She is vain, and she wheedles herself into favorable positions with her parents. Fussy, she will not go on the trip to church until her dress is just right. This is not to say that she is bad, but rather than she is human, not a figure of unqualified virtue, but one of human and therefore frail capacities. Perhaps this complexity lends even more pity to her destruction than if she had been shown as a simple figure on a tapestry.

[4]        The most complex characterization is that of the father, Herr Töre. It is Töre's lot to wreak vengeance on the three crazed herdsmen, and to make vows to build the church where his daughter was killed. Töre does not go easily to either task, however, for he performs a ritualistic cleansing before attacking the three men, and his regret and horror after his deed are made apparent. Similarly, his prayers alongside his daughter's corpse indicate his bewilderment, frustration, and incomprehension. His previous quiet, almost inarticulate manner is thus shown as covering greater, almost philosophic capabilities. He is a man thrust into situations that he cannot control or comprehend, and he tries to make his way as best he can. Of particular interest is his declaration of inability to understand God's ways. In view of this declaration his decision to build the church may be seen as a human commitment, a compromise solution, rather than an ordinary memorial act of devotion.

[5]        While these characterizations are important in illustrating the complexity of Bergman's treatment of the tale, the film's major strength is in the direction and in the filming. It was clearly Bergman's intention to dramatize through photography the complex, ambiguous, mysterious forces that swirl around the centers of human motivation. In what is in effect the epigraph of the film, for example, Bergman photographs the servant girl from above as she calls on Odin to assist her. This downward view conditions our subsequent attitudes toward the girl. When she meets the gnomic man in the woods, however, even she demonstrates uneasiness at the grotesque, distorted forces portrayed by the man. The same kind of mad force is suggested in the actions of the three herdsmen when they first see Karin riding through the woods. Their attitudes are

captured on film by an increasingly irrational and depraved set of actions, augmented by the closeups of the bizarre mute herdsman when he tries to speak. Even so, their violence is restrained until the frog is discovered in the bread. Here the forces that were enveloping the servant girl are unleashed on the herdsmen, for the appearance of the frog triggers their uncomprehending violence on the girl.

[6]     Such forces can be suppressed only by much greater, if equally vague, forces, and it is here that Bergman gains the utmost from camera and light. Clearly his views of Karin riding along the shore of the lake show beauty and innocence, but inability to control evil. Karin is clothed in light, and her horse is white. The lake is clear, and the scene is one of beauty. By contrast, when Bergman focuses the camera on Töre before the vengeance scene, he portrays a more complex and powerful set of forces. First, Töre is at the gate when the three herdsmen approach; he is in darkness and appears as a stolid, guardian-like figure. Later, Bergman shows him tearing up a young tree in preparation for his ritualistic bath and switching. Bergman in this scene captures a sense that Töre gathers strength directly from the earth. The scene is portrayed as a union of humanity, earth, and sky, in a vague, ghastly light, as though the forces conducing to rightness are equally as vast, as vague, and as ambiguous as those leading to evil.

[7]     In the face of this ambiguity, the virgin spring itself is to be seen as an affirmation of the difficulty and mystery of life. Bergman emphasizes the beauty of the gushing water in both sight and sound. It would be easy to accept this water as a new birth, a sign that horror and sacrifice are over. But it seems more reasonable, in view of the main actions of the film, to see the spring as a sign that there is value in making an effort to overcome hostile forces. The spring, like the tree, gives strength, and both come from the earth, which is shown throughout by Bergman as hill, vale, mud, and shore. As a symbol, the spring cannot guarantee that hostile forces can ever be eliminated, or that horror and violence can be stopped. The future will hold many reenactments of just such situations as Karin encounters on her innocent journey. But if persons like Töre make the commitment and the effort, evil at least will not prevail.

[8]     It is clear that Bergman has done well with a good script. At first one might wonder at the extent of Karin's preparations before her journey, but as the tale unfolds it may be seen that this preparation serves (a) to establish involvement with her character, and (b) to show her clothing, which later on becomes convincing evidence that the three herdsmen have murdered her. Similarly, the extensive movement of the three herdsmen when they first see Karin, which may seem unnecessary, creates an impression of their sinister irrationality. Logically, there is nothing done to excess, nor is there anything wanting in the film. In just about every technical matter from acting to photography and to editing, *Virgin Spring* is a major achievement in the art of the film.

★COMMENTARY ON THE THEME

Paragraph 1 gives essential background material about the film. It also includes a brief summary of the story.

In keeping with the first point of the thesis sentence, paragraphs 2, 3, and 4 discuss the characters. There is not much difference between these discussions and those that could be carried out for a story, novel, or play. The main difference is that the actions and decisions of the characters are all drawn from observation of the film, not from descriptions in a printed text. Paragraphs 5, 6, and 7 discuss the second aspect of the thesis sentence, namely Bergman's cinematic techniques. Paragraph 5 emphasizes camera angle and closeups. Paragraph 6 draws attention to the uses of light. Paragraph 7 treats the visual symbols of water and earth. The concluding paragraph evaluates the film in the light of Bergman's integration of scene and action.

# Taking Examinations
# on Literature

TAKING AN EXAMINATION on literature is not difficult if you prepare in the right way. Preparing means (1) studying the material assigned, studying the comments made in class by your teacher and by fellow students in discussion, and studying your own thoughts; (2) anticipating the questions by writing some of your own on the material to be tested and by writing practice answers to these questions; and (3) understanding the precise function of the test in your education.

You should realize that the test is not designed to plague you or to hold down your grade. The grade you receive is in fact a reflection of your achievement at a given point in the course. If your grades are low, you can probably improve them by studying in a coherent and systematic way. Those students who can easily do satisfactory work might do superior work if they improve their method of preparation. From whatever level you begin, you can improve your achievement by improving your method of study.

Your teacher has three major concerns in evaluating your tests (assuming literate English): (1) to see the extent of your command over the subject material of the course ("How good is your retention?"), (2) to see how well you are able to think about the material ("How well are you educating yourself?"), and (3) to see how well you can actually respond to a question or address yourself to an issue. This last point is preeminently important. If the question begins "Why does . . ." be sure to explain *why* the subject indeed *does*; do not just describe *what* is *done*. If you are asked to describe the organization of a literary work, be sure to describe the *organization*. Remember that a principal cause of low grades on exams is that many students do nothing but retell the story, without ever answering the questions asked. Look at the questions carefully, and answer them, trying always to deal with the issues in them. In this way, you can ensure success on your exam.

## Preparation

Your problem now is how to prepare yourself best to have a knowledgeable and ready mind at examination time. If you simply cram facts into your head for the examination in hopes that you will be able to adjust to whatever questions are asked, you will likely flounder.

Above all, keep in mind that your preparation should begin not on the night before the exam but as soon as the course begins. When each assignment is given, you should complete it by the date due, for you will understand your teacher's comments and the classroom discussion only if you know the material being discussed. Then, about a week before the exam, you should review each assignment, preferably rereading each assignment completely. With this preparation completed, your study on the night before the exam will be fruitful, for it might be viewed as a climax of preparation, not the entire preparation itself.

Go over your notes, referring constantly to passages from the text that were mentioned and studied in class by your teacher. A good idea is to memorize as many significant phrases from the passages as possible; then when you are writing your exam your knowledge of a small quotation from the text shows your teacher that you have a good knowledge of the material. As you study, it is good to think not only about main ideas but also about technical matters, such as organization and style. Any time you have a reference in your notes (or in your memory) to technical problems, observe or recall carefully what your teacher said about them, and about their relationship to ideas. Technique is always related to ideas, and if you show understanding of both, your exam is likely to be successful.

Your final preparation should consist of more than rereading your notes and reexamining key passages from the text. It should also contain writing and thinking, and here your ability to plan and practice your own questions and answers will be of great assistance. Make up some questions; perhaps you might rephrase a sentence from your notes into a question. Here is a brief fragment from some classroom notes on the subject of Dryden's *Absalom and Achitophel:* "A political poem — unintelligible unless one knows the politics of the time." Your sample question from this fragment might be: "Why is *Absalom and Achitophel* unintelligible without an understanding of the politics of the time?" Then you could spend fifteen or twenty minutes answering this question. Or you might look over a key passage from the text, decide what its subject is, and ask questions like "What does X say about _____ subject?" and "What is the effect of _____ in _____ ?" Spend as much time as possible in this way, making practice questions and answers on ideas and also on technique.

Let us try an example. Suppose you are reading Browning's "My Last Duchess." You might ask, "Why did the Duke give orders to have his former wife killed?" As you are writing an answer you would realize that the question is difficult and ambiguous: *why* applies either to the reasons given by the Duke or to the conclusions you yourself have made. You might, as a result, recast the question into two: (1) "What reasons does the Duke reveal for having given the orders to kill his wife?" and (2) "What, in your opinion, are the reasons for which the Duke gave these orders?" You could then write a satisfactory answer to either one of these questions separately, or could make them two parts of the original question. From problems like these you would gain experience not only in asking, answering, and organizing questions, but in knowing that the phrasing of questions is important.

Your questions may be of all types. You might study the organization of a work carefully and then ask yourself about that organization. Or you might become interested in a certain character and wish to practice on a question asking for an analysis of that character. Time spent in this way can never be wasted, for as you carry on your practice *you are in fact studying with great care.* In addition, this practice will surely make the examination less of a surprise to you than it would be otherwise. The less you are surprised, the better will be your performance. Possibly you could even anticipate the questions your teacher might ask.

Sometimes another view can augment your own understanding of the material to be tested. If you find it possible to study with a fellow student, both of you can benefit from discussing what was said in class. In view of the necessity for steady preparation throughout a course, keep in mind that regular conversations (over soda or some other beverage to your taste) well in advance of the examination are a good idea.

There are two types of questions that you will find on any examination about literature. Keep them in mind as you prepare. The first type is *factual,* or *mainly objective,* and the second is *general, comprehensive, broad,* or *mainly subjective.* In an English class, however, very few questions are purely objective, except possibility for multiple-choice questions.

### Factual Questions

MULTIPLE-CHOICE QUESTIONS.   These are the most purely factual questions. In an English class, your teacher will most likely reserve them for short quizzes, usually on days when an assignment is due, as a self-assurance that you are keeping up with the reading. Multiple choice can test your knowledge of facts, and it also can test your ingenuity in perceiving subtleties of phrasing in certain choices, but on a literature exam this type of question is rare.

IDENTIFICATION QUESTIONS. These questions are decidedly of more interest. They test not only your factual knowledge but also your ability to relate this knowledge to your understanding of the work assigned. This type of question will frequently be used as a check on the depth and scope of your reading. In fact, an entire exam could be composed of only identification questions, each demanding perhaps five minutes to write. Typical examples of what you might be asked to identify are:

1. *A Character,* for example, Maria in Joyce's short story "Clay." You would try to indicate her position, background, her importance in the story, and especially her significance in Joyce's design. You should always emphasize the second part, for it shows your understanding.

2. *Incidents,* which may be described as follows: "A woman refuses to go on tour with a traveling show" (assuming that either *Sister Carrie* by Dreiser or *The Big Money* by Dos Passos is being tested). After you locate the incident, try to demonstrate its *significance* in the story's main design.

3. *Things.* Your teacher may ask you to identify, say, an "overcoat" (Gogol's "Overcoat"), or "spunk water" (*Tom Sawyer*), or some other significant object.

4. *Quotations.* Theoretically, you should remember enough of the text to identify a passage taken from it, or at least to make an informed guess. Generally, you should try to locate the quotation, if you remember it, or else to describe the probable location, and to show the ways in which the quotation is typical of the work you have read, with regard to both content and style. You can often salvage much from a momentary lapse of memory by writing a reasoned and careful explanation of your guess, even if the guess is incorrect.

TECHNICAL AND ANALYTICAL QUESTIONS AND PROBLEMS. In a scale of ascending importance, the third and most difficult type of factual question is on those matters with which this book has been concerned: technique, analysis, and problems. You might be asked to discuss the *structure, tone, point of view,* or *principal idea* of a work; you might be asked about a *specific problem;* you might be asked to analyze a poem that may or may not be duplicated for your benefit (if it is not duplicated, woe to the student who has not read the assignments well). Questions like these are difficult, because they usually assume that you have a fairly technical knowledge of some important terms, while they also ask you to examine the text quite rigidly within the limitations imposed by the terms.

Obviously, technical questions will occur more frequently in advanced courses than in general ones, and the questions will become more subtle as the courses become more advanced. Teachers of general courses may frequently use main-idea or special-problem questions but will probably not use many of the others unless they specifically state their intentions to do so in advance, or unless technical terms have been studied in class.

Questions of this type are fairly long, perhaps with from fifteen to twenty-five minutes allowed for each. If you have two or more of these questions to write, try to space your time sensibly; do not devote 80 per cent of your time to one question and leave only 20 per cent for the rest.

## BASIS OF JUDGING FACTUAL QUESTIONS

In all factual questions, literate English being assumed, your teacher is testing (1) your factual command, and (2) your quickness in relating a part to the whole. Thus, suppose that you are identifying the incident "A woman refuses to go on tour with a traveling show." You would identify Sister Carrie as the woman, and say that she is advised by her friend Lola to stay in New York (where the big opportunity is) and not to go on tour, where nobody important will see her. You would also try to show that the incident occurs when Carrie is just a minor dancer, during her early years in show business. But, you should, more importantly, show that her decision leaves her in New York, where a new opportunity develops, quickly enabling Carrie to become a star. You should conclude by saying that the incident prepares the way for all Carrie's later successes and shows how far she has advanced above Hurstwood's deteriorating state, monetarily speaking. The incident can therefore be seen as one of the most significant in the entire novel.

Your answers should all take this general pattern. Always try to show the *significance* of the things you are identifying. *Significance* of course works in many directions, but in a short identification question you should always try to refer to (1) major events in the book, (2) major ideas, (3) the structure of the work, and (4) in a quotation, the style. Time is short; therefore you must be selective, but if you can set your mind toward producing answers along these lines, you will probably approach what your teacher expects.

Here are three answers that were written to an identification question. The students were asked to identify "The thing which was not," from the fourth voyage of Swift's *Gulliver's Travels*.

*Answer 1.* This quotation serves as an example of a typical saying in the language of the Houyhnhnms. It means that the thing was false. It shows their roundabout method of saying things.

*Answer 2.* This quotation is found in Chapter IV of "A Voyage to the Country of the Houyhnhnms." Gulliver is told this by his Master, one of the Houyhnhnms (a horse). It is brought out when the two of them are discussing their own customs and culture, and Gulliver is telling his Master how he sailed over to this country. The Master finds it hard to believe. He tells Gulliver that lying is altogether foreign to the culture of the Houyhnhnms. He says speech is for the purpose of being understood and he cannot comprehend lying and is unfamiliar with doubt. He goes on to say that if someone says "the thing which was not" the whole end of speech is defeated. I think what the Master has said to Gulliver clearly illustrates Swift's thought that people should use language as a means to communicate truth or otherwise its purpose is defeated. We can also see Swift's thought that this very beautiful concept of language and its use is not taken up by people. This degrades humanity.

*Answer 3. The thing which was not,* a variation on *"is* not," is used throughout the fourth voyage of *Gulliver* by the Houyhnhnm Master as a term for lying—telling a thing contrary to fact. The term is interesting because it shows a completely reasonable reaction (represented by that of the Houyhnhnm Master) toward a lie, with all the subtle variations on the word we have in English. By whatever term we use, a lie is *a thing which is not* (except in the mind of the person who tells it) and destroys the chief end of speech—truthful communication. The term is therefore an integral part of Swift's attack in *Gulliver* on the misuse of reason. A lie misleads the reason, and thereby destroys all the processes of reason (e.g., logic, science, law) by supplying it with nonexistent things. Because our civilization depends on the reasonable pursuit of truth, a lie about anything is thus actually an attack on civilization itself. Swift's Houyhnhnms have this value, then, that they provide us with a reasonable basis for judging elements in our own life, and for improving them where reason can improve them.

The first answer is not satisfactory, since it is inaccurate in sentences 1 and 3, and does not indicate much thought about the meaning of the quotation. The second answer is satisfactory; despite faults of style, it shows knowledge of the conditions under which the quotation is delivered, and also indicates some understanding of the general meaning of the quotation. The third answer is superior, for it relates the quotation to Swift's satiric purposes in *Gulliver's Travels* and also shows how lying actually becomes a perversion of language and reason. The distinguishing mark of the third answer is that it shows *thorough* understanding.

One thing is clear from these sample answers: *really superior answers cannot be written if your thinking originates entirely at the time you are faced with the question;* the more thinking and practicing you do before the exam, the better your answers will be. Obviously the writer of the third answer was not caught unprepared. You should reduce surprise on an exam to an absolute minimum.

The more extended factual questions also require more thoroughly developed organization. Remember that here your knowledge of essay writing is important, for the quality of your composition will inevitably determine perhaps a major share of your teacher's evaluation of your answers. It is therefore best to take several minutes to gather your thoughts together before you begin to write, because a ten-minute planned answer is preferable to a twenty-five minute unplanned answer. Surprising as this idea may seem, you do not need to write down every possible fact on each particular question. Of greater significance is the use to which you put facts you know and the organization of your answer. When the questions are before you, use a sheet of scratch paper to jot down the facts you remember and your ideas about them in relation to the question. Then put them together, phrase a thesis sentence, and use your facts to illustrate or prove your thesis.

It is always necessary, particularly when you are dealing with "problem" questions, to work key phrases from the original questions into your thesis sentence. Let us suppose that you are given the question: "What are some reasons for which Dick Diver loses his professional abilities and consequently drifts into oblivion?" (Fitzgerald's *Tender is the Night*). Your answer might begin in the following way: "Dick Diver loses his professional abilities for many reasons. Fitzgerald suggests that many of his energies are taken up by Nicole, but I believe that a more comprehensive reason is the paralysis of his self-esteem resulting from his superficial life among the international set. . . ." Presumably, your answer would then proceed to discuss the view you attribute to Fitzgerald and then your own. Notice that your first sentence clearly states the aims and limits of the answer, so that your answer will be completely self-contained. Whatever your method, however, do not simply start writing without reference to the question, for if the first sentence does not describe the answer to follow, teachers will probably feel that they are reading the answer in a vacuum. Your best approach to tests is to regard each answer as a small essay, demanding good writing, thinking, and organizing.

For comparison, here are two paragraphs from a twenty-five minute question on Fitzgerald's story "The Rich Boy." The question was: "What do Anson's two love affairs contribute to your understanding of his character?" Both paragraphs are about Anson's first love affair, with Paula Legendre:

| 1 | 2 |
|---|---|
| The Paula affair helps understand Anson. Paula best understood him through their relationship. Anson was searching for stability and security in life; he felt he could achieve these with Paula. This was shown through the following idea: if only he could be with Paula he would be happy. Paula saw him as a mixture | To show that Anson has a dual nature, Fitzgerald develops the Paula Legendre episode at great length. Paula represents everything that Anson's reliable side needs: conservatism, equality of social and economic position, earnestness of purpose, and love. Presumably, the lengthy, low conversations between the two are |

of solidity and self-indulgence and cynicism. She deeply loved him, but it was impossible for him to form a lasting relationship with her. The reason for this was his drinking, and his code of superiority. This was shown in the fact that he felt hopeless despair before his pride and his self-knowledge. His superiority can be further observed through his physical and emotional relationship with Paula. His entire relationship with Paula was based on his feelings that emotion was sufficient, and why should he commit himself? Her marriage greatly affected Anson; it made a cynic out of him. His attitude toward women influenced his relationship with Dolly, too.

presented to illustrate the positive, substantial character of Anson. But Fitzgerald is also illustrating the weakness of Anson's character—a weakness that he brings out by the relationship with Paula. As a result of a lifelong position of unchallenged wealth and status, without any real responsibility, Anson has developed into a man of shallow and superficial emotions, even though he *knows*, consciously, what mature emotions are. Thus, he cannot face the responsibility of marriage with Paula: he gets drunk and embarrasses her; he delays proposing marriage at the logical moment in the magic of love and moonlight, and therefore he lets Paula's mood vanish forever into the night. When Paula, who despite her wealth is more stable than Anson, marries another man, Anson's serious side is deeply disturbed, but his superficial side is made happy. Unfortunately, this division has made him a perpetual child, unable to cope with adult life. These same characteristics are also enforced by Fitzgerald in the affair with Dolly Karger.

It is easy to see that Column 2 is superior to Column 1. If Column 1 were judged as part of an outside-class theme, it would be a failure, but as part of a test it would probably receive a passing grade. Column 2 is clearer; it develops its point well and uses evidence more accurately to illustrate its point.

## General or Comprehensive Questions

General or comprehensive questions are particularly important on final examinations, when your teacher is interested in testing your total comprehension of the course material. You have much freedom of choice in deciding what to write, but you must constantly bear in mind that your teacher is looking for intelligence and knowledge in what you choose to say.

Considerable time is usually allowed for answering a comprehensive question, perhaps a full forty-five minutes, depending on the scope and depth that your teacher expects. The question may be phrased in a number of ways:

1. A direct question asking about philosophy, underlying attitudes, "schools" of literature or literary movements, main ideas, characteristics of style, backgrounds, and so on. Here are some typical questions in this category: "Define and characterize Metaphysical poetry," or "Discuss the influences of science on literature in the Restoration," or "Describe the dramatic prose of the Jacobean dramatists."

2. A "comment" question, usually based on an extensive quotation, borrowed from a critic or written by your teacher for the occasion, about a broad class of writers, or about a literary movement, or the like. Your teacher may ask you to treat this question broadly (taking in many writers) or may ask you to apply the quotation to a specific writer.

3. A "suppose" question, such as "Suppose Rosalind were in Desdemona's place; what would she do when Othello accused her of infidelity?" or "What would Pope say about Joyce's *Ulysses?*"

### BASIS OF JUDGING GENERAL QUESTIONS

In dealing with a broad, general question you are in fact dealing with an unstructured situation, and you yourself not only must supply an *answer* but—almost more important—must also create a *structure* within which your answer can have meaning. You might say that you make up your own question, which will be derived from the original, broadly expressed question. If you were asked to "Consider Shakespeare's thoughts about the ideal monarch," for example, you would do well to structure the question by narrowing its limits. A possible narrowing might be put as follows: "Shakespeare dramatizes thoughts about the ideal monarch by setting up a contrast between, on one side, monarchs who fail either by alienating their close supporters or by becoming tyrannical, and, on the other side, monarchs who succeed by securing faithful supporters and by creating confidence in themselves." With this sort of focus, you would be able to proceed point by point, introducing supporting data as you went. Without such a structure, you would experience difficulty.

As a general rule, the best method to adopt in answering a comprehensive question is that of comparison-contrast. The reason is that it is very easy in dealing with, say, a general question on Yeats, Eliot, and Auden to write *three* separate essays rather than one. Thus, you should force yourself to consider a topic like "The Treatment of Alienation," or "The Attempt to Find Truth," and then to treat such a topic point by point rather than author by author. If you were answering the question posed on Shakespeare's thoughts about the ideal monarch, you might try to show the failures of Richard II and Richard III against the successes of Henry IV and Henry V. It would also be relevant to introduce, by way of comparison and contrast, references to Antony, and even to King Lear or to Prospero (from *The Tempest*). By moving from point to point, you would bring in these references as they are germane to your topic. But if you treated each figure separately, your comprehensive answer would become diffuse and ineffective. For further ideas on this method, see Chapter 10.

In judging your response to a general question, your instructor is interested in seeing: (1) how intelligently you select material, (2) how well you organize your material, (3) how adequate and intelligent are the generalizations you make about the material, and (4) how relevant are the facts you select for illustration.

Bear in mind that in comprehensive questions, though you are ostensibly free, the freedom you have been extended has been that of creating your own structure. The underlying idea of the comprehensive, general question is that you, personally, possess special knowledge and insights that cannot be discovered by more factual questions. You must therefore try to formulate your own responses to the material and to introduce evidence that reflects your own particular insights and command of information.

# B

# *A Note on Documentation*

THIS NOTE does not attempt to present a complete discussion of documentation, but only as much as is necessary for typical themes about literature. You will find complete discussions in most writing handbooks and guidebooks to research, and in the latest edition of the *MLA Style Sheet*. Whenever you are in doubt about documentation, always ask your teacher.

In any writing not derived purely from your own mind, you must document your facts. In writing about literature, you must base your conclusions on material in particular literary works, and must document this material. If you refer to secondary sources, you must be especially careful to document your facts. To document properly you must use illustrative material in your discussion and mention your sources either in your discussion or in footnotes to it.

### Integration and Mechanics of Quotations

Ideally your themes should reflect your own thought as it is prompted and illustrated by an author's work. Sometimes a problem arises, however, because it is hard for your reader to know when *your* ideas have stopped and your *author's* have begun. You must therefore arrange things to make the distinction clear, but you must also create a constant blending of materials that will make your themes easy to follow. You will be moving from paraphrase, to general interpretation, to observation, to independent application of everything you choose to discuss. It is not always easy to keep these various elements integrated. Let us see an example in which the writer moves from a reference to an author's ideas — really paraphrase — to the writer's own independent application of the idea:

[1] In the "Preface to the Lyrical Ballads," Wordsworth stated that the language of poetry should be the same as that of prose.    [2] That is, poetic diction should not be artificial or contrived in any sense, but should consist of the words normally used by people in their everyday lives (pp. 791–93).    [3] If one follows this principle in poetry, then it would be improper to refer to the sun as anything but *the sun*.    [4] To call it a *heavenly orb* or the *source of golden gleams* would be inadmissible because these phrases are not used in common speech.

Here the first two sentences present a paraphrase of Wordsworth's ideas about poetic diction, the second going so far as to locate a particular spot where the idea is developed. The third and fourth sentences apply Wordsworth's idea to examples chosen by the writer. Here the blending is provided by the transitional clause, "If one follows this principle," and the reader is thus not confused about who is saying what.

Sometimes you will use short quotations from your author to illustrate your ideas and interpretations. Here the problem of distinguishing your thoughts from the author's is solved by quotation marks. In this sort of internal quotation you may treat prose and poetry in the same way. If a poetic quotation extends from the end of one line to the beginning of another, however, indicate the line break with a virgule (/), and use a capital letter to begin the next line, as in the following:

Wordsworth states that in his boyhood all of nature seemed like his own personal property. Rocks, mountains, and woods were almost like food to him, and he claimed that "the sounding cataract / Haunted . . . [him] like a passion" (76–80).

Making internal quotations still creates the problem of blending materials, however, for quotations should never be brought in unless you prepare your reader for them in some way. Do not, for example, bring in quotations in the following manner:.

The sky is darkened by thick clouds, bringing a feeling of gloom that is associated with the same feeling that can be sensed at a funeral. "See gloomy clouds obscure the cheerful day."

This abrupt quotation throws the reader off balance. It is better to prepare the reader to move from the discourse to the quotation, as in the following revision:

The scene is marked by sorrow and depression, as though the spectator, who is asked to "See gloomy clouds obscure the cheerful day," is present at a funeral.

Here the quotation is made an actual part of the sentence. This sort of blending is satisfactory provided the quotation is brief.

The standard should be not to quote within your own sentence any passage longer than twenty or twenty-five words. Quotations of greater length demand so much separate attention that they interfere with your own sentence. When your quotation is long, you should set it off separately, remembering to introduce it in some way. It is possible but not desirable to have one of your sentences conclude with an extensive quotation, but you should never make an extensive quotation in the middle of your sentence. By the time you finish such an unwieldy sentence your reader will have lost sight of how it began.

The physical layout of extensive quotations should be as follows: Leave three blank lines between your own discourse and the quotation. Single-space the quotation and make a special indention for it to set it off from the rest of your theme. After the quotation leave a three-line space again and resume your own discourse. Here is a specimen, from a theme about John Gay's *Trivia*, an early eighteenth-century poem:

> In keeping with this general examination of the anti-heroic side of life, Gay takes his description into the street, where constant disturbance and even terror were normal conditions after dark. A person trying to sleep was awakened by midnight drunkards, and the person walking late at night could be attacked by gangs of thieves and cutthroats who waited in dark corners. The reality must have been worse than Gay implies in his description of these sinister inhabitants of the darkened streets:
>
> > Now is the time that rakes their revels keep;
> > Kindlers of riot, enemies of sleep.
> > His scattered pence the flying Nicker flings,
> > And with the copper shower the casement rings.
> > Who has not heard the Scourer's midnight fame?
> > Who has not trembled at the Mohock's name?
> > —lines 321–326
>
> Gay mentions only those who have "trembled" at the Mohocks, not those who have experienced their brutality.

This same layout applies also when you are quoting prose passages. When quoting lines of poetry, always remember to quote them as lines; do not run them together. When you set off the quotation by itself as in the example above, you do not need quotation marks.

Whether your quotation is long or short, you will often need to change some of the material in it to conform to your own thematic requirements. You might wish to omit something from the quotation that is inessential to your point. Indicate such omissions with three spaced periods ( . . . ), but if your quotation is very brief, do not use spaced periods as they might be more of a hindrance than a help. See, for example, the absurdity of using spaced periods in a sentence like this one:

Keats asserts that ". . . a thing of beauty . . ." always gives joy.

If you add words of your own to integrate your quotation into your own train of discourse, or to explain words that may seem obscure, put square brackets around these words, as in the following passage:

> In the "Tintern Abbey Lines," Wordsworth refers to a trance-like state of illumination, in which the "affections gently lead . . . [him] on." He is unquestionably describing a state of extreme relaxation, for he mentions that the "motion of . . . human blood [was] / Almost suspended [his pulse slowed]" and that in these states he became virtually "a living soul" (lines 42–49).

Always reproduce your source exactly. Because most high school anthologies and texts modernize the spelling in works that are old, you may never see any old-spelling editions. But if you use an un-modernized text, as in many advanced courses, duplicate everything exactly as you find it, even if this means spelling words like *domestic* as *domestick* or *joke* as *joak*. A student once modernized the word *an* in the construction "an I were" in an Elizabethan text, spelling it *and.* Thus created a mistake, for the *an* really meant *if.* Mistakes like this one are rare, but you will avoid all such problems if you simply reproduce the text as you find it.

A word of caution: Do not use too many quotations. Always remember that you will be judged on the basis of your own thought, and on the continuity and development of your own theme. Concentrate on that, and use quotations only for illustration.

## Formal Documentation

It is essential to acknowledge any source from which you have derived factual or interpretive information. If you fail to grant recognition, you run the risk of being challenged for representing as your own the results of other people's work. To indicate the source of all derived material, you must, formally, use footnotes at the bottom of your page or at the end of your theme, or, informally, embody some form of recognition in the body of your paper. Although the care necessary for noting book titles and page numbers can be annoying, you should realize that footnotes and informal references exist to help your readers. First, your readers may want to consult your source in order to assure themselves that you have not misstated any facts. Second, they may dispute your conclusions and wish to see your source in order to arrive at their own conclusions. Third, they may become so interested in one of your points that they might wish to read more about it for their own pleasure or edification. For these reasons, you must show the source of all material that you use.

If you are using many sources in a research report, the standard method is to document your paper formally. The procedures discussed here will be sufficient for most papers requiring formal documentation. For especially difficult problems, consult the *MLA Style Sheet*, latest edition, or the section on documentation in your writing handbook.

The first time you quote from a source, or refer to the source, you should provide a footnote giving the following information in the order listed below.

### FOR A BOOK

1. The author's name, first name or initials first.
2. The title: in quotation marks for a story or poem; underlined for a book.
3. The edition (if indicated), abbreviated thus: *2nd ed., 3rd ed.*, etc.
4. The name of the editor or translator. Abbreviate "editor" or "edited by" as *ed.*; "editors" as *eds.* Use *trans.* for "translator" or "translated by."
5. The publication facts should be given in parentheses in the following order:
   (a) City of publication, followed by a colon (the state need not be included unless the city might be confused with another).
   (b) Publisher. This information is frequently not given, but it is wise to include it.[1]
   (c) Year of publication.
6. The page number(s), for example, *p. 65, pp. 65f., pp. 6–10*. For books commonly reprinted (like *Gulliver's Travels*) and for well-known long poems (like *Paradise Lost*) you should include the chapter or part number and the line numbers, so that readers using a different edition may be able to locate your quotation.

### FOR A MAGAZINE ARTICLE

1. The author, first name or initials first.
2. The title of the article, in quotation marks.
3. The name of the magazine, underlined.
4. The volume number, in Arabic numerals (no longer Roman).
5. The year of publication, within parentheses.
6. The page number(s), for example, *65, 65f., 6–10.* (It is not necessary to include *p.* or *pp.* when you have included the volume number of the periodical.)

To prepare for subsequent footnotes, mention at the end of the

---

[1] If faced with a choice, some editors prefer citing the publisher rather than the city of publication, on the assumption that several publishers in cities like London or New York will often have published editions of the same work. For identification purposes, citing the publisher is therefore more helpful than citing the city, but as yet this practice has not been widely adopted. Ask your instructor about his preferences, and be guided by his advice.

first footnote that you will hereafter use a shortened reference to the source, such as the author's last name, or the title of the work, or some abbreviation, according to your preference. This practice is illustrated in the sample footnotes below.

Footnotes may be positioned either at the bottom of each page (separated from the text by a line) or else at the end of the theme in a list. Some instructors request that each footnote go right into the text at the appropriate position, with lines setting the footnote apart from the text. Ask your instructor about the practice you should adopt.

The first line of a footnote should be paragraph indented, and continuing lines should be flush with the left margin of your theme. Footnote numbers are positioned slightly above the line. Generally, you may single-space footnotes unless you are preparing your paper for publication. Then, double-spacing is usually preferable. Once again, however, ask your instructor about how to proceed.

### SAMPLE FOOTNOTES

In the examples below, book titles and periodicals, which are usually italicized in print, are shown underlined, as they would be in your typewritten paper.

[1] Joseph Conrad, The Rescue: A Romance of the Shallows (New York: Doubleday & Co., Inc., 1960), p. 103. Hereafter cited as The Rescue.

[2] George Milburn, "The Apostate," An Approach to Literature, 3rd ed., Cleanth Brooks, John Thibaut Purser, and Robert Penn Warren, eds. (New York: Appleton-Century-Crofts, Inc., 1952), p. 74. Hereafter cited as "The Apostate."

[3] Carlisle Moore, "Conrad and the Novel as Ordeal," Philological Quarterly, 42 (1963), 59. Hereafter cited as Moore.

[4] Moore, p. 61.

[5] The Rescue, p. 171.

[6] "The Apostate," p. 76

As a general principle, you do not need to repeat in a footnote any material that you have already incorporated into your theme. For example, if in your theme you mention the author and title of your source, then your footnote should merely give the data about publication. Here is an example:

In *Charles Macklin: An Actor's Life,* William W. Appleton points out that Macklin had been "reinstated at Drury Lane" by December 19, 1744, and that he was playing his stellar role of Shylock.[7]

[7] (Cambridge, Mass.: Harvard University Press, 1961), p. 72.

## Informal Documentation

Sentiment today among many editors and most persons who pay printing bills is that writers should incorporate as much reference material as possible within the text of a paper. If you are using many sources, formal footnotes avoid much ambiguity, but even so you should make a point of including the names of authors, articles, and books in the body of your theme, as in the example just above.

When you are writing a theme based on only one work of literature, as is the case for most of your themes, it is possible to use only one footnote and then to rely on a completely informal system. The principle of informal documentation is to incorporate as much documentation as possible into your discussion to avoid the bother of footnoting.

In your first footnote, indicate that all later references to the source will be indicated in parentheses:

[1] Lucian, *True History and Lucius or the Ass,* trans. Paul Turner (Bloomington: Indiana University Press, 1958), p. 49. All parenthetical page numbers refer to this edition.

The next time you refer to the source, do the following:

1. For an indented (set off) quotation, indicate the page number, line number, or chapter number, preceded by a dash, immediately below the quotation, as follows:

    Nobody grows old there, for they all stay the age they were when they first arrived, and it never gets dark. On the other hand, it never gets really light either, and they live in a sort of perpetual twilight, such as we have just before sunrise.

    −p. 39

2. For a quotation run-in with your own discussion:

    (a) If your sentence ends with the quotation, put the reference in parentheses immediately following the quotation marks and immediately before the period concluding your sentence:

    Sidney uses the example that "the Romaine lawes allowed no person to be carried to the warres but hee that was in the Souldiers role" (p. 189).

    (b) If the quotation ends near the conclusion of your sentence, put the reference in parentheses at the end of your sentence before the period:

    William Webbe states that poetry originated in the needs for "eyther exhortations to vertue, dehortations from vices, or the prayses of some laudable thing"; that is, in public needs (p. 248).

(c) If the quotation ends far from the end of your sentence, put the reference in parentheses immediately following the quotation mark but before your own punctuation mark:

> If we accept as a truth Thomas Lodge's statement, "Chaucer in pleasant vein can rebuke sin vncontrold" (p. 69), then satire and comedy are the most effective modes of moral persuasion in literature.

## A SYSTEM OF ABBREVIATED TITLES

Some instructors have recommended a method of informal documentation even when many works are being used, as in an extended research theme. The mechanics are simple. First of all, a first page should contain the complete list of works used in the paper, arranged alphabetically according to abbreviations that stand for the works. All necessary bibliographical information should be included in this list. (For a book: author, last name first; title, underlined; place of publication; publisher; and date. For an article: author, last name first; title, in quotation marks; name of journal, underlined; volume number, in Arabic numerals; year of publication, within parentheses; and inclusive page numbers.) Here is a model entry:

Sp    Spacks, Patricia Meyer. An Argument of Images: The Poetry of Alexander Pope. Cambridge, Mass. Harvard University Press. 1971.

Whenever a reference to this book is necessary, the abbreviation *Sp* followed by the page number can be used within parentheses, for example: (Sp, p. 26). A typical list of references might look as follows:

ABBREVIATIONS OF WORKS USED IN THIS THEME

D    Dixon, Peter. The World of Pope's Satires. London. Methuen. 1968.

K    Kallich, Martin I. Heav'ns First Law. DeKalb, Ill. Northern Illinois University Press. 1967

N    Nicolson, Marjorie, and G. S. Rousseau. "This Long Disease, My Life," Alexander Pope and the Sciences. Princeton. Princeton University Press. 1968.

Sit    Sitter, John E. The Poetry of Pope's Dunciad. Minneapolis. University of Minnesota Press. 1971.

Sp    Spacks, Patricia Meyer. An Argument of Images: The Poetry of Alexander Pope. Cambridge, Mass. Harvard University Press. 1971.

> NOTE: When references are made to page numbers in these works, the abbreviations and the page numbers are given in parentheses.

Here is a sample paragraph showing how the abbreviation system might be used:

In the midst of fragmentation and disunity, Alexander Pope held to the ideal that the universe was a whole, an entirety, which provided a "viable benevolent system for the salvation of everyone who does good," as Martin Kallich has stated (K, p. 24). Pope's view was therefore positive, and for him the desirable goal of each human being was to pursue moral and intellectual wholeness. The "peculiar faculty of man" (N, p. 101) was reason, the single most important element leading to this wholeness. Not unnaturally, Pope saw a "common humanity" in life, as Patricia Meyer Spacks has observed (Sp, p. 149), and therefore he was amused and tolerant of people who were not capable of reason, like Sir Plume.

As long as all that you want from a reference is the page number of a quotation or of a paraphrase, the informal method is suitable and easy. It saves your reader the trouble of glancing down to the bottom of the page or thumbing through pages to seek a long list of footnotes. Obviously such an informal system is not adequate if you wish to add more details or to direct the reader to other source materials. In such cases, formal footnotes must be used.

## A Final Word

Whether you are using a formal or an informal system of documentation, there is an unchanging need to grant recognition to sources. As for the particular system you use in any of your papers, your instructor is your final authority.

# APPENDIX

# C

# A Perspective on Research Themes

RESEARCH, as distinguished from pure criticism, refers to using primary and secondary sources for assistance in solving a literary problem. That is, in criticizing a work, pure and simple, you consult only the work in front of you, whereas in doing research on the work, you consult not only the work but many other works that were written about it or that may shed light on it. Typical research tasks are to find out more about the historical period in which a work was written, or about prevailing opinions of the times, or about what modern (or earlier) critics have said about the work. It is obvious that a certain amount of research is always necessary in any critical job, or in any theme about a literary work. Looking up words in a dictionary, for example, is only a minimal job of research, which may be supplemented by reading introductions, critical articles, encyclopedias, biographies, critical studies, histories, and the like. There is, in fact, a point at which criticism and research merge.

It is necessary that you put the job of doing research in perspective. In general, students and scholars do research in order to uncover some of the accumulated "lore" of our civilization. This lore — the knowledge that presently exists — may be compared to a large cone that is constantly being filled. At the beginnings of human existence, there was little knowledge of anything, and the cone was at its narrowest point. As civilization progressed, more and more knowledge appeared, and the cone thus began to fill. Each time a new piece of information or a new conclusion was recorded, a little more knowledge or lore was in effect poured into the cone, which accordingly became slightly fuller and wider. Though at present our cone of knowledge is quite full, it appears to be capable of infinite growth. Knowledge keeps piling up and new disciplines keep developing. It becomes more and more difficult for

one person to accumulate more than a small portion of the entirety. Indeed, historians generally agree that the last person to know virtually everything about every existing discipline was Aristotle—2,400 years ago.

If you grant that you cannot learn everything, you can make a positive start by recognizing that research can provide two things: (1) a systematic understanding of a portion of the knowledge filling the cone,
and (2) an understanding of, and ability to handle, the methods by which
you might someday be able to make your own contributions to the filling of the cone. The principal goal of education is to help you to reach a
state where you are prepared to make your own contributions. Research
is a key method of reaching this goal.

Thus far we have been speaking broadly about the relevance of
research to any discipline. The chemist, the anthropologist, the ecologist,
the marine biologist—all employ research. Our problem here, however,
is literary research. A critical paper on a primary source without any external aids is one kind of research. In the sense usually applied in literature courses, however, research is the systematic study of library sources
in order to illuminate a literary topic.

## Selecting a Topic

Frequently your instructor will ask for a research paper on a specific topic. But if you have only a general research assignment, your first
problem is to select a topic. It may be helpful to have a general notion of
the kind of research paper you would find most congenial. There are
five types:

1. A paper on a particular work. You might treat character (for example,
"The Character of Strether in James's *The Ambassadors*," or "Kurtz as a
type of antihero in Conrad's *Heart of Darkness*") or tone, ideas, form,
problems, and the like. A research paper on a single work is similar to
a theme on the same work, except that the research paper takes into account more views and facts than those you are likely to have without
the research. This type of paper is particularly attractive if you are
studying a novelist or a playwright, whose works are usually quite long.

2. A paper on an idea, or some facet of style, imagery, tone, or humor of a
particular author, tracing the origins and development of the topic
through a number of different works by the author. An example might
be "The idea of the true self as developed by Frost in his poetry before
1920." This type of paper is particularly suitable if you are writing on a
poet whose works are short, though a topic like "Shakespeare's idea of
the relationships between men and women as dramatized in *The
Winter's Tale, All's Well That Ends Well, A Midsummer Night's Dream,*
and *As You Like It*" would also prove workable.

3. A paper based on comparison and contrast. There are two types here:

(a) A paper on an idea of some artistic quality common to two or more authors. Your intention might be to show points of similarity or contrast, or to show that one author's work may be read as a criticism of another's. A typical subject of such a paper might be "The 'hollow-man' theme in Eliot, Auden, and Dreiser," or "Goldsmith's *She Stoops to Conquer* as a response to selected sentimental dramas of the eighteenth century." Consult the second sample theme in Chapter 10 for an example of this type.

(b) A paper concentrating on opposing critical views of a particular work or body of works. Sometimes much is to be gained from an examination of differing critical opinions, say "The conflict over *Lolita*," "The controversy over Book IV of *Gulliver's Travels*," or "Pro and con over Lina Wertmüller's film *Swept Away*." Such a study would attempt to determine the critical climate of opinion and taste to which a work did or did not appeal, and it might also aim at conclusions about whether the work was in the advance or rear guard of its time.

4. A paper showing the influence of an idea, an author, a philosophy, a political situation, or an artistic movement on specific works of an author or authors. A paper on influences can be fairly cut-and-dried, as in "The influence of Italian army customs and operations on the details in Hemingway's *A Farewell to Arms*," or else it can be more abstract and psychological, as "The influence of the World War I psyche on the narrator in *A Farewell to Arms*."

5. A paper on the origins of a particular work or type of work. One avenue of research for such a paper might be to examine an author's biography to discover the germination and development of a work, for example, "*Heart of Darkness* as an outgrowth of Conrad's experience in the Belgian Congo." Another way of discovering origins might be to relate a work to a particular type or tradition: "*Hamlet* as revenge tragedy," or "*Mourning Becomes Electra* and its origins in the story of Agamemnon."

If you consider these types, an idea of what to write may come to you. Perhaps you have particularly liked one author, or several authors. If so, you might start to think along the lines of types 1, 2, and 3. If you are interested in influences or in origins, then types 4 or 5 may suit you better.

If you have not decided on a topic after rereading the works you have liked, however, then you should carry your search for a topic into your school library. Look up your author or authors in the card catalogue. Usually the works written by the authors are included first, followed by works written about the authors. Your first goal should be to find a relatively recent book-length critical study published by a university press. Use your judgment here: look for a title indicating that the book is a general one dealing with the author's major works, rather than just one work. Study those chapters relevant to your base work. Most writers of critical studies describe their purpose and plan in their introductions or first chapters. So read the first part of the book. If there is no separate chapter on the base work, use the index and go to the relevant pages. Reading in this way should soon supply you with sufficient knowledge about the issues and ideas raised by the base work to enable you to select a topic you will wish to study further. Once you have made your decision, you are ready to go ahead and gather a working bibliography.

## Setting Up a Bibliography

The best way to gather a working bibliography of books and articles is to begin with major critical studies of the writer or writers. Again, go to the card catalogue and pick out books that have been published by university presses. These books will usually contain selective bibliographies. Be particularly careful to read the chapters on your base work or works, and to look for the footnotes. Quite often you can circumvent many blind alleys of research if you record the names of books and articles listed in footnotes. Then refer to the bibliographies included at the ends of the books, and select any likely looking titles. Now, look at the dates of publication of the critical books you have been using. Let us suppose that you have been looking at three, published in 1951, 1963, and 1977. The chances are that the bibliography in a book published in 1977 will be fairly complete up through about 1974, for the writer will usually have completed his manuscript about three or four years before the book actually was published. What you should do then is aim at gathering a bibliography of works published since 1973 or 1974. You may assume that writers of critical works will have done the selecting for you of the most relevant works published before that time. If you are working on an advanced paper in a graduate course, however, you should be more thorough: recheck bibliographies for possible sources that the critics might have missed. If you are going forward with a thesis, check everything in sight, because a bibliography for a thesis should aim at exhaustiveness.

### BIBLIOGRAPHICAL GUIDES

Fortunately for students doing literary research, the Modern Language Association of America has been providing a virtually complete bibliography of literary studies for years, not just in English and American literatures, but in the literatures of most modern foreign languages. The Association started achieving completeness in the late 1950's, and by 1969 had reached such an advanced state that it divided the bibliography into four parts. The first volume of the *1973 MLA International Bibliography* is devoted to "General, English, American, Medieval and Neo-Latin, and Celtic Literatures," and it contains 14,783 entries. All four volumes are bound together in library editions, just as the earlier bibliographies were bound separately for reference-room use. Most university and college libraries have a set of these bibliographies readily available on open shelves or tables. There are, of course, many other bibliographies that are useful for students doing research, many more than can be mentioned here meaningfully. As an entry into the vast field of bibliography on English studies, you might consult Donald F. Bond, compiler, *A Reference Guide to English Studies* [A Revision of the *Bibliographical Guide to English Studies* by Tom Peete Cross] (Chicago: University of Chicago Press [Phoenix Books], 1962). This work lists a total of 1,230 separate studies and bibliographies on which further research may be based. Section VII lists 100 "Periodical Publications Containing Reviews and Bibliographies." There is more here than can be readily imagined. For most purposes, however, the *MLA International Bibliography* is more than adequate. Remember that as you progress in your reading, the footnotes and bibliographies in the works you consult also will constitute an unfolding bibliography.

The *MLA International Bibliography* is conveniently organized. If your author is Richard Wright, for example, look him up under "American Literature V. Twentieth Century," the relevant listing for all twentieth-century American writers. If your author is Shakespeare, refer to "English Literature VI. Renaissance and Elizabethan." So many books and articles appear each year on Shakespeare that the bibliography lists the separate plays alphabetically under the Shakespeare entry. Depending on your topic, of course, you will find most of the bibliography you need under the author's last name. Journal references are abbreviated, but a lengthy list explaining abbreviations appears at the beginning of the volume. Using the MLA bibliographies, you should begin with the most recent one and then go backward to your stopping point. Be sure to get the complete information, especially volume numbers and years of publication, for each article and book you wish to consult.

If your research carries you into a great number of primary sources, then you should rely on *The Cambridge Bibliography of English Literature,* in five volumes. The *CBEL* is selective for secondary sources, but is invaluable as a general guide to the canon and the various editions of individual authors' works. If you want to see a first edition of poems by the eighteenth-century poet Christopher Smart, for example, the *CBEL* will describe the edition, and it also will describe an acceptable or standard modern edition of the poems if you want the best reading edition.

You are now ready to consult your sources and to take notes.

## Taking Notes and Paraphrasing Material

There are many ways of taking notes, but the consensus is that the best method is to use note cards. If you have never used cards before, you might profit from consulting any one of a number of handbooks and special workbooks on research. Robert M. Gorrell and Charlton Laird present a lucid and methodical explanation of taking notes on cards in their *Modern English Handbook,* 6th ed. (Englewood Cliffs: Prentice-Hall, Inc., 1976), pp. 369–373. The principal virtue of using cards is that cards may be classified, numbered, renumbered, shuffled, used in different contexts, thrown away, and arranged in a useful order when you actually start writing your research paper. If some other system is more in line with your own feelings, however, and you are willing to sacrifice the flexibility and freedom of cards, so be it.

As you take notes, be sure always to get the sources and pages for every entry, no matter how short. Record only one thing on each card— one quotation, one paraphrase, one observation—never two or more. You lose flexibility if you put two things on a single card.

A major problem in taking notes, one that can cause grief later on in writing, is to distinguish copied material from your own words. Here you must be super-cautious. Always—*always*—put quotation marks around *every direct quotation you copy verbatim from a source.* Make the quotation marks immediately, before you forget, so that you will always know that the words of your notes within quotation marks are the words of another writer.

Often, as you take a note, you may use some of your own words and some of the words from your source. In cases like this it is even more important to be cautious. Put quotation marks around *every word* that you take directly from the source, even if you find yourself literally with a note that resembles a picket fence. At a later time, when you begin writing your paper, your memory of what is yours and not yours will become dim, and if you use another's words in your own paper, but do not grant recognition, you lay yourself open to the charge of plagiarism.

### PARAPHRASING

The best principle in taking extensive notes is to aim at rephrasing or paraphrasing the sources. A paraphrase is a restatement of resource material using your own words; it can never quite duplicate the source, and some people maintain that paraphrasing even at best is misleading. When you are doing research, however, you are responsible for getting down ideas and facts that you find, and therefore you must work on paraphrasing. Chapter 1 in this book has a full discussion of making a précis or abstract. If you master the technique in that chapter, you will be well prepared for paraphrasing for your research paper.

The biggest problem in paraphrasing is genuinely to put the ideas into words that are independent of the source. Often it is difficult to find any better words than those in the original. If you have already discovered this difficulty, do not be surprised. The writer of the original unquestionably put things in the best way he could. Improving on the original, or just stating the same ideas and facts as in the original, is therefore not easy. Your sole aim should be to make a short transcription of the substance of the original. Retain the ideas as faithfully as possible, and if you cannot avoid using some of the words in your source, or if your own words are in identical order with the original, be sure to use quotation marks and also to observe that your order coincides with that of the original.

To see the problems of paraphrase, let us look at a paragraph of original criticism, and then see how a student doing research might take notes on it. The paragraph is by Professor Maynard Mack, from an essay entitled "The World of Hamlet," originally published in *The Yale Review*, 41 (1952), and reprinted in *Twentieth Century Interpretations of Hamlet*, David Bevington, ed. (Englewood Cliffs: Prentice-Hall, Inc., 1968), p. 57:

> The powerful sense of mortality in *Hamlet* is conveyed to us, I think, in three ways. First, there is the play's emphasis on human weakness, the instability of human purpose, the subjection of humanity to fortune — all that we might call the aspect of failure in man. Hamlet opens this theme in Act I, when he describes how from that single blemish, perhaps not even the victim's fault, a man's whole character may take corruption. Claudius dwells on it again, to an extent that goes far beyond the needs of the occasion, while engaged in seducing Laertes to step behind the arras of a seemer's world and dispose of Hamlet by a trick. Time qualifies everything, Claudius says, including love, including purpose. As for love — it has a "plurisy" in it and dies of its own too much. As for purpose — "That we would do, We should do when we would, for this 'would' changes, And hath abatements and delays as many As there are tongues, are hands, are accidents; And then this 'should' is like a spendthrift's sigh, That hurts by easing." The player-king, in his long speeches to his queen in the play within the play, sets the matter in a still darker light. She means these protestations of undying love, he knows, but our purposes depend on our memory, and our memory fades fast. Or else, he suggests, we propose something to ourselves in a condition of strong feeling, but then the feeling goes, and with it the resolve. Or else our fortunes change, he adds, and with these our loves: "The great man down, you mark his favorite flies." The subjection of human aims to fortune is a reiterated theme in *Hamlet*, as subsequently in *Lear*. Fortune is the harlot goddess in whose secret parts men like Rosencrantz and Guildenstern live and thrive; the strumpet who threw down Troy and Hecuba and Priam; the

outrageous foe whose slings and arrows a man of principle must suffer or seek release in suicide. Horatio suffers them with composure: he is one of the blessed few "Whose blood and judgment are so well co-mingled That they are not a pipe for fortune's finger To sound what stop she please." For Hamlet the task is of a greater difficulty.

It is obvious that no note can do full justice to such a well-substantiated paragraph of criticism. There are subtleties and shades, and a mingling of discourse with interpretive and appreciative reminiscences and quotations from the play, that cannot be duplicated briefly, and which will be lost when put into other words. But if you wish to take notes at all you must make arbitrary decisions about what to transcribe. If you want mainly the topic of such a paragraph, the following type of note might be sufficient:

> *Hamlet* shows a mood of "mortality" in three ways. The first is an emphasis on human incapacity and "weakness." Corruption, forgetfulness, loss of enthusiasm, bad luck, misery — all these suit the mood of approaching death (Mack, p. 57).

This note is brief, concentrating on material in the early part of the paragraph rather than the middle and end. For such a short note, it is reasonable to paraphrase the *first* part of a paragraph of criticism, for it is there that the writer most often states his topic idea. Observe also that the note contains a sentence in which the note-taker has tried to describe in general terms the details substantiating the topic.

Let us suppose that you wish to take a fuller note, in anticipation of including in your paper not just the topic of the paragraph, but also some of the supporting detail. Such a note might look like this:

> Mack cites "three ways" in which a "powerful sense of mortality" is shown in *Hamlet.* The first is the showing of man's "weakness," "instability," and helplessness before fate. In support, Mack refers to Hamlet's early speech on a single fault leading to corruption, also to Claudius's speech (in the scene persuading Laertes to trick Hamlet). The player-king also talks about his queen's forgetfulness and therefore inconstancy by default. As slaves to fortune, Rosencrantz and Guildenstern are examples. Horatio is not a slave, however. Hamlet's case is by far the worst of all (Mack, p. 57).

When the time comes to write a paper, it would be appropriate to use any part of a note like this one. The note-taker's phraseology is almost completely his own, and the few quotations are within quotation marks. As long as the original writer is given proper credit for ideas used, and *the page number of the original is cited,* the note-taker could make almost any use he chose of the material in the notes.

With only a little practice, you should be able to paraphrase original criticism. Always keep in mind the objective of getting ideas into your own words, no matter how great the temptation to quote the original directly. Again, always be careful to use quotation marks when you retain original wording.

As you read the items in your bibliography, continue to take notes, and do not underestimate the value of making your own commentaries as you go. The best time to get your original ideas down on paper is precisely the moment when they occur to you as a result of your reading. Often you may notice a detail that the critic has missed, or you may see the hint of an idea that the critic does not develop. When such lucky chances occur, you should create your own note. Label it clearly as your own, and you may find that you are well on the way toward a major idea in your final theme.

## Planning Your Theme and Using Your Research

When you have finished taking notes on your reading, you are ready to go ahead with the job of planning and beginning your paper. Remember that research is a technique, and that all research papers do not necessarily have to be long. The length of your theme is usually a requirement of the assignment. Naturally, a short paper would require you to bring in fewer results of research than a longer paper.

The common problem in preparing and writing a research theme is to determine your own dependence on the sources. Should you base your theme entirely on the sources, or should you attempt to interpret them or argue with them? How many of your own ideas should you include in your theme? To what extent should you include interpretations of the base text that originally was the concern of the criticism and commentary you have read? These are the major questions that might occur to you as you plan your theme.

In fact, the research that you have done should not alter the form of the theme you write. The principal difference between what you write with this aid is (1) the ideas and facts you use from others, and (2) the ideas that others have caused you to have. There should theoretically be no difference in the type of theme you finally write, even though you are adding information from other sources. The real problem is that you must integrate your results into a coherent theme that is somehow still uniquely your own. Most problems in research themes are problems in composition.

There are accordingly a number of methods of employing research as you write. In most themes you will probably find that you may use them all. The one goal you should keep in front of you, however, is that the pattern of research should be to work from the *known* to the *unknown*. Remember the image of the cone. The research you have done is your examination of what already is in the cone, and the pattern of your use of this research is to arrive at conclusions that have not already existed—to add your own ideas to the cone. This is not to say that as a student you should expect your research work to create any new directions immediately, but that the *pattern* of your education should always point toward creativity and originality.

Here are some ways of incorporating research into a theme:

1. PROVIDING CONCLUSIONS AND FACTUAL INFORMATION FROM OTHERS.   The first use of research, and the most common, is to indicate what others have said by way of providing conclusions and/or factual information about a work or problem. It goes almost without saying that nobody can draw conclusions unless there is a factual basis for them. Facts cannot be imagined (though they often are), but must be discovered. For this reason you will constantly find yourself quoting primary and secondary sources for information to support your conclusions. Here is a fragment of material showing how research can bring information into a paper. The subject is Henry James's view of reality in his novel *The Ambassadors:*

> To a considerable degree in *The Ambassadors,* James writes out of a conviction that reality is psychological and internal, not objective and external. One commentator on the book has found in it a philosophical conviction which he traces to John Locke and the British empiricists, to whom "man's basic entity . . . was a mental substance . . . [and in] the mental substance alone a knowable reality."[1] In *The Ambassadors* James, by making Lambert Strether's mind and emotions the medium through which the world is seen, dramatizes just such a position. Form and content then complement one another perfectly, and their interaction creates a philosophical position which has properly been termed by one critic, Tony Tanner, "epistemological scepticism."[2] Tanner, one of the most perceptive critics on James, has observed that epistemology was one of James's primary interests. In Tanner's view, James was constantly facing the question not only of how human beings perceive the "endless flow of sensations" surrounding them "from the world," but also of how they "*should*" look at the world.[3]

> [1]John Henry Raleigh, "Henry James: The Poetics of Empiricism," *PMLA,* 66 (1951), 111. Hereafter cited as "Raleigh."
> [2]Tony Tanner, *The Reign of Wonder: Naivety and Reality in American Literature* (New York: Harper and Row, 1967), p. 288. Hereafter cited as *Tanner.*
> [3]*Tanner,* p. 267.

The major problem in using research in this way—as a supply of information and interpretation and as substantiation for argument—is that the writer too easily passes the responsibility for his own thinking onto the shoulders of his sources. How can your instructor judge your work if all you do is to describe what others have said? Clearly, *you must always attempt to create your own thoughts and observations, even when doing research.*

2. USING RESEARCH AS A SPRINGBOARD INTO ARGUMENT OR AGREE-
MENT WITH A CRITIC.    A second use of research—and a most important
one—is that of examining what one or several critics or commentators
have said in order (a) to dispute them, or (b) to agree with them. This
use forces you to be argumentative, and in this way you place the responsibility for thinking squarely where it belongs—on your own shoulders. As you create arguments, you are also fulfilling that pattern of
originality that should be your educational goal. You may not be filling
the cone, but you are doing what is necessary for filling it eventually.
Beethoven had to learn scales and harmony before he became a com-
poser. To the degree that you build upon the works of critics and commentators in order to show through your conclusions that they were
right or wrong, you are fashioning your thoughts in patterns that make
a contribution to knowledge.

An example showing the use of research as a springboard into argument follows. The example is about the character of Strether, the
narrator in James's *The Ambassadors*. The argument in the example is
one opposing the details first brought out, but the example would be
equally valid if the argument were in agreement. If a writer wrote in
agreement, however, he would presumably have to add to the arguments presented in the section laying out the details. If one argues in
disagreement, he can concentrate on rebutting arguments and furnish-
ing details to support his position. In the following example, the material representing the writer's attempt to be original by disputing an
established critical opinion will be italicized:

> Opinion is strong that Strether is to be taken with unreserved accept-
> ance. To some critics he possesses "the soul" of an artist, to use Leon
> Edel's words.[1] Since James admired art and the aesthetically responsive,
> proponents of this view assume that he admired Strether too. To others
> the argument for viewing Strether as having positive "meaning function"
> within the novel lies on James's conviction that the growth of conscious-
> ness is also a growth toward "beatitude."[2] Dorothea Brook, in her book
> *The Ordeal of Consciousness in Henry James,* speaks in religious terms of
> the "redemptive" quality of suffering when the sufferer has the "supreme
> gift of consciousness—specifically self-consciousness."[3] When Strether
> takes leave of Europe in the final pages of the book, a solid body of criti-
> cism has it that he has undergone a virtual apotheosis. Jay Martin, for
> example, claims that Strether has made a "divine ascension into a state
> beyond good and evil."[4]
> *But it is difficult to believe that James, in a mature novel like* The Ambassa-
> dors, *created major characters who were without fault. He was too relentlessly
> honest, too perceptive, and too concerned with the morally gray areas of life to
> see character so simplistically. It does not seem reasonable to separate the posi-
> tive nature of Strether's perceptions from the negative actions which he takes
> as a result of these perceptions. Above all, it is the Strether of the book with*

*whom we must deal, not the ideas toward art or morals which James may have expressed elsewhere. That James surrounds Strether so completely with ironies and comic circumstances makes the position untenable that Strether is a risen hero.*

[1]Henry James, *The Ambassadors,* Leon Edel, ed. (Boston: Houghton Mifflin Co., 1960), p. vii.
[2]John Henry Raleigh, "Henry James: The Poetics of Empiricism," *PMLA,* 66 (1951), 109.
[3](Cambridge, Eng.: Cambridge University Press, 1962), pp. 16, 22.
[4]*Harvest of Change: American Literature 1865–1914* (Englewood Cliffs: Prentice-Hall, Inc., 1967), p. 356.

This passage is no more than a fragment, but it is possible to see in it a desirable turn of mind. The writer is pushing beyond the frontier of established views. Presumably he would continue the line of dispute he is taking, and would draw on the original text for evidence to support his position. It might well be that the position you take may be open to dispute itself, but that does not really matter. What does matter is the pattern of pushing outward toward something new.

3. USING RESEARCH TO DISCOVER A NEW AREA OF DISCUSSION.   The third use of research, and one closely related to the second, is to discover and show what others have not yet done. Once you can show that a vacuum exists, then it follows that you can fill it. If you have studied a great number of sources, and have observed that none of these deals with a particular insight or interpretation that you have unearthed on your own, or if no critic deals with a major point of comparison that you have raised independently, it seems clear that you have staked out an original area for yourself. It is by such means that a great deal of scholarship is originated. Luckily, it frequently happens to many students that in reading a number of critics, such new ideas present themselves, and they can move in and build on them.

Many writers have done just that. If you examine much critical work, you will notice that writers often begin their studies with a rapid review of existing scholarship on their topic — "the state of the art" — and this method is true of all disciplines, not only of literary studies. The writer usually conducts this review as part of a strategy to show that his topic is going to be original and new. A sample of this technique is the following, a section from a paper that treats the subject of Kurtz, a major figure in Joseph Conrad's tale *Heart of Darkness:*

There is near unanimity among the critics that Kurtz represents the good man gone sour. T. S. Eliot in "The Hollow Men" quotes Conrad's phrase "Mistah Kurtz — he dead," as his epigraph, showing his belief that Kurtz is symbolic of the twentieth-century hollow man. Lilian Feder describes Marlow's voyage to recover Kurtz as having parallels with Aeneas's descent into the underworld as described in Book VI of Virgil's *Aeneid.*[1] Along similar lines, William L. Godshalk describes Kurtz as a "diabolical Christ" figure.[2] Both Douglas Hewett[3] and Albert J. Guerard[4] deal with the principle of evil represented by Kurtz. Frederick R. Karl describes Kurtz as a "god devil"[5] and claims that "the story is about the loss of responsible heart." It would probably be difficult to find a critic who did not deal with some aspect of the evil represented by Kurtz.

*None of the critics, however, treats the idea that Kurtz is a type derived from a long line of antiheroes who represent the reverse side of an optimistic coin. When the framers of the U.S. Constitution created our system of representative government, they were optimistic, but when they created the electoral college as a direct check on the popular vote, they must have been thinking that at the heart of people even in the new world there lurked the same darkness that possessed Kurtz. It is this same awareness that one can see in Swift's Yahoos and in Browning's satiric portrait of the Bishop in "The Bishop Orders His Tomb at St. Praxed's Church." It is worth exploring the parallels that Kurtz has with the Yahoos and with Browning's Bishop, together with other satirical portraits by Browning.*

[1]"Marlow's Descent Into Hell," *Nineteenth-Century Fiction,* 9 (1955) 280–292.
[2]"Kurtz as Diabolical Christ," *Discourse,* 12 (1969), 100–107.
[3]*Conrad: A Reassessment,* 2nd ed. (Chester Springs, Pa.: Dufour, 1969).
[4]*Conrad the Novelist* (Cambridge, Mass.: Harvard University Press, 1958).
[5]*A Reader's Guide to Joseph Conrad* (New York: Noonday Press, 1960), p. 138.

While you are likely to use this technique frequently at the beginning of your paper, and at the beginnings of various sections of a long research paper, it is equally useful anywhere as you progress in your various points. Here is a short fragment from the middle of an argument, on the same topic, Kurtz:

One may then see that Kurtz is shown surrounded by darkness, unrelieved by some of the light that Browning casts on the character of his Bishop. The point to make about the darkness is that it is *always* operative in human beings, nor is it ever absent. Some of the studies on Kurtz do not sufficiently recognize the permanence of the darkness. They fail to emphasize that Kurtz is to be seen as a typical human being, not a freak. The darkness seems to be accidental to them: they claim that Kurtz has sunk into an abyss "darker than savagery itself," in the words of Wilfred S. Dowden,[1] or else they speak of Kurtz's "corruption and disintegration," as does J. I. M. Stewart.[2] The assumption here is that Kurtz is different because he has fallen away from civilization, but in truth the critics have failed to make an important point. The only element distinguishing Kurtz from anyone else is that he has had the opportunity to indulge himself without fear of reprisal. In a position of power like that of St. Praxed's Bishop, he too — and so too, perhaps, alas, all of us — would burn the church to disguise his thefts. The darkness is always around us; the Yahoo is always a part of us.

[1]*Joseph Conrad: The Imaged Style* (Nashville: Vanderbilt University Press, 1970), p. 72.
[2]*Joseph Conrad* (New York: Dodd, Mead & Co., 1968), p. 77.

## Concluding Advice

Whenever you write a research theme, remember that research is a means to an end. The object of securing facts and opinions from other writers is to secure your own mind as you go ahead to construct your own views of the world. By studying literary and social historians and literary critics, you can learn their methods along with the things that they can teach you. When you write, you should apply their methods for your own purposes. A research paper is not meant to be only a recitation of what others have said. Think of it as an occasion for launching yourself into the pattern of human learning. In a way, you might look at your entire education as an experience in research. The goal is not just to acquire, but to build. If you are to be successful, you must see yourself as preparing for a future in which you will be supplying the facts and interpretations upon which others may build; you will have the responsibility of applying known facts and principles to problems for which as yet there are no solutions.

# Index